Instructor's Manual

to accompany

A Child's World
INFANCY THROUGH ADOLESCENCE

Ninth Edition

Diane E. Papalia

Sally Wendkos Olds

Ruth Duskin Feldman

Prepared by

Leslie A. Grout
and
Ron Mulson
both of Hudson Valley Community College

Boston   Burr Ridge, IL   Dubuque, IA   Madison, WI   New York   San Francisco   St. Louis
Bangkok   Bogotá   Caracas   Kuala Lumpur   Lisbon   London   Madrid   Mexico City
Milan   Montreal   New Delhi   Santiago   Seoul   Singapore   Sydney   Taipei   Toronto

McGraw-Hill Higher Education

A Division of The McGraw-Hill Companies

Instructor's Manual to accompany
A CHILD'S WORLD: INFANCY THROUGH ADOLESCENCE, NINTH EDITION
DIANE E. PAPALIA/SALLY WENDKOS OLDS/RUTH DUSKIN FELDMAN

Published by McGraw-Hill Higher Education, an imprint of The McGraw-Hill Companies, Inc.,
1221 Avenue of the Americas, New York, NY 10020. Copyright © The McGraw-Hill Companies,
Inc., 2002, 1999, 1996. All rights reserved.

This book is printed on acid-free paper.

1 2 3 4 5 6 7 8 9 0 QPD QPD 0 3 2 1

ISBN 0-07-241414-6

www.mhhe.com

Table of Contents

WELCOME TO YOUR INSTRUCTOR'S MANUAL

There is no more important course for undergraduates than the one you are about to teach. Your students may choose a variety of careers, some involving children, some not. But most of them will become parents. And the work you do to introduce them to concepts of child psychology can have far-reaching consequences. We have been teaching child psychology and child development courses for years across varied settings. While we do not profess to be experts, we are pleased to offer suggestions for creating a course that can be meaningful for you, your students, and the yet-unknown children in your students' future.

We hope you enjoy teaching your course using *A Child's World*, 9th edition. Papalia, Olds and Feldman have updated the text and included contemporary issues, applications, and research as well as classic material. The Instructor's Manual pulls together a variety of materials and strategies that have been classroom-tested over the years. It is not meant to be followed like a cookbook; rather, browse the ideas and choose something that fits your objectives and your style. All ideas are not for everyone or every class.

Keep in mind that Murphy's Law prevails in teaching, so it is always helpful to have more materials prepared than you think you will need. Whatever you don't use will be ready for the next class.

INTERACTIVE INSTRUCTION

Beginning teachers and experienced teachers alike will find it helpful to browse through this Manual for ideas that you can translate to immediate classroom practice. We have emphasized interactive instruction, so that students are engaged in the material from the very beginning. When they interact with you and with each other, they are more likely to learn and retain new information. They are also more likely to feel comfortable as contributing class members and therefore more likely to continue with the class, attend regularly, and connect the new material with their personal experiences.

Interactive instruction works best with small groups, but creating those groups can be a challenge in large lecture classes or in distance instruction formats. Have students in the lecture hall pair up to discuss topics, generate examples, or share experiences. Online classes which use course management software such as PageOut, BlackBoard or TopClass can use the discussion format to do many of the activities. In traditional classrooms of 20 – 40 students, the small group activities use four or five students. You may create work groups early in the semester, then restructure them after each test so that the highest achieving students are distributed throughout the groups, thus facilitating the learning of the less-skilled. Or students may form natural groups that work effectively. Do whatever you can do support small-group learning. The benefits will outweigh the complications!

FEATURES OF YOUR INSTRUCTOR'S MANUAL

The first page of each chapter highlights the text outline and includes the chapter contents.

1. TOTAL TEACHING PACKAGE OUTLINE

The Total Teaching Package Outline explicitly ties the strategies and ideas in the Instructor's Manual to the text materials. Within the Total Teaching Package Outline, we have connected the Learning Objectives to Teaching and Learning Activities. On the left side of the Outline, locate the text material you plan to cover. Move to the corresponding right side to see what Guideposts for Study, Learning Objectives, and Teaching and Learning Activities correspond to that material. You can always find additional materials on the McGraw-Hill website that is specific to *A Child's World*, 9th edition.

2. EXPANDED OUTLINE (TRANSPARENCY-READY)

Many instructors find it useful to prepare an outline of the chapter to facilitate helping their classes move through the material. We have prepared this expanded outline for you and created it so that you may photocopy it directly onto overhead transparency acetate and use it immediately.

3. GUIDEPOSTS FOR STUDY

These questions are drawn from the text and serve to assist students to preview material before they read it. Each is numbered and corresponds with a particular section of text.

4. LEARNING OBJECTIVES

Objectives are critical to assessment of teaching outcomes. In order to have learning objectives that are explicitly tied to the textbook, we have restructured the text's Checkpoint questions into objectives. Thus each objective corresponds directly to a Guidepost and to material in the textbook. In addition, by using the Total Teaching Package Outline, you can locate Teaching and Learning Activities to address specific Learning Objectives.

5. KEY TERMS

The chapter outline is built around the key terms. If students understand the chapter vocabulary, they will be able to apply and use the concepts. You may choose to highlight key terms for students, identify which ones to emphasize, or ask students to define and apply them.

6. TEACHING AND LEARNING ACTIVITIES

We have explicitly labeled instructional strategies as both teaching and learning. Beyond the obvious, both the instructor and the student teach and learn in an interactive classroom. We find that we invariably learn from our experiences of teaching; either learning new content or new strategies from our students. Yes, the most learning seems to come from the classroom experiences that do not appear to be very successful!

We have included a variety of teaching and learning activities.

LECTURE TOPICS

Lecture topics include information to enrich your classroom presentations in specific areas that are related to the textbook. Some material is best presented in a traditional "chalk-and-talk" format, so these topics are offered in this mode. Feel free to adapt materials to different teaching strategies; for example, some lecture topics may also serve as springboards to discussion.

DISCUSSION TOPICS

Your students are likely to come to class with some connection to the materials in the discussion topics. You may present some new information and ask them to integrate it with what they already know. Topics that may be addressed from multiple perspectives lend themselves well to discussion. Do not be afraid to play devil's advocate to challenge their thinking and their participation.

Discussion is what allows students to learn that everyone in the world does not see the world in the same way, and that the contexts from which people come may create dramatic differences in their views of the world. For some students, this is a remarkable new finding, and they need some preparation before encountering the variations of human experience. Remind them that each class member has a unique and important point of view, that such perspectives contribute to their education, and an atmosphere of tolerance and respectful interest will be helpful for everyone. With such attitudes, discussion can flourish and enrich the learning, as well as help students take ownership of the class.

INDEPENDENT STUDIES

Some students will want to go beyond the minimum class expectations, or you may choose to include independent research as a course requirement. The Independent Studies feature of the Instructor's Manual provides ideas for student work outside the classroom. The studies may become research papers or presentations, depending on your needs and the needs and interests of your students.

CHOOSING SIDES DEBATE TOPICS

The debate topics were chosen because they fit very specifically into the material of each chapter, because of their somewhat provocative nature, and because there is available evidence to support both sides. You may assign debates as a regular event, an extra credit option, or just an end-of-semester wrap-up activity. It usually is effective to assign a small group to the task of presenting each side. They will have to do some research in addition to what you can provide to them, and they will need to organize their arguments and present them in a persuasive manner. Decide in advance how long each side will have to present opening arguments, how long the rebuttal period will be, and provide the listening students with some idea of your expectations, so that they may make informed decisions when voting for the winning side.

KNOWLEDGE CONSTRUCTION ACTIVITIES

Research supports the use of group activities in the classroom. As a teaching strategy, activities are useful in addressing issues of intellectual and cultural diversity, supporting retention efforts, and generating a higher level of critical thinking than more traditional approaches. When students work in small groups, you will notice the following things happening. Instead of one person speaking and an entire classroom listening, more students will be involved in interaction at any given time. Students will tend to use examples that may be more relevant to their peers than the examples you might have used in the class discussion. (Can you name the characters in the highest rated television show that college-aged students watch? How about the top three songs in the college music polls?) If not, cohort effects are beginning to set in. Beware!)

While the groups are working, the instructor is also working. Group activity time is an opportunity for you to informally assess your students' understanding of the topic, observe the group dynamics in the classroom, and hear from students who would otherwise not be comfortable in addressing you.

Since activities are the heart of interactive instruction, we have included a host of activities for each chapter that are designed to help students to construct their own understanding of the material. The old Chinese proverb about learning is true for college students as well as for children:

> I hear and I forget.
> I see and I remember.
> I do and I understand.

We have given you lots of ways to help them to do and understand.

The Generative Terms activity is based on generative learning. This concept comes from the idea, supported by research, that elaboration on a concept is an excellent way to enhance memory for that concept. In the hierarchy of knowledge, a term or label for a concept is the most fundamental building block. As educators, we often settle for memorization when, with a little more creativity, we could have understanding. We have had students in the past that could recite a definition for a term verbatim from the book but really had little idea of what they were saying. Students who complete the Generative Terms activity must clearly understand the terms.

In this activity, students are asked to generate their own examples of terms, ideas, and concepts from the chapter. They may not use the instructor's examples or the textbook examples. A good way to lead into this is to finish covering the topics for the chapter and then ask the students if everyone understand the material. Invariably everyone assumes that they do, until you challenge them to apply their knowledge by generating an example. Then the fun begins for both you as an instructor and the students themselves as they work to apply what they have learned.

The last activity in each chapter is written to be free-standing and the language is directed toward the students. You may choose to photocopy this page and hand it out as an assignment. Most of these are small group activities that result in a product; a presentation, some data, or a brief paper. The activities move smoothly from small group into large group format; for example, after students collect and compile data from an observation in their small groups, they assign a reporter who helps to assemble data from the entire class. By putting these results on an overhead transparency, the blackboard, or a computer projection system, the entire class can see results across a number of observations. This experience is always instructive; if data are similar, students can clearly see a robust phenomenon. If they are dissimilar, the goal becomes explanation. Students can clearly see the effects of error, of culture and context, and different or unarticulated assumptions.

7. INSTRUCTOR RESOURCES

At the end of each chapter there is a brief list of books and journal articles and video resources that are relevant to the chapter. Some of these are useful in classroom presentation; others might be helpful to you or to your students if they are pursuing a particular topic.

LINKUPS

Provided by the authors of the main text, and appearing before chapters 6, 9, 11 and 14, these bulleted lists point to examples of the interaction of physical, cognitive, and psychosocial aspects of development.

TEACHING CHILD PSYCHOLOGY

SYLLABUS

Your syllabus is a document that states the relationship between your course and the student's grade. It basically serves as a contractual agreement between you and your students. Because it is very important, it makes sense to spend time carefully constructing it. Your institution may have guidelines for syllabus construction and it is helpful to look at models others have used. The Office of Teaching Resources in Psychology hosts an online archive of syllabi that you might find helpful. The Web address is http://www.lemoyne.edu/OTRP/index.html.

At the minimum, you will include contact information for yourself, the reference information for your textbook, a calendar of assignments and topics, a schedule for evaluation and specifics about that evaluation (tests, quizzes, etc.), and any term assignments that you plan to give. Students, especially in fall semester, are sometimes overwhelmed with the volume of work they are expected to complete, so it might be kind to include the fact of a term project but leave the specific details to discuss a bit later in the semester.

CLASS PARTICIPATION

Using this Instructor's Manual will support a high level of class participation. Involvement in class supports student learning, develops confidence and is a motivator for continued participation. By using small groups or developing interactive dyads in the large lecture class, you encourage participation. It is not necessary to offer grade points for participation; in fact, such extrinsic motivation may actually undermine the intrinsic motivation students have to work together in class. Your attitude and encouragement will go far in creating a climate in which student feel comfortable in interacting.

TESTS AND OTHER EVALUATIONS

The Test Bank for your textbook, available in print and on CD-ROM, will provide you with hundreds of questions from which to choose to evaluate student learning. The CD-ROM is remarkably flexible; you can easily edit questions and answers on the screen and save them to the test bank. The program will format and print your test and answer key; there is even a provision for online testing. Quiz questions may also be drawn from this resource. Please consult your McGraw-Hill representative about this and the availability of other supplementary materials for instructors including the Instructor's Resource CD-ROM; downloadable PowerPoints; and the Multimedia Courseware for Child Development. Additionally, for your students, please note the availability of a Study Guide as well as extensive online material at www.mhhe.com/papaliacw9.

Some students experience such anxiety around tests that their true knowledge is not assessed in that format. It is useful to have other means of assessment to complement testing. The research assignment can do just that.

RESEARCH ASSIGNMENT

We strongly encourage a research-based project that allows students to explore a topic of personal interest, connect published research to real-world experiences, and get an up-close view of child development. One goal of general education across the country is to enhance students' abilities to use the vast stores of information available on any given topic. Child psychology is no exception. Additionally, students often struggle with understanding that our knowledge of psychology comes from research activity; getting their hands into published research will help them to internalize this idea.

Research resources include databases published by the American Psychological Association (PsychInfo and PsychLit), the ERIC database, and the Child Development Abstracts published by the Society for Research in Child Development. Rapid changes in online reference materials make a complete list impossible; we spend time with our reference librarians each semester to find out what is new and what has disappeared from our landscape. Your library may also be able to schedule bibliographic instruction for your students to help them to learn what they will need in order to complete a research assignment.

A truly generative research assignment includes a review of published research and an experiential component; an interview, observation, or even collection of data with children, and an integrative summary. Our students have found this format to be flexible and often relevant to professional goals. They also produce papers that are interesting and fun to read.

A FINAL WORD

We have enjoyed putting these ideas together for you; we hope that you find them useful and that they serve as a springboard for your own ideas. Remember that none of these activities will work for every class and every situation. They are simply tools to have at your disposal in order to enable students to gain a greater understanding of the materials.

We would like to thank the text authors Diane E. Papalia, Sally Wendkos Olds, and Ruth Duskin Feldman, for their continued hard work and the materials they provided to us; Dana Gross, St. Olaf's College, for her welcome contribution to the Independent Studies feature; and our editor at McGraw-Hill, Rita Lombard, for her kindness, her patience and for her unflagging support.

We are grateful to our students who have taught us so much over our years of teaching, and to all of the children we have observed, taught, coached, and parented (Adrienne, Alex, Derek, Elliot, and the Princess Jess). What we do in the classroom, we do for children.

Now it is your turn. Enjoy!

Leslie A. Grout, Ph.D.
Ron Mulson

Hudson Valley Community College
Troy, NY

AUDIOVISUAL DISTRIBUTORS

ABC Merchandising (ABC)
American Broadcasting Co. TV
1330 Avenue of the Americas
New York, NY 10019

Ambrose Video Publishing, Inc.
28 W. 44th St. Ste 2100
New York, NY 10036-6600
(212) 768-7373
http://www.ambrosevideo.com/

American Journal of Nursing (AJN)
Educational Services Division
555 West 56th Street
New York, NY 10019-2925
http://www.ajn.org/

Beacon Films (BCN)
930 Pinter Avenue
Evanston, IL 60202
1 (800) 323-5448

Benchmark Films (BF)
145 Scarborough Road
Briarcliff Manor, NY 10510

Cambridge Documentary Films, Inc.
P.O. Box 390385
Cambridge, MA 02139-0004
(617) 484-3993
FAX (617) 484-0754
http://www1.shore.net/~cdf/contactus.html
http://www1.shore.net/~cdf/films1.html

Campus Film Distributors Corp.
24 Depot Square
Tuckahoe, NY 10107
(914) 961-1900

Cinema Guild
Division of Document Associates
1697 Broadway # 802
New York, NY 10019
(212) 246-5522

Corporation for Public Broadcasting
901 E. St. NW
Washington, DC 20004-2037
(202) 879-9600
http://www.cpb.org/
http://www.learner.org/collections/multimedia/
http://www.learner.org/channel/previews/

Coronet/MTI Film and Video Group (CORT)
Supplementary Education Group
Simon and Schuster Communications
108 Wilmot Road
Deerfield, IL 60015
1 (800) 323-5343

CRM/McGraw-Hill Films (CRM)
2215 Faraday Avenue
Carlsbad, CA 92008-7211
(760) 431-98800
http://www.crmfilms.com/
http://crmmedia.com/
http://crmpublishing.com/

Davidson Films (DAV)
668 Marsh Street
San Luis Obispo CA 93401
(805) 594.0422
FAX (805) 594.0532
http://davidsonfilms.com/

Educational Cable Consortium (ECC)
24 Beechwood Road
Summit, NJ 07901

Educational Development Center (EDC)
Distribution Center
55 Chapel Street
Newton, MA 02160

Far West Laboratory for Educational Research and Development (FWL)
Hotel Clairmont
41 Tunnel Road
Berkeley, CA 94705

Films for the Humanities and Sciences (FFHS)
P.O Box 2053
Princeton, NJ 08543-2053
1 (800) 257-5126
FAX (609) 275-3767
http://www.films.com/

Filmmakers Library, Inc. (FML)
124 East 40th Street, Suite 901
New York, NY 10016
(212) 808-4980
http://www.filmakers.com/SUBSTANCE.html

Films, Inc., Public Media Inc. (FI)
5547 Ravenswood Avenue
Chicago, IL 60640
1 (800) 323-4222

Harcourt Brace Jovanovich (HBJ)
176 West Adams Street
Chicago, IL 60603
(312) 853-3662
-or-
Harcourt Brace Publishing Company
5513 North Cumberland Avenue
Chicago, IL 60656
(773) 594-5110
FAX (773) 594-5170
http://www.harcourtbrace.com/
http://www.harcourtbrace.com/companies.htm
http://customerservice.harcourtbrace.com/

Health Sciences Communication Center (HSCC)
Case Western Reserve University
University Circle
Cleveland, OH 44106

Insight Media (IM)
2162 Broadway
New York, NY 10024-6620
1 (212) 721-6316
FAX (212) 799-5309
http://www.insight-media.com/

International Film Bureau
332 South Michigan Avenue
Chicago, IL 60604-4382
(312) 427-4545
Toll-free (800) 432-2241
FAX (312) 427-4550

Kent State University
Audio Visual Services
P.O. Box 5190
Kent, OH 44242-0001
(216) 672-3456
Toll-free (800) 338-5718
FAX (216) 672-3463

Magna Systems
P.O. Box 576
Itasca, IL 60143-0576
(708) 382-6477

Michigan State University (WK)
WKAR-TV
600 Kalamazoo Street
E. Lansing, MI 48824

Milner-Fenwick, Inc. (MF)
2125 Green Spring Drive

Timonium, MD 2093
National Film Board of Canada
1251 Avenue of the Americas, 16th Floor
New York, NY 10020-1173
(212) 596-1770
FAX (212) 596-1779

PBS Video (PBS)
1320 Braddock Place
Alexandria, VA 22314
1 (800) 344-3337
http://www.pbs.org/

Penn State Audio-Visual Services (PSU)
University Division of Media and Learning Resources
PCR: Films and video in the Behavioral Sciences
The Pennsylvania State University
Special Services Building
1127 Fox Hill Road
University Park, PA 16803-1824
Purchase/Preview Information: (814) 863-3102
Rental Scheduling: (814) 865-6314
Toll-free (800) 826-0132

Perrenial Education
1560 Sherman Avenue, Suite 1000
Evanston, IL 60201
(800) 323-9084, Ext. 113
FAX (708) 328-6706

Perspective Films Education Group (PER)
Simon and Schuster Communications
108 Wilmot Road
Deerfield, IL 60015

Polymorph Films, Inc. (PFV)
118 South Street
Boston, MA 02111

Psychological Films (PSYCHF)
3334 East Coast Highway, Suite 252
Corona Del Mar, CA 02625

Pyramid Film & Video (PF)
2801 Colorado Avenue
Santa Monica, CA 90404
1 (213) 828-7577

Research Press (RP)
Dept. W
P.O. Box 9177
Champaign, IL 61826
(217) 352-3273

Time-Life Film & Video (TLF)
100 Eisenhower Drive
Paramus, NJ 07652

University of California Extension Center
for Media and Independent Learning (UCEMC)
2000 Center Street, 4th Floor
Berkeley, CA 94704
(510) 642-0460
FAX (510) 643-9271

University of Minnesota Film & Video (UVF)
University of Minnesota
1313 Fifth Street S.E., Suite 108
Minneapolis, MN 55414-1524
(612) 627-4270
Minnesota Toll-free (800) 542-0013
Out-of-state toll-free (800) 847-8251
FAX (612) 627-4280

Video Learning Library (Videopolis)
http://www.videopolis.com/learning/s2110~1.htm

Ways of Knowing, Inc.
22D Hollywood Avenue
Hohokus, NH 07423
Toll-free (800) 666-9970

WGBH Boston Video
PO Box 2284-3213
South Burlington, VT 05407-2284
(800) 255-9424
FAX (802) 864-9846
http://www.boston.com/wgbh/shop/shoporderinfo.html
http://www.boston.com/wgbh/index.html
http://www.pbs.org/wgbh/shop/novavideo.html#educator
http://www.pbs.org/wgbh/shop/videdu02mind.html
http://www.boston.com/wgbh/search/

1 *STUDYING A CHILD'S WORLD*

THE STUDY OF CHILD DEVELOPMENT: THEN AND NOW
Early Approaches
Studying the Life Span
New Frontiers
An Emerging Consensus

THE STUDY OF CHILD DEVELOPMENT: BASIC CONCEPTS
Developmental Processes: Change and Stability
Domains of Development
Periods of Development

INFLUENCES ON DEVELOPMENT
Heredity, Environment, and Maturation
Major Contextual Influences
Normative and Nonnormative Influences
Timing of Influences: Critical or Sensitive Periods

In This Chapter of Your Instructor's Manual You Will Find:
1. Total Teaching Package Outline
2. Expanded Outline (transparency-ready)
3. Guideposts for Study
4. Learning Objectives
5. Key Terms
6. Teaching and Learning Activities
   Lecture Topics
   Discussion Topics
   Independent Studies
   Choosing Sides
   Knowledge Construction Activities
7. Resources for Instructors

1. TOTAL TEACHING PACKAGE OUTLINE

Chapter 1: The Study of Child Development: Then and Now

The study of child development: early approaches	**Guidepost for study 1.1**
Early approaches	**Guidepost for study 1.1** **Learning objective 1.1** **Lecture topic 1.4, 1.5**
Studying the life span	**Knowledge construction activities 1.2, 1.3, 1.5** **Box 1.1 (textbook p. 14)**
New frontiers	**Learning objective 1.2**
An emerging consensus	**Learning objective 1.3** **Choosing sides 1.1**
The study of child development: Basic concepts	**Guidepost for study 1.2, 1.3** **Knowledge construction activity 1.1**
Developmental processes: Change and stability	**Learning objective 1.4, 1.5** **Lecture topic 1.1**
Domains of development	**Learning objective 1.6** **Independent study 1.1**
Periods of development	**Learning objective 1.7** **Discussion topic 1.1**
Influences on development	**Guidepost for study 1.4**
Heredity, environment, and maturation	**Learning objective 1.8** **Lecture topic 1.2**
Major contextual influences	**Learning objective 1.9** **Discussion topic 1.2** **Knowledge construction activity 1.1, 1.3**
Normative and nonnormative influences	**Learning objective 1.10** **Independent study 1.2** **Knowledge construction activity 1.4**
Timing of influences: critical or sensitive periods	**Learning objective 1.11** **Lecture topic 1.3** **Box 1.2 (textbook p. 15)**

Please check out the online learning center located at www.mhhe.com/papaliacw9 for further information on these and other topics. There you can also access downloadable PowerPoints tailored to each chapter of the text and containing useful teaching notes as well as images and tables from the text itself.

2. EXPANDED OUTLINE (TRANSPARENCY READY)

I. The Study of Child Development: Then and Now
  A. Early approaches
    1. Baby biographies
    2. Developmental aspects
    3. Nature and nurture
    4. Pioneers in the field
  B. Studying the life span
    1. Developmental psychology
  C. New frontiers
    1. Evolution of the scientific approach
    2. Influence of technology
  D. An emerging consensus
    1. Domains of development are interrelated.
    2. Development includes individual differences.
    3. Children help shape their own development.
    4. Historical and cultural contexts strongly influence development.
    5. Early experience is important, but not binding.
    6. Development in childhood is connected to lifespan development.

II. The Study of Child Development: Basic Concepts
  A. Developmental processes: Change and Stability
    1. Quantitative change
    2. Qualitative change
  B. Domains of development
    1. Physical development
    2. Cognitive development
    3. Psychosocial development
  C. Periods of development
    1. Prenatal period
    2. Infancy and toddlerhood
    3. Early childhood
    4. Middle childhood
    5. Adolescence

III. Influences on Development
    A. General influences
        1. Individual differences
        2. Heredity
        3. Environment
        4. Maturation
    B. Major contextual influences
        1. Nuclear family
        2. Extended family
        3. Socioeconomic status
        4. Risk factors
        5. Culture and ethnicity
    C. Normative and nonnormative influences
        1. Cohort
    D. Timing of influences
        1. Critical periods
        2. Sensitive periods
        3. Plasticity

3. GUIDEPOSTS FOR STUDY

1.1 What is child development and how has its study evolved?

1.2 What are six fundamental points on which consensus has emerged in the study of child development?

1.3 What do developmental scientists study?

1.4 What are the three major aspects and five periods of child development?

4. LEARNING OBJECTIVES

Upon completing the study of the Introduction and Chapter 1, the student should be able to:

1.1   Define child development and describe how its study has evolved.

1.2   Generate examples of practical applications of research on child development.

1.3   List six fundamental points on which consensus has emerged in the study of child development.

1.4   Describe what it is that developmental scientists study

1.5   Distinguish between qualitative and quantitative development, giving an example of each.

1.6   Identify three major domains of development and describe how they are interrelated.

1.7   Name five periods of child development and list several key issues of events of each period.

1.8   Explain why individual differences tend to increase with age.

1.9   Construct examples of the influences of family and neighborhood composition, socioeconomic status, culture, ethnicity, and historical context.

1.10 Construct examples of normative age-graded, normative history-graded, and non-normative influences.

1.11 Explain the concept of critical period and give an example.

5. KEY TERMS

Child development
Quantitative change
Qualitative change
Social construction
Individual differences
Heredity
Environment
Maturation
Nuclear family
Extended family
Socioeconomic status
Risk factors
Culture
Ethnic group
Normative
Nonnormative
Cohort
Critical period
Plasticity

6. TEACHING AND LEARNING ACTIVITIES

LECTURE TOPICS

LECTURE TOPIC 1.1: CONNECTEDNESS

One of the most common beliefs about human development is that our infant and early-childhood qualities are predictive of what we will be like as adolescents and adults. Freud, for example, believed that our adult personality was basically formed by the time we were six years old. Back in 1905, Thorndike said, "Every event of a man's mental life is written indelibly in the brain's archives, to be counted for or against him." Many psychologists believe not only that a new structure or process depends on an earlier one, but also that aspects of earlier structures are present in later stages. For example, our musical preferences as adults are shaped by the music we were exposed to as toddlers. Or, as Freud speculated, strict, anxious toilet training results in an adult who is stingy, obstinate, and compulsively clean.

On the other hand, some theorists believe that there is a good deal of discontinuity in human development. Even when some sequences seem to be set (crawling occurs before the child stands), one can not say that the first event is necessary for the second event to occur (if prevented from crawling, the child would still learn to stand at the appropriate time). Kagan argues that the mere fact that behavior X always happens before behavior Y does not necessarily prove that behavior Y cannot occur without behavior X's appearing first. Because of our strong belief that early-childhood personality and experiences contribute heavily to who we are as adults, we see more relationships between phenomena than really exists.

Research on the stability of personality characteristics tends to be done with children over a 2 or 3 year period. Within this short time period, some characteristics (such as aggressive behavior

6

in boys) appear to be stable. Yet if infant and early childhood qualities are used to predict personality in early childhood and adolescence, there seems to be little continuity. For example, a 1983 study showed that the correlation between aggression at age eight and age thirty was 0.3 for men and only 0.2 for women. With aggression, and with most other characteristics, we tend to acquire the qualities that our environment shapes in us rather than remaining bound to the psychological qualities we exhibited during our first years.

Reference

Kagan, J. (1984). The nature of the child. New York: Basic Books.

LECTURE TOPIC 1.2: THE GENAIN QUADRUPLETS

Twin studies are helpful in assessing the relative importance of heredity and environment in personality development. Most studies of twins with mental disorders, for example, show that both monozygotic twins are more likely to suffer from mental illnesses than are both dizygotic twins. These findings suggest a hereditary basis for mental illness, though other explanations are still possible.

However, psychologists have done a longitudinal study that is more telling even than the twin studies: They have studied the Genain Quadruplets, four sisters who have all been diagnosed as schizophrenic. Now in their fifties, the sisters were studied by David Rosenthal at the National Institute of Mental Health (NIMH) more than 20 years ago, and recently by Allan Mirsky.

Nora, Iris, Myra, and Hester Genain are pseudonyms given by Rosenthal to protect the quadruplet's identities. Genain comes from the Greek words for "dire birth." Their first names come from the acronym for the National Institute of Mental Health. Childhood popularity, including a sister song-and-dance routine, turned into special problems during their high school years. Hester dropped out of high school with symptoms of destructiveness, irritability, depression, vomiting, and odd mannerisms. The others graduated but had increasing problems. In their twenties all had been diagnosed as schizophrenic and were studied by NIMH.

The heaviest of the quadruplets at birth was Nora at 4.5 pounds. They spent their first 6 weeks in the hospital. During their entire childhood and adolescence they had to deal with a father who did not allow them to have playmates or to leave home.

There are differences in their schizophrenic symptoms. Hester and Iris (the smallest infants at birth) take the most antipsychotic drugs, and each has spent more than 15 years in the hospital. Nora and Myra have both held jobs, but only Myra married and had children. The recent follow-up study of the quadruplets has allowed the use of CAT and PET scans. The goal was to examine which characteristics were not hereditary. Because the sisters' genes are identical, any physical, mental, or social differences can be attributed to environmental causes.

Although the Genains have different lifestyles, different levels of symptoms, and different histories of treatment and hospitalization, all four of the CAT scans showed no brain shrinkage. In the PET scans, the Genains all showed high energy use in the visual areas, whereas normal brains have high energy use in the frontal lobes. The quadruplets all had less alpha brain wave activity than is normal (one possible reason might be hallucinations).

References

Buchshaum, M. S. (August 1984). The Genain quadruplets. *Psychology Today*, 46-51.

Rosenthal, D. (1963). *The Genain quadruplets*. New York: Basic Books.

LECTURE TOPIC 1.3: CRITICAL PERIODS: MATERNAL AND FAMILIAL DEPRIVATION AND INTELLECTUAL RETARDATION

The early years are assumed to be critical years for later development. This is true for intellectual factors as well as maternal and family deprivation. In 1979, Michael Rutter, focusing on maternal and family deprivation, explored the critical period in relation to social and intellectual development. Presentation and discussion of his observations on intellectual retardation and parenting deprivation follow:

a. It is thought that many intellectual deficits have their roots in early childhood. A number of studies have shown that children from very poor or deprived parental environments do not necessarily maintain depressed IQ scores. This is especially evident in children who have been removed from miserable circumstances. These children, who have suffered at least 6 or 7 years of deprivation, have very low IQs at discovery, but their scores increase dramatically to near normal after intervention. Koluchova studied twins who both had IQs of 40 at age 7 and IQs of 100 at age 14. Dennis found that Lebanese orphans (age 6) who were moved from a poor institution to a higher-quality one increased 30 points in IQ. Kagan similarly found Guatemalan village children who were extremely isolated and deprived as infants but performed normally (compared to U.S. children) at age 8. These studies imply that major environmental improvements in middle childhood can make up for earlier disadvantages. This does not mean deprivation has no effect. The differences may not be reflected in particular tests, or, as is often the case, social or personality problems develop (for example, Harrow's surrogate-raised monkeys were terrible mothers).

b. If the early years are the critical periods for development, then good development during these years should protect against later deprivations. Apparently there is little evidence that favorable early experiences act as insurance against poor later experiences.

c. It is not known whether early improvements in a child's familial circumstances have a greater effect than later improvements. Children adopted in later years do not improve as much intellectually as earlier-adopted children. Due to many factors, such as incomparable amount or length of deprivation and differences in parent-child interaction with a younger versus older adopted child, it is difficult to determine just what causes less advancement in the older child.

Clearly, at all ages of childhood, environmental factors associated with parents (mothers in particular) can affect intellectual performance. The amount of effect and the actual cause of the effect are not known.

References

Hunt, J. McV. (1979). Psychological development: Early experience. *Annual Review of Psychology*, 103-143.

Kagan, J., Klein, R. E., Finley, G., Rogoff, B., & Nolan, E. (1979). A cross-cultural study of cognitive development. *Monographs of the Society for Research in Child Development*, (5 Serial No. 180).

Rutter, M . (1979). Maternal deprivation, 1972-1978: New findings, new concepts, new approaches. *Child Development*, <u>50</u>, 283-305.

LECTURE TOPIC 1.4: HISTORICAL PERSPECTIVES

A brief history of attitudes toward children is generally interesting and shocking to most students. Medical writings before the seventeenth century rarely mentioned specific treatment for children. The health of children was the responsibility of midwives, not physicians. Physicians appeared content with this separation; children did not seem to respond to medical treatment anyway (for example, blood letting, purges, and changes in climate). We do not have much information on infant mortality prior to the eighteenth century when public records began to be kept. The statistics from England and Europe are quite appalling. Before 1750, the chances of a child living to be 5 years old were 3 to 1 against the child! In London, there was not a 50-50 chance of survival beyond the age of 5 until the end of the eighteenth century. Disease, infection, lack of cleanliness, and abandonment all contributed to the problem.

Abandonment has been documented as a tremendous problem in Paris. A foundling home was established by Vincent de Paul about 1640. Mothers from all over France began bringing their children to this *Hospice des enfants trouvés* because there were strict laws against infanticide and because they hoped that the children's chances of survival would be better there. In the mid-eighteenth century, one child was abandoned at the hospice for every three births registered in Paris. Grossly understaffed and unprepared for such numbers of children, foundling homes themselves became plagued by infant mortality. One of the worst recorded cases was at a foundling home in Dublin, where 10,272 infants were admitted between 1775 and 1800. Only 45 survived.

About this same time a letter was published by a physician, William Cadogan, in which he attempted to change some of the normal eighteenth-century practices of infant care. One practice was to wrap babies and often encase them in girdles with stays to keep their limbs straight. To keep them warm, mothers often wrapped newborn infants in layers of cloth equal to the weight of the infant. Another belief was that clean linen and swaddling cloths robbed the babies of nourishing juices. Cadogan suggested the revolutionary idea of removing excess wrapping and changing the baby at least once a day! One widespread general feeding practice was to give the baby at birth butter and sugar, a little oil, some spiced bread and sugar, and a warm drink of gruel mixed with wine or ale. Cadogan wrote that, for their first 3 months, infants needed nothing but their mother's milk.

In spite of attempts at reform, the mid-eighteenth century saw the growth of the factory system, which caused a tremendous demand for cheap labor. Children essentially became slaves, often working, eating, and sleeping at their machines. On Sunday, the only day the factories were closed, the children could be found, ragged and dirty, playing in the streets. Sunday schools were instituted to keep them out of the way and to save them for God.

In 1833, England finally passed a statute regulating child labor in spite of vigorous opposition by factory owners. This law limited the number of hours a child could work per week to 48 if they were between the ages of 9 and 13, and to 68 hours if they were between the ages of 13 and 18. A child younger than 9 was not to be employed at all. However, this applied only in cotton, woolen, and other factories. In the 1840s, children of 5 and 6 could be found working 14 hours a day in the coal mines. The excavations were commonly 2 to 3 feet high with little ventilation and such poor drainage that the children stood or crawled in mud and water to work.

Profound changes have occurred in the past 150 years. Medical science and laws to protect children have reduced the infant mortality rate and stimulated humane treatment of the developing child. But childhood as we now know it is of relatively recent origin.

References

Coontz, S. (1992). *The way we never were: American families and the nostalgia trap*. New York: Basic Books.

Kessen, W. (1965). *The Child*. New York: Wiley.

LECTURE TOPIC 1.5: A SECOND LOOK AT THE HISTORY OF CHILDHOOD

Lloyd deMause maintains that, "the history of childhood is a nightmare from which we have only recently begun to awaken. The further back in history one goes, the lower the level of child care, and the more likely children are to be killed, abandoned, beaten, terrorized, and sexually abused." deMause emphasizes the prevalence of child neglect and abandonment, abuse (both physical and sexual), infanticide, and exploitation. (Remember, however, that the historical records of childhood and child-rearing practices from before the eighteenth century are sparse and generally inspire much conjecture on the part of social historians.)

deMause has identified six modes of parent-child relations from antiquity to the present. Until the fourth century, *infanticide* was commonly practiced. Infanticide did not begin to be reduced until the Middle Ages, and the killing of illegitimate children, though unlawful, still occurs today. deMause believes that, in the period from the fourth to the thirteenth century, *abandonment* replaced infanticide as a common way in which parents related to their children. The abandonment included giving child-rearing responsibility for the care of the child to others as well as emotional abandonment at home. The mode that gained prominence during the period from the fourteenth to the seventeenth century deMause characterizes as *ambivalence*. During this third period, parents were advised that children were like clay forms that could be physically shaped by their parents. At the beginning of the eighteenth century there evolved an *intrusive mode* in which parents sought not only to physically shape the child but also to gain control of the child's will.

The fifth mode deMause proposes, the *socialization mode*, prevailed from the nineteenth century to the mid-twentieth century. According to deMause, "the raising of a child became less a process of conquering its will than of training it, guiding it into proper paths, teaching it to conform, socializing it." During this period of parent-child relations, the father began to assume a definite role.

In the mid-twentieth century, the present *helping mode* began. "The helping mode involves the proposition that the child knows better than the parent what it needs at each stage of its life, and fully involves both parents in the child's life as they work to empathize with and fulfill its expanding and particular needs. There is no attempt at all to discipline or form habits. Children are neither struck nor scolded, and are apologized to if yelled at under stress. The helping mode involves an enormous amount of time, energy, and discussion on the part of both parents, especially in the first six years, for helping a young child reach its daily goals means continually responding to it, playing with it, tolerating its regressions, being its servant rather than the other way around, interpreting its emotional conflicts, and providing the objects specific to its evolving interests. Few parents have yet consistently attempted this kind of child care." However, deMause is convinced that this approach "results in a child who is gentle, sincere, never depressed, never imitative or group oriented, strong-willed, and unintimidated by authority."

You should recognize that even though the historical record is slim, parents of earlier centuries were not all ignorant, mean-spirited, lacking in compassion, and continually abusing of their children. Indeed, some historical documents do record the kindness and affection of parents of earlier eras towards their children. The obvious fact is that, even though infant mortality rates were high until recent times, across the centuries the world's population increased as more and more children survived to adulthood. The social historians may not be able to agree on the conditions of these children's lives, but clearly progressive improvement in child-rearing practices supported the population increase.

References

Borstelmann, L. J. (1983) Children before psychology: Ideas about children from antiquity to the late 1800s. In W. Kessen (ed), *Handbook of child psychology: Vol 1. History, theory and methods*. New York: Wiley.

deMause, L.(1974). The evolution of childhood. In L. deMause (ed.), *The history of childhood*. New York: Harper & Row.

Pollock, L. (1983). *Forgotten children: Parent-child relations from 1500 to 1900*. Cambridge, England: Cambridge University Press.

DISCUSSION TOPICS
DISCUSSION TOPIC 1.1: PERIODS OF CHILDHOOD

When presenting the periods of childhood that are reviewed in the text, raise the issue of other periods that have been proposed. For example, Kenniston has proposed a stage of youth following adolescence that some people pass through on their way to adulthood. Is this a useful period to include? Does it help us better understand our development? Ask the class to speculate about what other periods may be added in the future. Retail merchants already aim advertising at the preteen group. Will this become a legitimate period in our lifetime?

DISCUSSION TOPIC 1.2: FOLKWAYS AND PARENTING ADVICE/ CROSS CULTURAL FOLKWAYS

Now, at the beginning of the course, is a good time to start dealing with the folk wisdom on how best to rear children that has been passed down from one generation to the next. Elicit from your class the common-sense information they know about children. If class members are slow to express themselves, offer the piece of advice that picking up the baby every time it cries will spoil the child. Almost everyone seems to believe this, although developmental studies have shown that babies who have caregivers who respond quickly and consistently to their cries actually cry less at 1 year of age than babies who are left to "cry it out." Discuss how folk wisdom comes into existence and how developmental studies may debunk some folk wisdom as myth but may confirm the value of other traditional pieces of advice to parents. This is a good time to compare subcultures in your region.

Examine the ways different subcultures explain child behavior. How would these beliefs influence the family's use of information received from the pediatricians, psychologist, or parenting class?

INDEPENDENT STUDIES
INDEPENDENT STUDY 1.1

Try to observe one or more examples of (a) an infant learning to walk, and (b) a teenage learning to drive. (If you cannot find examples to observe, think about examples you have observed in the past.) Compare the roles played by physical, cognitive, and psychosocial factors in each of these developmental milestones. How much influence does each of the three domains have on each milestone? In each case, is one domain more influential than he others, or are the three domains equally influential? Is the relative influence of the domains similar or different in the two situations?

INDEPENDENT STUDY 1.2

Thinking about your own life, give examples of the following kinds of influences: normative age-graded, normative history-graded, and nonnormative. How have these influences help make you the person you are today? Which of the three kinds of influences has been most important in your life? Compare your answers with those of one or two classmates. Discuss the normative history-graded influences you identified and determine whether there is a clear consensus about the defining historical events for your cohort.

CHOOSING SIDES
CHOOSING SIDES: SCIENTIFIC CHILD REARING

It has become folk wisdom in our society that, like the minister's son who becomes a determined hellion, the children of child psychologists and other experts on child development (professional or amateur) are half expected to become social and emotional misfits. The cause of this outcome is alleged to be the reliance of these "experts" on books and theories rather than common sense, religion, and tradition. The larger issue is whether the research findings of scientists and professionals should affect the way our society treats children. Students can consider this issue from historical, philosophical, religious, cultural, and scientific perspectives without having a great deal of expertise. An interesting and animated debate might arise over the following proposition: decisions concerning the education, training, and care of children should be based on scientific findings rather than on philosophy, religion, or personal feelings.

Pros: Children have often been victims of the whims of societal fashion and adult convenience. It is essential to establish the basics of child development through careful observation and controlled studies. Parents who know the medical, intellectual, familial, emotional, and other requisites for optimal growth can give the child the best opportunity for survival and a productive life. Current society, especially, needs rational decisions based on proven evidence as presented by individuals who specialize in the study and treatment of children.

Cons: The system of values governing society and the treatment of children by that society is the result of years of human experience. The ideals, religions, philosophies, and traditions of society are the most valuable guidelines for rearing children. Western civilization guarantees the freedom to follow diversified methods according to individual dictates. Scientific findings are often cyclical, contradictory, and limited in their scope. We simply do not know enough about the complexities of human behavior to make correct decisions on a scientific basis. By following the dictates of so-called experts, our society will experience confusion, the destruction of religious rights, and the establishment of pseudoscientific governing laws.

The following lists give arguments to support each side of the debate.

Pros: Scientific Guidelines
1. Superstitious behavior causes the mistreatment of children, especially those who have a deficiency or abnormality.
2. Better treatment of children is directly attributable to scientific advances that have bettered the overall human condition (for example, sanitation, machinery, and medicine).
3. Medicine and health care practices are primarily responsible for the increased survival rate of children (for example, vaccinations, pasteurization, and obstetrics).
4. Only through the scientific method can cause-and-effect relationships be proved.
5. The rights of children will be better protected if we know what is best for their development irrespective of religion, tradition, and laws.
6. Scientists, psychologists, physicians, and child-care professionals are better educated, more enlightened, and better able to weigh complex evidence to find the underlying principles that govern behavior.
7. Religions deny children the advantages of many modern advances in education (evolution theories), medicine (blood transfusions), and entertainment (dancing, music, etc.).

Con: Nonscience
1. The experts in child rearing and education do not agree about the correct ways in which to treat children.
2. Scientific studies of children will exploit them and their parents (for example, denying control groups special care and treatments).
3. Scientific facts are cold and not tempered by human feelings, traditions, and values.
4. It is too expensive and time consuming to investigate spurious research findings, complex human feelings, and diverse methods of treating children.
5. Modern society is not necessarily a better society because of scientific advances.
6. Implementation of scientific theories would infringe on human rights.
7. Scientific findings give general rules but cannot explain the exceptions to the rules.
8. When conducting research and interpreting findings, scientists cannot divorce themselves from the prevailing mood and trend of their own society, and are therefore biased.

References
Eckardt, G., Bringmann, W. G., & Sprung, L. (eds.) (1985). *Contributions to a history of developmental psychology*. Berlin: Mouton.
Gallagher, J. J. (ed.) (1987). *The malleability of children*. Baltimore, MD: Brookes.
Kessen, W. (1965). The Child. New York: Wiley.
Lerner, R. M. (ed.) (1983). *Developmental psychology: Historical and philosophical perspectives*. Hillsdale, NJ: Erlbaum.
Lomax, E., Kagan, J., & Rosenkrantz, B. (1978). *Science and patterns of child care*. San Francisco: Freeman.
Mussen, P. (ed.) (1983). *Handbook of child psychology*. New York: Wiley.

KNOWLEDGE CONSTRUCTION ACTIVITIES
KNOWLEDGE CONSTRUCTION ACTIVITY 1.1: GENERATIVE TERMS

This activity will use the principles of generative learning as explained in the introduction to assist students in gaining a better understanding of terms. Divide the class into groups of four or five. Assign each group the task of generating an example for a term from this chapter. The example that each group creates cannot be one that has been used in the class or in the book. They must think of a new application for the term that they are given. Groups are allowed to use their books and notes. By creating their own example of the term, they demonstrate an understanding of the term to the level of application. There are several approaches that can be used in this exercise. Students may be given the entire list at once, but often one group will finish far ahead of the others and topics will get out of sequence. Another strategy is to give all of the groups the same term to create an example and then go around the room to discuss outcomes. This has been very successful, but also takes the most time. A third approach is to give each group a different term and see what examples they can generate.

Some generative terms for Chapter 1
Quantitative change
Qualitative change

Physical development

Cognitive development

Psychosocial development

Maturation

Heredity effects

Cohort

Critical period

Plasticity

KNOWLEDGE CONSTRUCTION ACTIVITY 1.2:
DEVELOPMENTAL AUTOBIOGRAPHY

Have students write a developmental autobiography in which they trace their physical, intellectual, and personality/social/emotional development from conception through adolescence. This may be accomplished in several ways: (1) Students may share informally what they know and are willing to reveal about each of their developmental periods in class discussions or in small-group discussions. This will work best in classes where good rapport already exists. (2) Students may be asked to collect anecdotal records of their past development and mention them at appropriate times throughout the course. (3) Or the project may be undertaken as a major paper to be completed shortly before the end of the course, after a majority of the material that covers development to young adulthood has been presented. Students should be reassured that you do not have a voyeuristic interest in their personal lives, but that the project is a meaningful way to relate the content of the course to their individual lives. For some students this may be the first time that they learn about the circumstances of their prenatal development and early childhood. For others, particularly adoptees, information about their early development may not be possible to obtain. Students who do not wish to recount traumatic past experiences in their lives should under no circumstances be encouraged to do so. Generally students resist what appears to be a rather awesome task (especially older, returning students). Present the task in a positive light, and you will find that most students discover that it is a very rewarding project.

KNOWLEDGE CONSTRUCTION ACTIVITY 1.3: DEVELOPMENTAL LIFE-LINE

This activity can be used as a first day icebreaker. It helps students to conceptualize a lifespan approach to development Draw a long horizontal line on the chalkboard. On the left side, make a mark and ask students when development begins. They will probably respond either at birth or at conception. Mark the milestone on the line. Then go to the other end of the line and ask when development ends. Usually students say death, so mark that on the board. If someone suggests that there is development after death, suggest that the science of psychology only studies people up until death. Then hand the chalk to a student and ask him to put a developmental milestone on the line, anything they want, and then pass the chalk to another students. Continue passing the chalk until every student has had a chance to put a milestone on the lifeline. I have them give their names as they do it, and we talk about the nature of some of the milestones. After students have finished, I mark of the lifeline in terms of major stages, and ask students to categorize some of the milestones (some are biological, some dictated by social clock, some are idiosyncratic).

KNOWLEDGE CONSTRUCTION ACTIVITY 1.4: COHORT DIFFERENCES

To investigate cohort influences, assign small groups of students to interview different age groups about the history-graded influences of their generation. Age groups can start as young as 8 and 9 years olds and should go through old age. Students may generate lists of societal events from the past hundred years. When a common list has been formed, students should interview people in their assigned age group about how they have been influenced, and how much, by each of the events. Be sure to discuss not only the results of the interviews, but also the interviewing process as a research method. Have students compile the results to serve as a database for future class discussions and projects.

KNOWLEDGE CONSTRUCTION ACTIVITY 1.5:
TREASURE HUNT AT THE LIBRARY

Note: This activity will need to be revised or tailored to library resources available at specific institutions.

This assignment is designed to give students experience locating research articles and utilizing various resources available at the library.

1. Using an electronic database such as PsychInfo, how many "results" do you get when looking up *self-esteem*?

2. How many electronic databases are listed under Child Development and Family Studies on the library electronic resources page?

3. If you wanted to look up information on *influenza*, which database(s) would be most appropriate?

4. If you wanted to locate information about *infant mortality* rates in the United States, which would be the most appropriate database to use?

5. Using a database such as SocSciAbs you want to locate the number of abstracts listed pertaining to *genetic engineering*. How many do you find?

6. Using the library online catalog, locate all the books by Jean Piaget. How many did you find listed?

7. How many bibliographies does our library own about child development?

8. Using ERIC, how many "results" are there for *motivation*? What other databases might you use for this topic?

9. You have located an article you think will provide you with good information about your topic. Unfortunately our library does not own the journal it is in. Describe how you would proceed to get the article. Is there a charge for this service?

10. You have heard about the extensive collection our library has about children and learning. What hours are they open on Saturday?

11. Where can you find a copy of the most recent edition of *APA Publication Manual*? Is there an online version or resource for this available and if so how do you locate it?

12. There are a number of electronic journals available online. Locate the *Journal of Adolescence* April 1998 edition and you will discover there is an article in this issue about risk-taking patterns of female adolescents. How many participants provided information in this study? Print a copy of the abstract and attach it to this assignment.

13. You discover an article you want to read which is available at the library but is stored on microfilm. Can you make a copy of this article and if so, how much does it cost per page?

14. Identify the most weird, unusual, "they've got a journal about that!" journal title you can find.

7. RESOURCES FOR INSTRUCTORS

Books and Journal Articles

Kagan, J. (1984). *The nature of the child*. New York: Basic Books.

Miller, P.H. (1993). *Theories of developmental psychology; third edition*. New York: W.H. Freeman.

Mussen, P.H., editor. (1983). *Handbook of child psychology*. New York: John Wiley & Sons.

Video Resources
Title, date, and running time are given. Addresses for the video suppliers are in the front section of this manual.

Child development. (IM, 1992, video, 30 min.) Presents a historical overview of the contributions of Locke, Rousseau, Freud, Erikson, Bowlby, Watson, Gessell, Piaget, and modern theorists to the field of developmental psychology.

Culture, Time, and Place. (IM, 1992, 30 min.) Shows how language, school, and relationships bring about acculturation about attitudes, values, and beliefs.

Development and Diversity. (IM, 1992, 30 min.) Explores historical and cultural definitions of childhood. Probes the prolongations of infancy and childhood; looks at children in different countries.

Infancy to adolescence. (IM, 1990, video, 2 volumes, 60 min. each) David Hartman and eminent researchers in psychology, biology, anthropology, and sociology investigate major theories of human development.

2 *A CHILD'S WORLD:*

HOW WE DISCOVER IT

BASIC THEORETICAL ISSUES
Issue 1: Which Is More Important—Heredity or Environment?
Issue 2: Are Children Active or Passive in Their Development?
Issue 3: Is Development Continuous, or Does It Occur in Stages?
An Emerging Consensus
THEORETICAL PERSPECTIVES
Perspective 1: Psychoanalytic
Perspective 2: Learning
Perspective 3: Cognitive
Perspective 4: Ethological
Perspective 5: Contextual
How Theory and Research Work Together
RESEARCH METHODS
Sampling
Forms of Data Collection
Basic Research Designs
Developmental Research Designs
Ethics of Research

In this chapter of your Instructor's Manual You Will Find:
1. Total Teaching Package Outline
2. Expanded outline (transparency-ready)
3. Guideposts for study
4. Learning Objectives
5. Key terms
6. Teaching and Learning Activities
    Lecture Topics
    Discussion Topics
    Independent Studies
    Choosing Sides
    Knowledge Construction Activities
7. Resources for Instructors

1. Total Teaching Package Outline

Chapter 2: A Child's World: How We Discover It

BASIC THEORETICAL ISSUES	Guidepost for study 2.1, 2.2 Learning objectives 2.1, 2.2
Issue 1: Which is More Important—Heredity or Environment?	Lecture topic 2.3
Issue 2: Are Children Active or Passive in Their Development?	Guidepost for study 2.2
Issue 3: Is Development Continuous, Or Does It Occur in Stages?	Guidepost for study 2.2
An Emerging Consensus	Lecture topic 2.1
THEORETICAL PERSPECTIVES	Guidepost for study 2.3 Discussion topic 2.1
Perspective 1: Psychoanalytic	Learning objective 2.3
Perspective 2: Learning	Learning objectives 2.4, 2.5, 2.6, 2.7
Perspective 3: Cognitive	Learning objectives 2.8, 2.9, 2.10, 2.11, 2.12, 2.13
Perspective 4: Ethological	Learning objective 2.14
Perspective 5: Contextual	Learning objective 2.15, 2.16, 2.17
How Theory and Research Work Together	Knowledge construction activity 2.8
RESEARCH METHODS	Guidepost for study 2.4 Learning objective 2.18 Discussion topic 2.2 Knowledge construction activity 2.2
Sampling	Learning objective 2.21 Knowledge construction activities 2.5, 2.7
Forms of Data Collection	Learning objective 2.19

Basic Research Designs	**Discussion topic 2.2, 2.3, 2.4** **Knowledge construction activity 2.6**
Developmental Research Designs	**Learning objective 2.20** **Lecture topic 2.2** **Knowledge construction activity 2.4**
Ethics of Research	**Guidepost for study 2.5** **Learning objective 2.21** **Independent study 2.1** **Discussion topic 2.2** **Choosing Sides 2.1** **Knowledge construction activity 2.3**

Please check out the online learning center located at www.mhhe.com/papaliacw9 for further information on these and other topics. There you can also access downloadable PowerPoints tailored to each chapter of the text and containing useful teaching notes as well as images and tables from the text itself

2. EXPANDED OUTLINE (TRANSPARENCY READY)

I. Basic Theoretical Issues and Development
  A. Theory
  B. Hypothesis
  C. Issues
    1. Heredity or environment
    2. Active or passive
    3. Continuous or stages
II. Models of Development
  A. Mechanistic
  B. Organismic
III. Theoretical Perspectives
  A. Psychoanalytic
    1. Psychosexual theory (Freud)
      a. Stages of development: oral, anal, phallic, latency, genital.
      b. Parts of personality: id, ego, superego.
    2. Psychosocial theory (Erikson)
      a. Eight stages of development
  B. Learning
    1. Behaviorism
      a. Classical conditioning (Pavlov, Watson)
      b. Operant conditioning (Skinner)
        i. Positive reinforcement
        ii. Negative reinforcement
        iii. Punishment
    2. Social Learning (Bandura)
      a. Social cognitive
      b. Observational learning

C. Cognitive
    1. Cognitive stage theory (Piaget)
        a. Organization
        b. Schemes
        c. Adaptation
           i. Assimilation
           ii. Accommodation
        d. Equilibration
    2. Information-processing
        1. Mental processes
    3. Cognitive neuroscience
D. Ethological (Bowlby)
    1. Biology and evolution
E. Contextual
    1. Bioecological (Bronfenbrenner)
        a. Microsystem, mesosystem, exosystem, macrosystem, chronosystem
    2. Sociocultural (Vygotsky)
        a. Zone of proximal development
        b. Scaffolding
IV. Research Methods
  A. Scientific method
    1. Operational definitions
  B. Sampling
    1. Sample
    2. Population
  C. Data Collection
    1. Self-reports
        a. Journals
        b. Interviews
        c. Questionnaires

2. Behavioral and Performance Measures
   a. Tests
      i. validity
      ii. reliability
      iii. standardization
3. Observations
   a. Naturalistic
   b. Laboratory
D. Basic Research Designs
   1. Case study
   2. Ethnographic study
   3. Correlational study
      i. Positive and negative
   4. Experiment
      i. Causation
      ii. Experimental group
      iii. Control group
      iv. Independent variable
      v. Dependent variable
E. Developmental research designs
   1. Longitudinal
   2. Cross-sectional
   3. Sequential
F. Ethics
   1. Beneficence
   2. Respect
   3. Justice

3. GUIDEPOSTS FOR STUDY

2.1 What purposes do theories serve?

2.2 What are three basic theoretical issues on which developmental scientists differ?

2.3 What are five theoretical perspectives on child development, and what are some theories representative of each?

2.4 How do developmental scientists study children, and what are some advantages and disadvantages of each research method?

2.5 What ethical problems may arise in research on children?

4. LEARNING OBJECTIVES

Upon completing the study of this chapter, the student should be able to:

2.1 State three basic issues regarding the nature of child development.

2.2 Contrast the mechanistic and organismic models of development

2.3 Describe psychoanalytic perspectives on development, contrasting the theories of Freud and Erikson.

2.4 Identify the chief concerns, strengths, and weaknesses of the learning perspective.

2.5 Describe the differences between classical and operant conditioning, giving an example of each.

2.6 Distinguish among positive reinforcement, negative reinforcement, and punishment, giving an example of each.

2.7 Compare behaviorism and social learning (social-cognitive) theory and generate examples of observational learning.

2.8 Contrast Piaget's assumptions and methods with those of classical learning theory.

2.9 List three interrelated principles that bring about cognitive growth, according to Piaget, and generate an example of each.

2.10 Identify the contributions and criticisms of Piaget's theory.

2.11 Describe what information-processing researchers do and tell three ways in which such research can be applied.

2.12 Tell how Case's theory draws from both Piaget and the information-processing approach.

2.13 Explain how brain research can contribute to the understanding of cognitive processes.

2.14 Tell what kinds of topics ethological researchers study and generate potential uses of their methods.

2.15 Name Bronfenbrenner's five systems of contextual influence and give examples of each.

2.16 Explain how Vygotsky's central focus differs from Bronfenbrenner's and Piaget's.

2.17 Tell how Vygotsky's theory applies to educational teaching and testing.

2.18 Compare the use and drawbacks of case studies, ethnographic students, correlational studies, and experiments.

2.19 Distinguish among laboratory, field, and natural experiments.

2.20 List advantages and disadvantages of longitudinal, cross-sectional, and cross-sequential research.

2.21 Name three principles that govern decisions about inclusion of participants in research.

5. KEY TERMS

Theory
Hypothesis
Mechanistic model
Organismic model
Psychoanalytic perspective
Psychosexual development
Psychosocial development
Learning perspective
Learning
Behaviorism
Classical conditioning
Operant conditioning
Reinforcement
Punishment
Social-learning theory
Observational learning
Cognitive perspective
Organization
Schemes
Assimilation
Accommodation
Equilibration
Information-processing approach
Cognitive neuroscience approach
Ethological perspective
Contextual perspective
Bioecological theory
Microsystem, mesosystem, exosystem, macrosystem, chronosystem
Sociocultural theory
Zone of proximal development
Scaffolding
Scientific method
Sample
Operational definitions
Naturalistic observation
Laboratory observation
Case study
Ethonographic study
Participant observation
Correlational study

6. TEACHING AND LEARNING ACTIVITIES

LECTURE TOPICS

LECTURE TOPIC 2.1: PRESENTING RESEARCH ON HUMAN DEVELOPMENT

It would be impossible to present everything that has been surmised and investigated concerning human development in one course. One of the primary problems is the prodigious amount of social science research relevant to human development. There has been an explosion in research interest in human development. The Society for Research in Child Development publishes the *Child Development Abstracts and Bibliography*, a collection of abstracts of research and scholarly articles covering the life span up through adolescence. In 1962, this journal searched an already impressive 133 journals for appropriate articles. In 1979, the same abstracting journal had to search 293 international journals in order to adequately present references to literature on child development. Similarly research in the life-span segments beyond adolescence is booming. There is no way a single textbook and a single course can adequately summarize the diversity of the research and the complexity of the conclusions. Therefore, the instructor must impress on the student the enormity of the task, the satisfaction of searching for the "truth," and the challenge of applying what we think we know. Students should finish this course wanting to know more about their unfolding lives and wanting to continually update their reading.

Fortunately for textbook authors, instructors, and students alike, the scientific study of human development is relatively recent (beginning in the late 1800s), and human characteristics and behavior have not changed markedly since that time (one need only read the Bible, Greek drama, and Shakespeare to realize this). It is interesting to compare the work of early researchers such as G. S. Hall with current work in developmental psychology. Hall and his colleagues at Clark University, between 1894 and 1915, circulated numerous questionnaires to gather data about the developmental problems of that time. The following are examples of the breadth and variety of their questionnaire studies: anger, dolls, the early sense of self, peculiar and exceptional children, moral education, religious experience, adolescence and its phenomena in body and mind, memory, motor education, mathematics in the early years, education of women, dreams, the language interest in children, motherhood, emotional reactions to the moon, children's ideas of death, and the junior high school. Although more sophisticated research methodologies have been developed since Hall's time, and each decade has its research fads, most of these topics (couched in current jargon) are still fervently researched.

The answers to all the questions about human development are not available in the current research literature, but we do know a great deal more than Hall and his associates and have a great many more questions. A survey of the major journals--*Child Development, Developmental Psychology*, and *Monographs of the Society for Research in Child Development*--from January 1979 to March 1980, roughly classified approximately 300 articles into basic categories of research themes. The themes, clearly reflected in the Papalia and Olds chapter topics, include cognitive processes/abilities, language processes, physical development, socialization /personality/ affect, and teaching/education. The most common topics in cognitive processes (a total of 132 articles) were perception (45), logic-reasoning, categorizing (29), and memory (18). Language processes (23) focused mainly on semantics--meaning (14). Physical development and teaching/education had relatively few articles (15). The largest number of studies were in socialization/personality/affect (136), including child interaction with peer, parent, and adult (35), moral development (20), achievement (14), prosocial behavior/ altruism/ cooperation (15), and emotion/anxiety/fears (14). Of course, specialized journals focus on more specific or even different topics. But the general overlapping with topics important in Hall's day is clear. Most conspicuous in its absence is religion. Perhaps in the next few years we will see a reemergence of investigation on that topic.

References

Child development abstracts and bibliography. (1962-1963, pp. 36-37, pp. 236-238) and (1979, p. 53, XXIV-XXVII).

Garbarino, J. (1992) *Children and families in the social environment.* New York: Aldine deGruyter.

Lomax, E., Kagan, J., & Rosenkrantz, B. (1978). *Science and patterns of child care.* San Francisco: Freeman.

LECTURE TOPIC 2.2: TERMAN'S LONGITUDINAL STUDY OF HIGH-IQ CHILDREN

No longitudinal studies compare in length and uniqueness than to the study started by Lewis Terman in 1921. Using his newly devised Stanford-Binet intelligence test in 1922, Terman tested 250,000 students in California and selected 1,528 of them for his study of "genius." These 3 to 19-year-old students had IQs above 135. Terman wanted to demonstrate that "early ripe, early rot" was not true for the intellectually gifted. His early studies clearly demonstrated that the sample, on the whole, had better school performance, social adjustment, athletic prowess, and health than their contemporaries. They were definitely a unique group. Not only were they from the top 1 percent in terms of IQ, but the sample also had characteristics not shared by the general population. For example, too high a proportion were from white middle-class and professional families, and all were from California. Also, they experienced the Depression and World War II. Nevertheless, repeated testings over nearly 60 years reveal some interesting life-span findings about intelligence and development.

In 1960, a comparison was made between the 100 most successful (A group) and the 100 least successful (C group) men. In general, members of the A group were richer, healthier, and better emotionally and socially adjusted. In the investigator's effort to find predictors of differences in these middle-aged men, several early characteristics seemed important. For example, in grade school, members of the A group skipped more grades and graduated early from high school. They also tended to join more clubs, participate in sports, and be involved in more activities such as hobbies and collecting. The A group came from more advantaged families; there were fewer parental divorces, and the parents encouraged independence and accomplishment. Members of the A group and C group focused on persistence as a reason for their success or relative failure. Members of the A group sought higher education and were more likely to become professionals.

Interestingly, the richest of the groups tended to have the least amount of formal education.

In 1972, the entire sample was asked to reflect on what gave them the most satisfaction in life: occupation, family life, friendship, richness of cultural life, service to society, or their overall joy in living. The men had different responses in comparison to the women. The men rated family life number one in providing satisfaction, followed by occupational satisfaction. This is somewhat surprising, considering the higher amount of ambition and worldly skill possessed by these men. Also interesting is the tendency for the men in earlier career points to rate occupation number two, whereas in later career, joy in living was rated two rather than three. Friends, cultural life, and service were consistently rated four, five, and six, respectively. Rating family number one was best predicted by a happy home life as a child; a favorable attitude toward the father seemed especially important. Approximately 70 percent of the men had unbroken marriages--comparable to the national norms at 60 years of age. The approximately 21 percent who were divorced tended to remember unhappy conflicts with parents during childhood. Most of the men valued and wanted a happy family. Interestingly, having a working wife correlated with having a less happy family.

The women agreed that the family was their number-one satisfaction. However, occupation was rated number five. Instead, friends, joy, and culture were rated two, three, and four, respectively. Friends and cultural richness were especially more important to the women than the men. In general, for the women as well as the men, money was not the source of life satisfaction; but remember they were above the national median on income. Those women who were satisfied with their parents and early lives tended to be satisfied at later stages and had consistently good self-concepts. Fewer than half of the women worked. However, at age 62 almost all the women said they would have liked to work except when raising children. Career women (having a career was best predicted by high math ability in school and ambition) showed a very strong, high satisfaction with life. Almost the opposite of a representative national sample, the working women who were single were the most satisfied, followed by childless married women, divorced women, married women with children, and widows. Families seemed to become less important prerequisites for satisfaction. However, in terms of general happiness, married women with or without children were the happiest.

Robert Sears (himself a Terman subject) and Pauline Sears are carrying on three analyses of the sample. An exhaustive comparison of earlier data and data collected in 1977 is not yet completed. Overall, the achievement of the Terman sample is impressive and has definitely eliminated the belief that extreme scores on the IQ test have no predictive value. Yet, it must be remembered that although the group on the whole did well, the IQ test did not predict those who did comparatively poorly. In addition, from among the 1,528 "geniuses," no recognized Nobel prize winner, Picasso, or Mozart has emerged.

References

Coleman, D. (February, 1980) 1,528 little geniuses and how they grew. *Psychology Today*, 28-43.

Sears, P. S., & Barbee, A. H. (1978). Career and life satisfaction among Terman's gifted women. In *The Gifted and the creative: Fifty-year perspective*. Baltimore: Johns Hopkins Press.

Terman, L. M. (1925). Mental and physical traits of a thousand gifted children. In L. M. Terman (Ed.), *Genetic studies of genius*, vol. 1. Palo Alto, CA: Stanford University Press.

Terman, L. M., & Oden, M. H. (1947). The gifted child grows up. In L. M. Terman (Ed.), *Genetic studies of genius*, vol. 4. Palo Alto, CA: Stanford University Press.

LECTURE TOPIC 2.3 HEREDITARY INFLUENCES ON BEHAVIOR

A large body of recent human behavioral genetic research indicates that individual differences in behavioral development are substantially influenced by hereditary factors. The following are a sampling of studies investigating different behaviors.

Two longitudinal studies of cognitive development, the Louisville Twin Study and the Colorado Adoption Project, have found that genetic influences on IQ scores increase significantly during childhood and that genetic influences on IQ during early childhood correlate highly with genetic influences on adult IQ.

In the area of mental retardation, recent research has focused on the chromosomal condition known as the fragile X syndrome. Fragile X syndrome is important because it is inherited as a recessive trait. This means that females with two X chromosomes have a buffer if only one X chromosome is defective, whereas males with a fragile X chromosome have no buffer and are at risk. Fragile X syndrome is estimated to be the second most common chromosomal cause of mental retardation and a major reason for the higher levels of mild mental retardation observed in males.

Another area of research has been the inheritance of attitudes and beliefs. Traditionalism, the tendency to follow rules and authority, to believe in high moral standards, and to believe in strict discipline, was found in studies of twins reared together and apart to have a substantial genetic influence.

For additional summaries of recent research, see Plomin and McClearn, 1993.

References

Defries, J. C., Plomin, R., & LaBuda, M. C. (1987). Genetic stability of cognitive development from childhood to adulthood. *Developmental Psychology* 23, 4-12.

Martin, J. B., Eaves, L. J., Heath, A. C., Jardine, R., Feingold, L. M., & Eysenck, H. J. (1986). Transmission of social attitudes. *Proceedings of the National Academy of Sciences 83*, 4364-4368.

Nussbaum, R. L.,& Ledbetter, D. H.(1986) Fragile X syndrome: A unique mutation in man. *Annual Review of Genetics 20,* 109-145.

Plomin, R. (1988). The nature and nurture of cognitive abilities. In R. J. Sternberg (Ed.), *Advances in the psychology of human intelligence* (Vol. 4, pp. 1-33), Hillsdale, NJ: Erlbaum.

Plomin, R. (1989). Environment and genes: Determinants of behavior. *American Psychologist 44*, 105-111.

Plomin, R. & McClearn, G.E. (Eds), (1993). *Nature, Nurture & Psychology*. Washington, D.C.: American Psychological Association.

30

Tellegen, A., Lykken, D. T., Bouchard, T. J., Wilcox, K., Segal, N., & Rich, S. (1988). Personality similarity in twins reared apart and together. *Journal of Social and Personality Psychology 54*, 1031-1039.

Wilson, R. S. (1983). The Louisville Twin Study: Developmental synchronies in behavior. *Child Development 54*, 298-316.

DISCUSSION TOPICS

DISCUSSION TOPIC 2.1: DEVELOPMENTAL PERSPECTIVES

If most of the students have previously taken an introductory psychology class, present the different perspectives as a review lesson. Divide the class into groups of three or four students and ask them to list names, terms, and facts that they associate with each perspective. You could also include a biological perspective for added discussion of heredity and environmental factors. After allowing adequate time for this exercise, investigate which perspectives the students are most familiar with and why. Conclude with a discussion of the similarities and differences among the perspectives.

DISCUSSION TOPIC 2.2: METHODS FOR STUDYING CHILD DEVELOPMENT/ ETHICS OF RESEARCH

Although each of the theoretical perspectives inspires different questions and research techniques, the principles of the scientific method are critical to any scientific inquiry.

There are two major methods for studying people: nonexperimental and experimental. Nonexperimental studies depend upon observation of people in natural settings, with no effort to alter behavior. The nonexperimental methods include the case study, naturalistic observation, laboratory observation, interviews, the clinical method, and correlational studies. Experimental studies can be divided into three types: laboratory experiments that are very controlled; field experiments in which a change is introduced in a familiar setting, and natural experiments involving naturally occurring events that cannot ethically be produced, such as malnutrition. These three types of experimental studies differ in the degree of control by the researchers and the extent to which the findings are generalizable.

The two major methods of data collection are longitudinal designs and cross-sectional designs. Because each has advantages and disadvantages, cross-sequential designs have been developed to try to overcome the drawbacks of the other two methods.

In studying children, investigators must consider certain ethical issues and balance possible effects on participants with potential benefit to the field of child development. Major ethical issues include the right to privacy, the right to informed consent, and the right to self-esteem.

DISCUSSION TOPIC 2.3: LIMITATIONS OF CORRELATIONAL STUDIES.

A very good example of the dangers and limitations of psychological research is the Bettleheim work on the causes of infantile autism. Bettleheim was a proponent of the psychoanalytic perspective and strongly believed that the parent-child interaction had a great influence on the child's psychological development. He began to study the causes of infantile autism, a disorder in which the child is severely limited in ability to respond to the environment. What he observed was that the mothers of these infants seemed cold and distant in their interactions with their babies. They did not seem to show the warmth, connectedness, and love that a "normal" mother would display. Bettleheim labeled these women "refrigerator mothers" and concluded that this detached parenting style was the cause of infantile autism. Because of Bettleheim's stature in psychology, initially this work was well received. Upon closer analysis, however, there were a number of problems in the structure of the research. Eventually more scientific studies revealed that infantile autism is actually influenced by genetics. There is a very high concordance rate among monozygotic twins and far more males are affected with infantile autism than females. Bettleheim, in inferring causation from a correlation and without firm, rigorous experimentation to control for other variables, caused a number of parents to feel needless guilt and pain because they had been led to believe that they were responsible for their child's abnormality.

DISCUSSION TOPIC 2.4: QUESTIONABLE CORRELATIONS

Often in class the limitations of correlational results can be pointed out by using examples of correlations that are obviously not causational. One that demonstrates this would be the correlation between the number of elephants in American cities and the number of murders in those cities. Are the elephants really causing the murders? Another that works is the rate of ice cream consumption per capita and the crime rate per capita in American cities. Does eating ice cream cause criminal behavior or could there be another factor influencing both?

INDEPENDENT STUDIES

INDEPENDENT STUDY 2.1: ETHICAL RESEARCH

Have individual class members create a list of topics, age groups, and behaviors they think that developmental psychologists cannot ethically investigate. Then have the students compare their lists for similarities and differences. The more homogeneous your student population, the more similar the lists should be. The differences can be used to illustrate the value differences that exist in our society which effects researchers in human development.

CHOOSING SIDES

CHOOSING SIDES 2.1: ETHICS AND ANIMAL RIGHTS

Harold Herzog suggests summarizing at least two arguments often used by animal rights activists. The utilitarian argument uses the principle of equality to oppose the use of animals in research. The second argument is that at least some nonhuman animals have fundamental rights.

This argument is based on inherent value and respect for animals. To facilitate thinking about these issues, Herzog has students decide which of the following hypothetical research projects should be conducted. Students are to imagine that they are on the Institutional Review Board or the committee for Animal Care and Use at their university and they must provide rationales for which experiments can be conducted and why. If done in groups, they should be encouraged to reach consensus rather than a majority vote.

Case 1: Dr. Howard is a psychobiologist working on the frontiers of a new and exciting research area of neuroscience, brain grafting. Research has shown that neural tissue can be removed from the brains of monkey fetuses and implanted into the brains of monkeys that have suffered brain damage. The neurons seem to make the proper connections and are sometimes effective in improving performance in brain-damaged animals. These experiments offer important animal models for human degenerative diseases such as Parkinson's and Alzheimer's. Dr. Howard wants to transplant tissue from fetal monkey brains into the entorhinal cortex of adult monkeys; this is the area of the human brain that is involved with Alzheimer's disease.

   The experiment will use 20 adult rhesus monkeys. First, the monkeys will be subjected to ablation surgery into the entorhinal cortex. This procedure will involve anesthetizing the animals, opening their skulls, and making lesions using a surgical instrument. After they recover, the monkeys will be tested on a learning task to make sure their memory is impaired. Three months later, half of the animals will be given transplant surgery. Tissue taken from the cortex of monkey fetuses will be implanted into the area of the brain damage. Control animals will be subjected to sham surgery, and all animals will be allowed to recover for 2 months. They will then learn a task to test the hypothesis that the animals having brain grafts will show better memory than the control group.

   Dr. Howard argues that this research is in the exploratory stages and can only be done using animals. She further states that by the year 2000 about 2 million Americans will have Alzheimer's disease and that her research could lead to a treatment for the devastating memory loss that Alzheimer's victims suffer.

Case 2: Dr. Fine is a developmental psychobiologist. His research concerns the genetic control of complex behaviors. One of the major debates in his field concerns how behavior develops when an animal has no opportunity to learn a response. He hypothesizes that the complex grooming sequence of mice might be a behavior pattern that is built into the brain at birth, even though it is not expressed until weeks later. To investigate whether the motor patterns involved in grooming are acquired or innate, he wants to raise animals with no opportunity to learn the response. Rearing animals in social isolation is insufficient because the mice could teach themselves the response. Certain random movements could accidentally result in the removal of debris. These would then be repeated and could be coordinated into the complex sequence that would appear to be instinctive but would actually be learned. To show that the behaviors are truly innate, he needs to demonstrate that animals raised with no opportunity to perform any grooming like movements make the proper movements when they are old enough to exhibit the behavior.

Dr. Fine proposes to conduct the experiment on 10 newborn mice. As soon as the animals are born, they will be anesthetized and their front limbs amputated. This procedure will ensure that they will not be reinforced for making random grooming movements that remove debris from their bodies. The mice will then be returned to their mothers. The animals will be observed on a regular schedule using standard observation techniques. Limb movements will be filmed and analyzed. If grooming is a learned behavior, then the mice should not make grooming movements with their stumps as the movements will not remove dirt. If, however, grooming movements are innately organized in the brain, then the animals should eventually show grooming-like movement with the stumps.

In his proposal, Dr. Fine notes that experimental results cannot be directly applied to human behavior. He argues, however, that the experiment will shed light on an important theoretical debate in the field of developmental psychobiology. He stresses that the amputations are painless and the animals will be well treated after the operation.

KNOWLEDGE CONSTRUCTION ACTIVITIES

KNOWLEDGE CONSTRUCTION ACTIVITY 2.1: GENERATIVE TERMS

This activity will use the principles of generative learning as explained in the introduction to assist students in gaining a better understanding of terms. Divide the class into groups of four or five. Assign each group the task of generating an example for a term from this chapter. The example that each group creates cannot be one that has been used in the class or in the book. They must think of a new application for the term that they are given. Groups are allowed to use their books and notes. By creating their own example of the term, they demonstrate an understanding of the term to the level of application. There are several approaches that can be used in this exercise. Students may be given the entire list at once, but often one group will finish far ahead of the others and topics will get out of sequence. Another strategy is to give all of the groups the same term to create an example and then go around the room to discuss outcomes. This has been very successful, but also takes the most time. A third approach is to give each group a different term and see what examples they can generate.

Some generative terms for Chapter 2
Classical conditioning
Operant conditioning
Positive reinforcement
Negative reinforcement
Punishment
Observational learning
Assimilation
Accommodation
Case study
Ethnographic study
Sample
Population

KNOWLEDGE CONSTRUCTION ACTIVITY 2.2: POPULARIZED RESEARCH

Have students review parenting magazines and other popular magazines to collect examples of popularized research in human development. Each student should bring two or three articles from different sources to class. Analyze these articles in terms of:

a. Informational value to parents, educators, the public, and so on.
b. General topics or themes shared by articles.
c. Distribution across the three theories of human development defined in the text: learning theory, cognitive, and psychoanalytic.
d. General viewpoints on the nature-nurture controversy.
e. Reliance on scientific findings to support conclusions. If possible, determine the methodology of the studies (naturalistic observation, survey, experiment, etc.).
f. Validity of conclusions and advice in the article.
g. Age span involved.

KNOWLEDGE CONSTRUCTION ACTIVITY 2.3: ETHICS

Have students investigate the ethical standards, if any, established for research at their particular institution. Is there a review board to determine whether proposed research projects meet ethical criteria? What ethical criteria are used? How do they compare with the published guidelines from the National Commission for the Protection of Human Subjects of Biomedical and Behavioral Research, or from the American Psychological Association's Committee on Ethical Standards in Psychological Research.

KNOWLEDGE CONSTRUCTION ACTIVITY 2.4:
OBSERVING CHILDREN'S BEHAVIOR

Assign students to observe and compare children's behavior in different settings such as in a shopping mall, at a park, at a preschool, and on public transportation. Ask the students to look for similarities and differences in behavior across the settings. In class, discuss with the students the problems associated with conducting effective, naturalistic observational studies.

KNOWLEDGE CONSTRUCTION ACTIVITY 2.5:
THE NORMAL CURVE AND COMPILING DATA

To help students understand how the normal curve is established and how to collect data, an exercise that is effective is as follows. Divide the class into groups of two. Working in pairs, each group flips a coin 10 times. One student flips the coin, while the other student keeps a record of how many times heads comes up out of the ten flips. Repeat this at least four times for each group of students. It does not hurt to bring a bag of pennies into class for this exercise. After the flips are completed, eleven people in the class are assigned the task of tallying the results. Each person is assigned a number from 0 to 10. They are to compile the total number of times that the number they are assigned came up in the tallying. When these data are compiled, display them on the board in the form of a frequency polygon or a histogram. As you are aware, probabilities are that 5 out of 10 will be the most common finding, and the further that you get from 5, the less frequent the occurrence of that event.

KNOWLEDGE CONSTRUCTION ACTIVITY 2.6: EXPERIMENTAL METHOD

To illustrate the procedures and challenges of using the experimental method, propose a hypothesis and allow time for small groups to design an experiment to test it. A good hypothesis to test is that classrooms that are too hot have a negative effect on student learning. Students will have to consider operational definitions as they specify what they mean by too hot and learning. Have students list their variables, experimental group, and control group. How can extraneous variables be controlled so that at the end to the experiment, causation can be established?

KNOWLEDGE CONSTRUCTION ACTIVITY 2.7:
TEACHING ABOUT SAMPLING USING M & M'S

Bring to class a small package of plain M & M's (snack size) for each student. If students are told to bring calculators to class it will be easier for them. Students should be told that their M&M's are an "intact random sample." Instruct them to open the package and count the contents by color. You might caution them against premature mortality from consumption! Have them convert their raw data into percentages. Ask each student to generate a hypothesis about the distribution of plain M&M's based on their sample. Then have students form pairs or small groups and pool their data. Finally, pool the data for the entire class.

Typically, this demonstration is an effective way to show how larger samples are more accurate. Mars, Inc. published information that states plain M&M's are 30% brown, 20% each red and yellow, and 10% each green, orange, and blue.

Reference
Smith, R.A. (1999). A tasty sample(r): Teaching about sampling using M& M's. In Benjamin, L.R., Nodine, B.F., Ernst, R.M., & Broeker, C.B. (Eds.), *Activities handbook for the teaching of psychology, Vol. 4*. Washington, D.C.: American Psychological Association.

KNOWLEDGE CONSTRUCTION ACTIVITY 2.8: CONTEXTUALIZING THEORIES

In order to develop meaningful comparisons between theoretical perspectives, ask students to consider the historical contexts in which each emerged. Divide students into small groups and provide them with important dates and historical events for each of the perspectives; i.e., founding of Wundt's experimental laboratory, publication date for Freud's Interpretation of Dreams, the 1938 publication of Skinner's The Behavior of Organisms: An Experimental Analysis, George Miller's research of the 1950's, and the separate but parallel existences of Jean Piaget and Lev Vygotsky. Students will discuss how the historical events of the times influenced the development of each perspective.

KNOWLEDGE CONSTRUCTION ACTIVITY 2.9: TESTING PROVERBS

By either using the proverbs listed below or using one of your own, formulate a testable hypothesis based on the meaning of the proverb. Discuss what theory you think would best support your hypothesis and, discuss how you might design a study to test the hypothesis. Identify the following components of research as they apply to your study.

1. Hypothesis:

2. Type of study:

3. Independent variable:

4. Dependent variable:

5. Experimental group:

6. Control group:

7. Sampling method:

Potential research topics
All you need is love
Like father like son
One bad apple spoils the barrel
Can't teach an old dog new tricks
Blood is thicker than water
Opposites attract
The early bird catches the worm
http://www.cj.5c.com/ Famous Proverbs
http://www.bartleby.com/99/index.html Bartlett's Book of Quotations
http://www.smackem.com/quotes/index2.html The quotation site

7. RESOURCES FOR INSTRUCTORS

Books and Journal Articles

Abelson, R.P. (1995). *Statistics as principled argument.* Hillsdale, NJ: Erlbaum.

Campbell, D.T. & Stanley, J.C. (1963). *Experimental and quasi-experimental designs for research.* Boston: Houghton Mifflin.

Cook, T.D. & Campbell, D.T. (1979). *Quasi-experimentation: Design and analysis issues for field settings.* Boston: Houghton Mifflin.

Damon, W. & Lerner, R. (2000). Theoretical models of human development. *Handbook of Child Psychology, Vol.1.* New York: Wiley

Meltzoff, J. (1998). *Critical thinking about research: Psychology and related fields.* Washington, D.C.: American Psychological Association.

Miller, P.H. (1993). *Theories of developmental psychology; third edition.* New York: W.H. Freeman.

Slife, B. D. & Williams, R.N. (1995). *What's behind the research? Discovering hidden assumptions in the behavioral sciences.* Sage: London.

Stanovich, K.E. (1998). *How to think straight about psychology.* New York: Longman.

Turkewitz, G. & Devenny, D.A. (Eds.) (1993). *Developmental time and timing.* Hillsdale, NJ: Erlbaum.

Vygotsky, L.S. (1978). *The mind in society: The development of higher psychological processes.* Cambridge, MA: Harvard University Press.

Video resources

Learning. (IM, 1990, 30 min.) Presents information about classical and operant conditioning. A special focus is material on helping hyperactive children with operant conditioning

B. F. Skinner on behaviorism. (IM, 1977, video, 28 min.) B. F. Skinner discusses behavior modification, behavioral technology, and the uses of positive reinforcement in shaping human behavior.

Cognitive Development. (IM, 1990, 30 min.) Focuses on Piaget's theory and criticisms of that theory to describe stages of cognitive development. Looks at development of thought, reasoning, memory, and language.

Erik Erikson: A Life's Work. (Davidson, 1991, 38 minutes). Uses biography and interviews to introduce Erikson's theory. Best known for his identification of the eight stages of the life cycle, Erikson spent a lifetime observing and studying the way in which the interplay of genetics, cultural influences, and unique experiences produce individual human lives.

Everybody rides the carousel. (YU, 1982, approximately 25 min.). Describes Erikson's theory of life-span personality development.

Freud: The hidden nature of man. (IM, 1970, video, 29 min.) Using dramatized interviews with Sigmund Freud, this video assesses the psychologist's theories of psychoanalysis, the Oedipus complex, the unconscious, and the id, ego, and superego.

Piaget's Developmental Theory: An Introduction. (Davidson, 1989, 25 min.) Using both archival photographs of Dr. Piaget and newly shot footage of Dr. Elkind conducting interviews with children of varying ages, this film presents an overview of Piaget's developmental theory, its scope, and content. This video can serve as an introduction to Piaget's work or a review of it.

The Ecology of Development. (IM, 1992, 30 minutes) Profiles children of 12 families in five countries to illustrate the influence of family, peers, school, culture, and history on development. Defines the terms of Bronfenbrenner's ecological theory.

Vygotsky's Developmental Theory: An Introduction. (Davidson, 1994, 28 min.) With Deborah Leong, Ph.D. and Elena Bodrova, Ph.D. The video illustrates four basic concepts integral to his work: Children construct knowledge, learning can lead to development, development cannot be separated from its social context, and language plays a central role in cognitive development.

Research methods. (IM, 1975, video, 35 min.) This program addresses the impact psychological research can have on the average person. It explains what sound scientific research methods are and what makes these methods so important.

Research Methods for the Social Sciences. (IM, 1995, no time given) Covers types of experimental designs and their uses; deals with basic features of experiments as well as clinical, correlation, and field methods. Lays out 7 steps of the scientific method, interpretation of data, and ethical issues.

Statistics: Decisions through Data, Part 1. (IM, 1992, 3 volumes, 60 min. each) Basic descriptive statistics, their calculations, and various graphing methods. Uses graphics and animation to integrate real work examples. Includes a discussion of correlation.

Statistics: Decisions through Data, Part 2. (IM, 1992, 2 volumes, 60 min. each) Experimental design; discusses causation and sampling; deals with confidence intervals and statistical significance.

3

FORMING A NEW LIFE: CONCEPTION, HEREDITY, AND ENVIRONMENT

BECOMING PARENTS
Conception
What Causes Multiple Births?
Infertility

MECHANISMS OF HEREDITY
The Genetic Code
What Determines Sex?
Patterns of Genetic Transmission
Genetic and Chromosomal Abnormalities
Genetic Counseling and Testing

NATURE AND NURTURE: INFLUENCES OF HEREDITY AND ENVIRONMENT
Studying the Relative Influences of Heredity and Environment
How Heredity and Environment Work Together
Some Characteristics Influenced by Heredity and Environment

In This Chapter of Your Instructor's Manual You Will Find:
1. Total Teaching Package Outline
2.   Expanded outline (transparency-ready)
3. Guideposts for study
4. Learning Objectives
5. Key terms
6. Teaching and Learning Activities
        Lecture Topics
        Discussion Topics
        Independent Studies
        Choosing Sides
        Knowledge Construction Activities
7. Resources for Instructors

1. Total Teaching Package Outline

Chapter 3: Forming a New Life: Conception, Heredity, and Environment

Becoming parents	
Conception	**Guidepost for study 3.1** **Learning objective 3.1** **Knowledge construction activity 3.2**
What causes multiple births?	**Guidepost for study 3.2** **Learning objective 3.2**
Infertility	**Guidepost for study 3.3** **Learning objective 3.3** **Discussion topics 3.1, 3.2** **Knowledge construction activity 3.3** **Box 3.1 (textbook p. 52)**
Mechanisms of heredity	
The genetic code	**Guidepost for study 3.4** **Learning objective 3.4** **Lecture topics 3.1, 3.2** **Knowledge construction activity 3.1**
What determines sex?	**Learning objective 3.4** **Choosing sides 3.1**
Patterns of genetic transmission	**Learning objective 3.4** **Lecture topic 3.3**
Genetic and chromosomal abnormalities	**Guidepost for study 3.5** **Learning objective 3.5** **Independent study 3.1** **Box 3.2 (textbook p. 63)**
Genetic counseling and testing	**Learning objective 3.5** **Choosing sides 3.2** **Knowledge construction activity 3.5**
Nature and nurture: Influences of heredity and environment	
Studying the relative influences of heredity and environment	**Guidepost for study 3.6** **Learning objective 3.6**
How heredity and environment work together	**Guidepost for study 3.7** **Learning objective 3.7** **Knowledge construction activity 3.6**
Some characteristics influenced by heredity and environment	**Guidepost for study 3.7** **Learning objective 3.8**

Please check out the online learning center located at www.mhhe.com/papaliacw9 for further information on these and other topics. There you can also access downloadable PowerPoints tailored to each chapter of the text and containing useful teaching notes as well as images and tables from the text itself.

2. EXPANDED OUTLINE (TRANSPARENCY READY)

I. Becoming Parents
  A. Conception
  B. Clone
  C. Fertilization
  D. Zygote
      1. Dizygotic twins
      2. Monozygotic twins
          a. Temperament
  E. Infertility

II. Mechanisms of Heredity
  A. Deoxyribonucleic acid
  B. Genetic code
  C. Chromosomes
  D. Genes
  E. Human genome
  F. Genetic transmission
      1. Autosomes
      2. Sex chromosomes
      3. Alleles
      4. Homozygous
      5. Heterozygous
      6. Dominant inheritance
      7. Recessive inheritance
      8. Quantitative trait loci
      9. Multifactorial transmission
      10. Phenotype
      11. Genotype

III. Birth Defects and Disorders
   A. Mutations
   B. Natural selection
   C. Sex-linked inheritance
   D. Down syndrome
   E. Genetic counseling

IV. Heredity and Environment
   A. Behavioral genetics
   B. Heritability
   C. Concordant
   D. Reaction range
   E. Canalization

3. GUIDEPOSTS FOR STUDY

3.1 How does conception normally occur and how have beliefs about conception changed?
3.2 What causes multiple births?
3.3 What causes infertility and what are alternative ways of becoming parents?
3.4 What genetic mechanisms determine sex, physical appearance, and other characteristics?
3.5 How are birth defects and other disorders transmitted?
3.6 How do scientists study the relative influences of heredity and environment and how do heredity and environment work together?
3.7 What roles do heredity and environment play in physical health, intelligence, and personality?

4. LEARNING OBJECTIVES

After completing the study of this chapter, the student should be able to:
3.1 Describe conception.
3.2 Discuss multiple births, including the degree of genetic overlap in monozygotic and dizygotic twins.
3.3 List three causes of infertility and two alternative ways of becoming parents.
3.4 Explain the process of genetic transmission of traits, including dominant, recessive, sex-linked, and multifactorial inheritance.
3.5 Give an example of an inherited birth defect and explain how such a defect is transmitted. Discuss how genetic counseling can help parents make reproductive decisions.
3.6 Describe methods used in the study of behavioral genetics.
3.7 Define and give an example for reaction range, genotype-environment interaction, genotype-environment correlation (or covariance), and niche-picking.
3.8 Discuss the relative contributions of heredity and environment to obesity, temperament, intelligence, longevity, and schizophrenia.

5. KEY TERMS

Clone
Fertilization
Zygote
Dizygotic twins
Monozygotic twins
Temperament
Infertility
Deoxyribonucleic acid (DNA)
Genetic code
Chromosomes

Genes
Human genome
Autosomes
Sex chromosomes
Alleles
Homozygous
Heterozygous
Dominant inheritance
Recessive inheritance
Quantitative trait loci

Multifactorial transmission   Sex-linked inheritance
Phenotype   Down syndrome
Genetype   Genetic counseling
Mutations   Genetic testing
Natural selection

6. TEACHING AND LEARNING ACTIVITIES
LECTURE TOPICS
LECTURE TOPIC 3.1: ABNORMAL SEX CHROMOSOME PATTERNS
Present the following conditions to illustrate chromosomal patterns.

Kleinfelter's syndrome: Some males have an XXY pattern or an additional X chromosome. Physical characteristics include above average height and long arms and legs. Other physical characteristics includes possible breast development during puberty, a high-pitched voice, and light beard growth. Sometimes intellectual functioning is impaired and Kleinfelter males are sterile.

Turner's syndrome: Some females are missing the Y chromosome and have an XO pattern. Physical characteristics include a short and immature appearance, webbed necks, eyelid fold, receding chins, and a broad chest. Supplemental estrogen therapy during adolescence does stimulate breast development and other secondary sex characteristics though Turner females are sterile. There is little or no impairment in intellectual ability and some show above average IQ.

The double Y syndrome: About 1 out of every 1000 males has an extra Y chromosome or an XYY pattern. This phenomenon first attracted attention when it was reported that a disproportionate segment of the prison population were XYY men, and it was rumored that this syndrome led to increased violence. Current evidence indicates that the rate of violent crimes for the double Y syndrome men is lower than that for other prison inmates. It is associated with intellectual impairment and height that exceeds even that of Kleinfelter's syndrome.

Reference
Berch, D., & Bender, B. (1987, December). Margins of sexuality. *Psychology Today*, 54-57.

LECTURE TOPIC 3.2: DOWN SYNDROME
Since 1866 when Langdon Down first made medical records of what has sometimes been known as mongolism, much genetic, medical, and psychological research has focused on this syndrome. Although the exact cause of the chromosomal aberration responsible for the condition is not known, it is known that 97 percent of the cases are due to chance abnormalities during meiosis, the production of gametes. It is thought that, for some reason, chromosome 21 duplicates itself twice instead of once, does not divide properly when forming the gamete, or does not assemble into the correct cluster of chromosomes. As a result, an individual with Down syndrome receives from one parent a duplicate chromosome 21, resulting in a condition known as

trisomy 21. Apparently this cause of Down syndrome is usually due to abnormalities in the mother's ovum. The syndrome occurs in all races equally (and in chimpanzees). As early as 10 years after Down's 1866 report, it was noted that mothers who are older when they bear children are more likely to have children with Down syndrome. Thus suspicion centers on aging effects and the meiotic process in females. Before birth, the number of possible ova is fixed in the ovaries. In addition, meiosis has partially occurred and is interrupted until just before ovulation. Thus a 45-year-old woman has ova that have been held in suspension at a very critical stage of chromosomal division for 45 years. Although the Down syndrome attributable to these causes cannot be traced through family histories or predicted in any other way, mothers who are older also have a greater recurrence risk (about 3 times the risk of a mother of the same age who has not had a Down child).

There is a second way in which Down syndrome occurs: It can be caused by genetic transmission by the sperm as well as the ovum. This accounts for the other 3 percent of affected children. Due to a structural abnormality in chromosomes called translocation, males as well as females can receive abnormal chromosome 21. They show no physical abnormalities. A karyotype of these individuals can reveal that they carry only 45 functioning chromosomes. When the sperm and ova are produced, some will contain duplicate chromosome 21 and thus increase the risk of having Down syndrome children. Interestingly, female carriers of this genetic problem have a higher proportion of Down syndrome children than do male carriers.

Though not all affected children have the same physical characteristics, there are usually enough telltale characteristics to make syndrome diagnosis correct. The following are often present: epicanthic fold, a fold of skin above the tear duct; hypotonia, a relaxed condition of the muscles (often evident in the face); a large, furrow-surfaced tongue that often protrudes because the mouth cavity is smaller than normal; small stature, somewhat chubby; flat face with broad nose; stumpy hands that may have a straight crease across the palm (simian crease); irregular, abnormal set of teeth; sparse pubic hair; malformed ears; a gap between the first and second toes; and heart or other internal defects. Most affected children used to succumb to illness (usually respiratory infection) in the first year. Mainly due to antibiotics, many now survive until their late twenties and some until age 40 or 50 or older. Of the aging Downs population, a larger percentage have Alzheimer's disease, which has led to the discovery of genes on the 21st pair being linked to this disorder.

Today the Down syndrome child's most severe handicap is his or her mental retardation. Most individuals (60-70 percent) are either severely retarded (IQ = 25-49) or profoundly retarded (25-40 percent: IQ = 0-24). However, some have normal or above-average intelligence and can perform school work adequately. It is reported that one exceptional individual became an admiral in the British navy. These children are often quite affectionate and good humored, which is fortunate for them because they require a great deal of care and expensive medical attention from sympathetic others. However, personality differences make each person unique. They benefit greatly from home care but do cause considerable strain on the family.

References

Hartl, D. L. (1977). *Our uncertain heritage: Genetics and human diversity.* New York: J. B. Lippincott.

Horgan, J. (June 1993). Eugenics revisted. *Scientific American.*

Smith, D. W., & Wilson, A. A. (1973). *The child with Down syndrome*. Philadelphia: Saunders.

LECTURE TOPIC 3.3: GENETIC ENGINEERING

The use of genetic engineering to affect offspring is not new. In the broadest sense, genetic engineering is the passive or active attempt to systematically control the regeneration of organisms. Marrying a tall man instead of a short one will have genetic consequences, as will aborting a fetus that is found to be abnormal. The current implications of advances in genetic engineering can be better understood by looking at the wide variety of techniques involved.

Eugenics, or selective breeding, is the process whereby phenotypic characteristics are changed by selectively mating parents to obtain desired gene combinations. Most domestic animals and hybrid "miracle plants" are obtained in this manner. In theory, this method is equally applicable to humans. We could definitely increase desirable traits, such as intelligence, in children. However, societal norms of what is desirable change. And furthermore, encouraging one trait may make the human more susceptible to other dangers, such as disease. Certain high-yield grains are highly vulnerable to disease because common genetic heritage and inbreeding have reduced hetero-geneity. A recent product of selective breeding is featherless chickens—economically valuable, but biologically vulnerable.

Sperm banks freeze and store sperm. It is a simple process to impregnate the female artificially with this sperm. An infertile father's physical characteristics may be matched as closely as possible with the characteristics of a donor. Or a semisterile male may store his sperm until enough is collected for fertilization. Or a father who plans to have a vasectomy may store sperm in the event that he later wants children. It would be possible to store gametes from exceptional individuals, such as Nobel Prize winners, and generate more such individuals.

Sex determination is somewhat controllable because of the differing weight characteristics of X and Y sperm. Y sperm apparently swim faster because they carry less genetic material; so after a miniature test-tube race, they could be separated from the X sperm. Unfortunately, many chromosomally aberrant sperm have either one more or one fewer chromosome and thus (because of mass differences) might also be concentrated in numbers by such techniques.

Test-tube fertilization involves combining the sperm and the egg in a culture outside of the womb and then inserting the zygote in the mother's uterus. This technique has already proved successful and is in great demand by persons who otherwise could not have children. Objections to the technique include the "unnaturalness" of the procedure and the possible volunteer destruction of the zygote before implantation if it did not have the desired genotypic characteristics. Complete development of the fetus in a test tube is improbable because of the enormous complexity of the prenatal environment. Parthenogenesis is the process in which a single cell without fertilization produces a new individual. Such pregnancies do not occur in humans. However, this process does occur in plants and can be caused in turkeys.

Cloning is the process wherein an ordinary somatic nucleus is stimulated to produce a new individual. This new individual will have exactly the same genetic makeup as the original. If it were possible, this precise control of the genetic similarity of individual humans would certainly allow scientists to solve the nature-nurture controversy. Having copies made of yourself would not only appeal to egotistic tendencies but would also make available perfect donors for nonrejectable organ transplants. By removing the nucleus of a frog egg and replacing it with the cell nucleus of an adult frog, scientists have produced clones in the laboratory. It is also feasible to divide a zygote before cell specialization has occurred and let the resultant cells develop into identical individuals (the same basic process of monozygotic twinning).

Euphenics is the changing of the phenotype by altering the early developmental processes. By having brain cells divide one more time, investigators can double the number of neurons in the brain. Abnormal development due to drugs (such as thalidomide) or other factors could be reversed. There already is some evidence that mothers who take male hormones during pregnancy have girls who perform better on IQ tests.

Most recently it has become possible to actually change chromosomal structure and perform gene surgery. For example, it is possible to put a human gene on the chromosome of a bacterium. This is now being done to identify the location and functions of genes on the chromosomes. The implication is that it may become possible to remove defective genes or improve DNA in existing ones and thus rid humankind and the gene pool of genetic defects. However, the danger of uncontrollable mutant viruses and other organisms arising from such research has led scientists to voluntarily restrict and even abandon much research in this area.

Some other processes include in vitro implantation into a surrogate mother. Women may have a fertilized egg from a donor female implanted (this allowed a woman over age 60 to become pregnant in Italy in 1992).

Some of the horrifying processes described in Huxley's *Brave New World* are becoming feasible. Society must decide where genetic research should be directed and what values should guide it. Scientists are already expressing grave concerns. Students should learn the possibilities and become prepared to make some decisions on moral issues.

References

Huxley, A. (1946). *Brave new world.* New York: Harper & Row.

Karp, L. (1976). *Genetic engineering: Threat or promise*? Chicago: Nelson-Hall.

Wray, H., Sheler, J., & Watson, T. (March 10, 1997). The world after cloning. *US News & World Report.*

Zimmerman, B. K. (1984). *Biofuture: Confronting the genetic era.* New York: Plenum Press.

DISCUSSION TOPICS

DISCUSSION TOPIC 3.1: INFERTILITY: ON THE RISE?

The ending section of the chapter examines the issue of infertility and the technology that has developed to counteract it. Investigate with your class additional reasons for the rise in infertility in our present society. Has the declining birthrate and the rise in the number of couples who actively choose not to have children simply made us more sensitive to those couples with fertility problems? Were the estimates of infertility in the past inaccurately low because there were no services or advanced technology to help those individuals and they therefore told no one of their difficulties? Are there social and psychological factors that lead to infertility as well as the physical ones mentioned in the text? Is our society more stressful, and is a result of this stress infertility? Is there any relationship between changing gender roles for men and women and the rate of infertility?

DISCUSSION TOPIC 3.2: THE AVAILABILITY OF REPRODUCTIVE TECHNOLOGY

With infertility rates at their highest recorded levels, the demand for access to modern reproductive technologies is also great. Explore with your students the ethical and socioeconomic concerns surrounding this issue. Currently, the procedures are expensive. Should they be made available only to those with the ability to pay for them? How much coverage should be provided by medical insurance? Should access be limited only to childless offspring? Should single individuals be allowed to use the modern technologies to sire or bear offspring? Who is liable if the baby conceived by way of modern technology has a birth defect?

INDEPENDENT STUDIES

INDEPENDENT STUDY 3.1

Select three of the genetic and chromosomal abnormalities mentioned in this chapter. Try to include one or more abnormalities with cognitive as well as physical effects. Then, using your favorite search engine, explore the World Wide Web to identify support groups or organizations for parents whose children have these particular abnormalities. On the basis of the information you find in the Web pages for these organizations, compare the psychosocial impacts of the three abnormalities you have chosen. Are similar or different issues highlighted for each?

CHOOSING SIDES

CHOOSING SIDES 3.1: SELECTING THE GENDER OF THE FETUS

Technology has developed many methods for sex determination. Divide the class into two groups and have them discuss the pros and cons of such practices. Encourage cross-cultural information such as the one-baby rule of China and the preference for girls in India.

Pros:
1. Allows X or sex-linked disorders to be controlled by choosing girls
2. Reduces world population—fertility rates are based on the number of fertile females, so the reduction of female births will control population
3. Allows choices and might reduce negative consequences for unwelcome gender

Cons:
1. Allows girl fetuses to be aborted at high rate
2. Encourages sexist practices
3. Encourages abortion for socially questionable purposes

CHOOSING SIDES 3.2: FETAL RIGHTS

Propose the following scenario to the class: A young woman has been arrested for the third time for the use of cocaine. At that time she is 4 months pregnant. Law enforcement officials are trying to decide whether or not to incarcerate her for the remainder of her pregnancy. Their reasoning is that she is abusing her child by taking the drugs, and by keeping her in detention, they are preventing the child abuse.

Do the authorities have the right to intervene? Put students in groups of four or five to discuss this issue. Each group is to come to a consensus, then present their argument to the rest of the class. The following background material may be helpful.

Background material

Back in 1973 the *Roe v. Wade* decision affirmed the legality of abortion and stated that U.S. law never saw the fetus as a legal person. It did, however, allow states to protect the fetus during the last trimester because the fetus was then viable. This aspect of the *Roe v. Wade* decision has led to many legal battles over fetal rights.

In most areas of medical treatment, the courts have been giving patients more rights. Adults can refuse medicines, surgery, and blood transfusions. Yet under the concept of protecting potential human life, some courts are acting as "enforcers" of doctors' prenatal orders. Some doctors have gotten court orders that force women to have cesarean sections that they don't want for reasons ranging from fear of surgery and religious objections to disagreement with the doctor's position. Those who object to this intervention by the courts believe it consists of treating pregnant women as though they were incapable of making choices and were mere carriers of the fetus.

The medical profession can keep a brain-dead woman's body alive for weeks using life-support systems so that a fetus is able to survive after a cesarean section. So far, this has been done only when the family wishes: How would the courts rule if the family did not want life-support systems used? Should laws be passed that would exclude pregnant women from "natural death" statutes?

Legal issues abound. Some advocates of fetal rights favor the passage of legislation allowing doctors to require what they believe is necessary fetal surgery. Others want to make it a criminal offense to smoke or drink during pregnancy. At the same time, parents are not legally required to risk their own lives (for instance, by donating one of their organs) for their born children. In another arena, the Michigan highest court allowed a father to sue the mother of their son because a drug she took during pregnancy discolored the son's teeth.

In the workplace, some jobs are barred to all women of childbearing years because of some hazard. Critics make two points here. First, why do we bar women from well-paying careers instead of making the working conditions safe? Second, why has this been done only for well-paying positions while we let nurses and x-ray technicians be exposed to radiation?

One final area of concern is in criminal cases. Many state courts allow "wrongful death" lawsuits when a fetal death has been caused by a negligent third party, such as during a car accident. In an emotional case in 1981, Robert Hollis decided his wife shouldn't have a child. He forcibly disrupted her pregnancy and destroyed the fetus. Because the fetus was then in its 29th week, it was viable. Hollis was indicted for first-degree assault against his wife and first-degree murder of the fetus. The question is whether the fetus is a person who can be murdered. The circuit court judge said no, but the appeals court ruled yes; because of viability, states can regulate protection for the third-trimester fetus. In 1983 the Kentucky Supreme Court ruled no because the unborn have never been considered persons under the homicide act. Some individuals, however, are pushing for "feticide laws." They claim that society has both emotional and ethical obligations toward the fetus, and they believe that these obligations should be translated into fetal rights.

Reference

Gallagher, J. (September 1984). The fetus and the law: Whose life is it anyway? *Ms.*, 62-66, 134, 135.

KNOWLEDGE CONSTRUCTION ACTIVITIES

KNOWLEDGE CONSTRUCTION ACTIVITY 3.1: GENERATIVE TERMS

This activity will use the principles of generative learning as explained in the Introduction to assist students in gaining a better understanding of terms. Divide the class into groups of four or five. Assign each group the task of generating an example for a generative term from this chapter. The example that each group creates cannot be one that has been used in the class or in the book. They must think of a new application for the term that they are given. Groups are allowed to use their books and notes. By creating their own example of the term, they demonstrate an understanding of the term to the level of application. There are several approaches that can be used in this exercise. Students may be given the entire list at once, but often one group will finish far ahead of the others and topics will get out of sequence. Another strategy is to give all of the groups the same term to create an example and then go around the room to discuss outcomes. This has been very successful, but also takes the most time. A third approach is to give each group a different term and see what examples they can generate.

Some generative terms for Chapter 3 are listed below.

Homozygous	Phenotype
Heterozygous	Genotype
Dominant inheritance	Natural selection
Recessive inheritance	Sex-linked inheritance
Multifactorial transmission	Reaction range

KNOWLEDGE CONSTRUCTION ACTIVITY 3.2: CHOOSING PARENTHOOD

Would I make a good parent? As the text points out, the impact of pregnancy can be tremendous. The decision to have a child is one of the most important decisions a person can make. Consider some of the following questions in terms of the stressful impact childbearing could have.

a. Do I like doing the things parents generally do?

b. Would I expect my child to take care of me in my old age?

c. Could I find happiness in teaching and guiding a child, a teenager, or a young adult?

d. Am I financially able to support a child?

e. Would a child interfere with my freedom or educational plans?

f. Would I be willing to devote a large part of 18 years of my life to being a parent?

g. Could I accept and love a child who was physically or mentally abnormal?

Reference

Questions are adapted from Am I Parent Material? a pamphlet available from the National Organization for Non-Parents, 3 North Liberty St., Baltimore, MD 21201.

KNOWLEDGE CONSTRUCTION ACTIVITY 3.3:
INFERTILITY OPTIONS: ADOPTION

Some couples choose not to have children because of the risk of genetic abnormalities. Other couples are infertile and cannot have children. Have students investigate the option of adoption for such persons. In your state, what are the legal requirements for adoption? Who can adopt a child? Are there standards for age, weight, health, and so on, of the parents? Can single persons adopt? Must there be a racial match between parent and child? What is the availability of infants, older children, minority-group children, and handicapped children?

KNOWLEDGE CONSTRUCTION ACTIVITY 3.4:
INFERTILITY OPTIONS AND EMBRYO RIGHTS

A recent divorce case involved legal questions about frozen embryos. While married, the couple had attempted to have children. They finally availed themselves of modern reproductive techniques in which conception was achieved outside the womb. Several of the resulting embryos were frozen, awaiting the future needs of the couple. The legal questions focused on who had rights to the embryos when the marriage was dissolved. Assign students to research the topic and to prepare pro and con arguments for a debate. Several debates can be held in class, or a competition among written "position papers" could be held to judge the various arguments.

KNOWLEDGE CONSTRUCTION ACTIVITY 3.5:
GENE/ENVIRONMENT INTERACTION

The following exercise is to demonstrate the connection between genotype-environment interaction, genotype-environment correlation, and niche-picking. First, assign students to groups of four or five and assign each person to write down an example of a positive environmental factor that played a major role in the direction that his or her life took. After students have written down the environmental factor, ask them to identify any abilities or talents that they have that may have influenced them to be involved in that environment. Students in groups will share ideas. For example, a musical student may have taken a trip to Washington DC with the school band, and thereby became interested in government, ultimately majoring in political science. Arguably, without a musical talent (genetic influence) the student might have never made that trip.

KNOWLEDGE CONSTRUCTION ACTIVITY 3.6:
THINKING ABOUT GENETIC TESTING

If you were going to have a baby, would you want to know in advance the sex of the child?

Genetic testing allows people to discover a lot of information about their children before those children are even born. But not everyone wants to know everything!

Get together with three to four other students in a group. Construct a set of situation cards for each group member and decide where and how you will collect your data. Because of the sensitive nature of some of the scenarios, you might limit your participants to people that you know well.

> **Directions for situation cards:** Place the following information on ten 3 x 5 index cards:
>
> Your baby is likely to grow up to be very neurotic (anxious).
> Your baby is likely to be very extroverted.
> Your baby is likely to be autistic.
> Your baby is likely to be a genius.
> Your baby is like to be a genius and neurotic (anxious).
> Your baby is likely to be musically very talented but also likely to be poor at verbal tasks.
> Your baby is likely to be just average.
> Your baby is likely to be dyslexic.
> Your baby is likely to grow up to be just like you.

Ask your participants to read the diagnosis aloud and then asked if their child-rearing practices would change knowing this information in advance. Would they try to alter some outcomes more than others? Take notes on the responses you get from participants.

When you return to your group, compile your responses by diagnosis. How much influence do people think that the environment has? How much influence derives from genetics?

Based on your findings, what do you think people believe about genetic predisposition and the effect of the environment? What do you think about the value of prenatal diagnosis for the kinds of situations described in the cards?

Reference
Ely, R. (1999). Bringing genetic screening home. In L. R. Benjamin, B. F. Nodine, R. M. Ernst, & C. B. Broeker (eds.), *Activities handbook for the teaching of psychology* (vol. 4), Washington, DC: American Psychological Association.

RESOURCES FOR INSTRUCTORS

Books and Journal Articles

Glazer, E.S. & Cooper, S.L. (1988). *Without child: Experiencing and resolving infertility.* New York: Lexington.

Greer, G. (1984). *Sex and destiny: The politics of human fertility.* New York: Harper & Row.

Halpern, S. .(January/February 1989). Infertility: Playing the odds. *Ms*, 147-151.

Hartmann, B. (1987). *Reproductive rights and wrongs.* New York: Harper & Row.

Sandelowski, M. (1993). *With child in mind: Studies of the personal encounter with infertility.* Philadelphia: University of Pennsylvania Press.

Tietze, C., Henshaw, S. K., & the Alan Guttmacher Institute (1986). *Induced abortion: A world review,* 6th ed. New York: The Alan Guttmacher Institute

Video resources

Developmental phases before and after birth (FFHS, 1994, video, 30 min.). This program examines the development of the fetus in utero and the child during the first year.

Fetal rights (FFHS, 1994, video, 28 min.). An examination of the obligations of the mother to her unborn child and her rights to privacy and control over her own body.

Genetic counseling I and II: Heredity and birth defects and amniocentesis (MF, 11 min. each). Presents basic genetic principles, human inheritance, and genetic counseling techniques.

Genetic screening (FFHS, 1994, video, 26 min.). The role of genetic screening in detecting abnormalities in adult genes, which in turn can predict whether genes in a child might be affected.

Genetics (FFHS, 1994, video, 30 min.). The medical advances and the ethical issues developing from the human genome project.

Heredity and prenatal development (CRM, 25 min.). Diagrams and drawings showing meiosis, fertilization, and prenatal development. Film also briefly discusses genetic and environmental factors in personality development.

4 *PREGNANCY AND PRENATAL DEVELOPMENT*

PRENATAL DEVELOPMENT: THREE STAGES
Germinal Stage (Fertilization to 2 weeks)
Embryonic Stage (2 to 8 weeks)
Fetal Stage (8 weeks to birth)

PRENATAL DEVELOPMENT: ENVIRONMENTAL INFLUENCES
Maternal Factors
Paternal Factors

MONITORING PRENATAL DEVELOPMENT
Prenatal Assessment
Prenatal Care

In This Chapter of Your Instructor's Manual You Will Find:
1. Total Teaching Package Outline
2. Expanded Outline (transparency-ready)
3. Guideposts for Study
4. Learning Objectives
5. Key Terms
6. Teaching and Learning Activities
    Lecture Topics
    Discussion Topics
    Independent Studies
    Choosing Sides
    Generative Learning Activities
7. Resources for Instructors

1. TOTAL TEACHING PACKAGE OUTLINE

Chapter 4: Pregnancy and Prenatal Development

Prenatal development: Three stages	
Germinal stage (fertilization to 2 weeks)	**Guidepost for study 4.1** **Learning objective 4.1** **Discussion topic 4.1** **Knowledge construction activity 4.1**
Embryonic stage (2 to 8 weeks)	**Guidepost for study 4.1** **Learning objective 4.2, 4.3** **Discussion topic 4.1** **Knowledge construction activity 4.1**
Fetal stage (8 weeks to birth)	**Guidepost for study 4.1, 4.2** **Learning objective 4.4** **Discussion topic 4.1** **Knowledge construction activity 4.1**
Prenatal development: Environmental influences	
Teratogens	**Guidepost for study 4.3** **Learning objective 4.6** **Lecture topics 4.3, 4.4** **Knowledge construction activity 4.1, 4.2, 4.3, 4.4** **Choosing sides 4.1**
Maternal factors	**Guidepost for study 4.3** **Learning objectives 4.5, 4.7** **Lecture topics 4.1, 4.2, 4.3** **Box 4.1 (textbook p. 81)**
Paternal factors	**Guidepost for study 4.3** **Learning objective 4.8** **Knowledge construction activity 4.1**
Monitoring prenatal development	
Prenatal assessment	**Guidepost for study 4.4** **Learning objective 4.9** **Knowledge construction activity 4.2** **Independent study 4.1** **Box 4.2 (textbook p. 89)**
Prenatal care	**Guidepost for study 4.4** **Learning objective 4.10** **Knowledge construction activity 4.1, 4.5**

Please check out the online learning center located at www.mhhe.com/papaliacw9 for further information on these and other topics. There you can also access downloadable PowerPoints tailored to each chapter of the text and containing useful teaching notes as well as images and tables from the text itself.

2. EXPANDED OUTLINE (TRANSPARENCY READY)

I. Prenatal Development
   A. Cephalocaudal principle
   B. Proximodistal principle
II. Stages of Development
   A. Germinal stage
   B. Embryonic stage
      1. Spontaneous abortion
   C. Fetal stage
      1. Fetal activity, sensory development, and memory
III. Environmental Influences
   A. Teratogenic Influences
      1. Drugs
      2. Alcohol
         a. fetal alcohol syndrome
      3. Nicotine
      4. Caffeine
   B. Maternal nutrition
IV. Sexually Transmitted Diseases
   A. Acquired Immune Deficiency Syndrome
V. Prenatal Assessment
   A. Ultrasound
   B. Amniocentesis
   C. Chorionic villus sampling
VI. Parental Factors
   A. Maternal Age
   B. Paternal factors
VII. Outside Environmental Hazards
   A. Chemicals
   B. Radiation

3. GUIDEPOSTS FOR STUDY

4.1 What are the three stages of prenatal development and what happens during each stage?

4.2 What can fetuses do?

4.3 What environmental influences can affect prenatal development?

4.4 What techniques can assess a fetus' health and well-being and what is the importance of prenatal care?

4. LEARNING OBJECTIVES

After completing the study of Chapter 4, the student should be able to:

4.1 Identify two principles that govern physical development and give examples of their application during the prenatal period?

4.2 Describe how the zygote becomes an embryo.

4.3 Explain why defects and miscarriages are most likely to occur during the embryonic stage.

4.4 Describe findings about fetal activity, sensory development, and memory.

4.5 Summarize recommendations concerning an expectant mother's diet and physical activity.

4.6 Describe the short-term and long-term effects on the developing fetus of a mother's use of medical drugs, alcohol, tobacco, caffeine, marijuana, opiates, and cocaine during pregnancy.

4.7 Summarize the risks of maternal illness, delayed childbearing, and exposure to chemicals and radiation.

4.8 Identify three ways in which environmentally caused defects can be influenced by the father.

4.9 Describe several techniques for identifying defects or disorders in an embryo or fetus and discuss their advantages and disadvantages.

4.10 Tell why early, high-quality prenatal care is important and how prenatal care in the United States could be improved.

5. KEY TERMS

Cephalocaudal principle
Proximodistal principle
Germinal stage
Embryonic stage
Spontaneous abortion
Fetal stage

Ultrasound
Teratogenic
Fetal alcohol syndrome
Acquired immune deficiency syndrome
(AIDS)

6. TEACHING AND LEARNING ACTIVITES

LECTURE TOPICS

LECTURE TOPIC 4.1:
MATERNAL WEIGHT GAIN AND OUTCOME OF THE PREGNANCY

Medical advice about mothers' weight gain during pregnancy has varied over the years. A few decades ago, pregnant women were told to minimize weight gain because of concern about toxemia and delivery complications; women were advised to gain fewer than 20 pounds. The current medical guidelines recommend a weight gain of 25 to 35 pounds. The guidelines do not recommend weight reduction even for overweight women.

In 1980, 20 percent of pregnant black women and 10 percent of pregnant white women gained fewer than 16 pounds during the course of their pregnancies. On the other hand, 60 percent of pregnant white women and 50 percent of pregnant black women gained over 26 pounds.

Pregnant women at least 35 years old were more likely than younger women to gain fewer than 16 pounds and were less likely to gain at least 26 pounds. Pregnant teenagers were another group whose weight gain was lower than average. However, older pregnant women were likely to gain less during pregnancy because they weighed more at the start of pregnancy, whereas pregnant teens tended to gain little because of inadequate food consumption.

Other factors associated with low maternal weight gain included being unmarried, fewer years of schooling, low income, and smoking. The number of low-weight-gain women dropped in half as income went from $9,000 to $30,000. Mothers who smoked during pregnancy were 40 percent more likely to gain less than 16 pounds.

As women gained weight during pregnancy, the risk of giving birth to a low-birthweight baby decreased. This association was strongest for women who weighed less than 110 pounds before becoming pregnant.

Teenagers were most likely to give birth to low-birthweight babies, but as teenagers gained more weight during pregnancy, the birthweight increased substantially. About 1 in 5 teenagers who gained less than 16 pounds during pregnancy gave birth to a baby who weighed less than 5.5 pounds.

Surprisingly, about 1 in 4 pregnant women continued to smoke during pregnancy. Compared to babies of nonsmokers, babies of smokers weigh 7 ounces less. The fetal death ratio is 20 percent higher for women who smoke during pregnancy than for nonsmokers.

References
Taffel, S. M. (March/April 1986). Association between maternal weight gain and outcome of pregnancy. *Journal of Nurse Midwifery, 31*, 78-81.

LECTURE TOPIC 4.2: LONG-TERM EFFECTS OF PRENATAL MALNUTRITION

The long-term effects of prenatal malnutrition are influenced greatly by the adequacy of the child's diet after birth. When children continue with an inadequate diet after birth, they exhibit long-term physical and intellectual deficits. If the pregnant woman receives dietary supplements during the last half of her pregnancy, or if her newborn child receives dietary supplements, the harmful long-term effects are reduced.

The solution is more complex than simply supplementing the diets of malnourished pregnant women and their newborn children. Fetally malnourished infants often are apathetic and unresponsive and, when they are aroused, become irritable. These qualities put such children at risk in another way—they often receive less interaction and emotional support from the caregivers.

Zeskind and Ramsey maintain that fetally malnourished infants need both dietary supplements and supportive-care environments to counteract the negative long-term effects of fetal malnourishment. They tested this hypothesis in a longitudinal study in which fetally malnourished 3-month-old infants were assigned to two conditions (early intervention and nonintervention). In the early-intervention condition, the infants participated in a day care program (8 hours per day, 50 weeks per year) that emphasized the acquisition of basic cognitive, language, and social skills. The nonintervention groups did not attend this program. Nutrition and medical care were the same for both groups. At regular intervals during the first 3 years, the children were administered IQ and social-responsiveness tests and were observed interacting with their mothers at home.

There were no differences in test scores at the beginning of the experiment, but the two groups diverged greatly in their performances. The early-intervention group eventually exhibited a nearly normal pattern of cognitive development, whereas the nonintervention groups exhibited progressive declines in intellectual functioning. The mothers in the early-intervention group became more responsive to their children, while the opposite occurred with mothers in the nonintervention group. Emotionally, the children who attended the day care program at age 3 were less anxious, more friendly, and more self-assured than their counterparts in the nonintervention group. These results show that the effects of fetal malnourishment are complex and are compounded over time. Both dietary and social intervention are necessary to overcome the intellectual and social deficits that fetal malnutrition produces.

References

Winick, M. (1976). *Malnutrition and brain development*. New York: Oxford University Press.
Zeskind, P. S., & Ramsey, C. T. (1978). Fetal malnutrition: An experimental study of its consequences in two caregiving environments. *Child Development, 49,* 1155-1162.
Zeskind, P. S., & Ramsey, C. T. (1981). Preventing intellectual and interactions sequelae of fetal malnutrition: A longitudinal, transactional, and synergistic approach to development. *Child Development, 52,* 213-218.

LECTURE TOPIC 4.3:
LONG-TERM EFFECTS OF SMOKING DURING PREGNANCY

Monroe Lefkowitz completed a study of 233 mothers and their 241 children to see whether there were any significant differences at 10 years of age between the children of smokers and those of nonsmokers. In a face-to-face interview, mothers of 10-year-olds were asked whether they had smoked during pregnancy. There were 133 nonsmokers and 100 smokers. Consistent with other studies that have found children of smokers average 200 g less at birth, the smokers' babies weighed an average of 196 g less than the nonsmokers' babies.

Floyd found many negative consequences for smoking, including the risk of poor attention span and learning problems at school age, along with an increase in behavioral problems. Nicotine has been found to be linked to poor attention span, attentional problems, learning problems, lower IQ scores, and social adjustment problems. These findings have been supported by others, indicating that nicotine has a devastating impact upon brain development.

References

Floyd, R. L., Rimer, B. K., Giovino, G. A., Muller, P. D., & Sullivan, S. E. (1993). A review of smoking in pregnancy: Effects on pregnancy outcomes and cessation efforts. *Annual Review of Public Health, 14,* 379-411.

Lefkowitz, M. M. (1981). Smoking during pregnancy: Long-term effects on offspring. *Developmental Psychology, 17,* 192-194.

LECTURE TOPIC 4.4: TERATOGENS

The monitoring of birth defects did not start in the United States until 1970, and the monitoring only covers 25 percent of the nation's newborns. The monitoring is done by the National Centers for Disease Control, and it costs $1.3 million of the CDC's $380 million annual budget.

Since 1970 the specific deformities that are monitored have tended to show some significant increases. A few (Down syndrome, neural tube defects, clubfoot, cleft palate, cleft lip) have not increased. However, limb reductions are up 20 percent, a heart defect called patent ductus arteriosus is up 300 percent and renal agenesis (missing kidney) is up 50 percent. Other defects that are up at least 20 percent are ventricular septal defect (a hole between major heart chambers), displaced hip, hypospadias (abnormal opening on the penis), and tracheo-esophageal fistula (hole between windpipe and esophagus).

It has been estimated that 25 percent of the birth defects are caused by chromosomal aberrations or mutations, 5 to 8 percent have definitely been identified as caused by teratogens, and the rest have not been diagnosed. Teratogens (from the Greek word *terato* meaning "monster") are agents such as drugs, chemicals, and viruses that cause birth defects through mutations of DNA in reproductive cells. Well-known teratogens include thalidomide, lead, and agent orange (dioxin).

The geographical distribution of birth defects is not an even one. There are hundreds of known birth defect clusters, and about 50 of them are added each year. Of all the new clusters of birth defects, only 3 or 4 are even investigated. One birth defect cluster is in Woburn, Massachusetts, which has a childhood cancer rate that is 2½ times the average. It was found that the high rate of birth defects occurred only in a part of town where buried toxic wastes had infiltrated the drinking wells. In Love Canal, New York, 56 percent of children born near the toxic dump were mentally or physically disabled.

One of the thorniest problems in research on birth defects is that a teratogen can cause many different birth defects, and any defect can be caused by a variety of teratogens. The typical research procedure has been to do animal research to study teratogens, yet only twice has the cause of human birth defects been found first in an animal. There is a tremendous need to do more examining of human populations. Another study involving Vietnam veterans and agent orange showed that the highest rate of birth defects was found among offspring of the "Ranch Hand" veterans—those who had sprayed the herbicide. As a country, we need to offer better public education so that both men and women can avoid teratogens, put stronger warnings on drugs, do better basic research including fetal autopsies, train our medical doctors on the topic (none of our medical schools has a teratology specialty), and reduce environmental pollutants.

References

Merewood, A. (April 1991). Sperm under siege. *Health*.

Norwood, C. (January 1985). Terata. *Mother Jones*.

Plomin, R. (1990). *Nature and nurture: An introduction to human behavioral genetics*. Pacific Grove, CA: Brooks/Cole.

DISCUSSION TOPICS

DISCUSSION TOPIC 4.1:
REVIEW OF THE PRINCIPLES OF PRENATAL DEVELOPMENT

After presenting the material about the stages of prenatal development, you can hold a useful review of developmental principles. Ask your students to give examples from prenatal development that illustrate the following principles: Development is orderly with quantitative and qualitative changes. Development is directional (cephalocaudal and proximodistal). Physical precedes behavioral development (readiness). Critical periods are a part of development.

INDEPENDENT STUDIES

INDEPENDENT STUDY 4.1

How have prenatal care and advice to expectant parents changed over the years? To find out, go to your school library or the public library near you. Possible sources to investigate are books about the history of obstetrics, books of child-care information, and popular magazines, particularly those aimed at women. Look at the earliest sources you can find, dating back to the early twentieth century or even earlier. Compare the information in these sources with the information about prenatal care and newborn behavior in Chapter 4.

CHOOSING SIDES

CHOOSING SIDES 4.1

Alcohol is a potent teratogen. It is also a legal substance when used by adults. In some states, a bartender can be subject to punishment if he or she serves alcohol to a visibly pregnant woman. This prohibition is designed to protect the fetus; some may argue that it violates the woman's civil rights. Give students a scenario. They are working in a bar; a woman customer comes in whom they suspect may be pregnant. Can they ask her if she is pregnant? Should they serve her if she says she is not pregnant, but they still suspect that she is? If she says that she is pregnant, but still demands to be served, what do they do? Is the woman's right to privacy being violated by this line of questioning?

KNOWLEDGE CONSTRUCTION ACTIVITIES

KNOWLEDGE CONSTRUCTION ACTIVITY 4.1: GENERATIVE TERMS

This activity will use the principles of generative learning as explained in the Introduction to assist students in gaining a better understanding of terms. Divide the class into groups of four or five. Assign each group the task of generating an example for a generative term from this chapter. The example that each group creates cannot be one that has been used in the class or in the book. They must think of a new application for the term that they are given. Groups are allowed to use their books and notes. By creating their own example of the term, they demonstrate an understanding of the term to the level of application. There are several approaches that can be used in this exercise. Students may be given the entire list at once, but often one group will finish far ahead of the others and topics will get out of sequence. Another strategy is to give all of the groups the same term to create an example and then go around the room to discuss outcomes. This has been very successful, but also takes the most time. A third approach is to give each group a different term and see what examples they can generate.

Listed below are some generative terms and examples for Chapter 4.

Teratogens
Describe a development that takes place during the germinal stage.
Describe a development that takes place during the embryonic stage.
Describe a development that takes place during the fetal stage.
Generate an appropriate daily menu for an expectant mother.
Generate a cause of a spontaneous abortion.
Describe a possible outcome of prenatal exposure to rubella.
Describe a possible outcome of prenatal exposure to nicotine.
Describe a possible outcome of prenatal exposure to alcohol.
Describe a possible outcome of prenatal exposure to caffeine.
Describe a possible outcome of prenatal exposure to maternal cocaine.
Describe a possible outcome of prenatal exposure to paternal cocaine.
Describe a possible influence of advanced paternal age.
Describe a possible influence of advanced maternal age.

KNOWLEDGE CONSTRUCTION ACTIVITY 4.2: PRENATAL ASSESSMENT

Divide the class into groups of four or five to work on the following activity. Give the following directions: "You are a medical group planning assessment and treatment for your pregnant patients. Recommend a procedure to assess each of the following conditions or situations. There may be more than one appropriate assessment." You will have best results if students are given each condition one at a time.

Gestational age
Tay-Sachs
Down syndrome
Spina bifida
Genetic disorders
Sickle-cell anemia
Multiple pregnancies

KNOWLEDGE CONSTRUCTION ACTIVITY 4.3:
IDENTIFICATION OF TERATOGENS

A teratogen is a substance that causes a malformation or deviation from the normal structural development of the fetus. Students should select a specific teratogen and conduct library research on its effects. Some examples might include thalidomide, DES, alcohol, tobacco, marijuana, cocaine, amphetamines, and other drugs taken during pregnancy. One of the functions of the Food and Drug Administration is to ensure the safety of the chemicals used in food, medications, and cosmetics on the market today. Have students investigate the FDA procedure, if any, for testing possible teratogens. A related concern might be to inquire about the FDA process for approving contraceptive devices. What must be the harmful effects on mother and child before such substances are removed from the market? The text comments on social drugs such as cigarettes and alcohol, which many pregnant women take without considering them drugs or thinking about how they might harm their fetus. Students might consider some alternative ways of educating the public about the possible effects. How might we, as a democratic society, decrease the consumption of social drugs during pregnancy? How do other countries deal with these issues? Visit the local March of Dimes office for information and class presentations.

KNOWLEDGE CONSTRUCTION ACTIVITY 4.4: FETAL ALCOHOL SYNDROME

Create groups of four or five students within the classroom to do the following activity: Search the popular literature (books, magazines, Internet, etc.) for information on the effects of alcohol on a developing fetus. Then based on your research and the information provided in the book, create a questionnaire that would test someone's knowledge of Fetal Alcohol Syndrome. Type up your questionnaire, photocopy it, have each member of your group administer it to five college students. DO NOT ask for anyone's name to be placed on the questionnaire. Summarize the responses you receive within your group by creating a table of answers. Report to the entire class on the student population's understanding of FAS.

Students will find all aspects of this activity challenging and fun. It provides an opportunity for playing with a common methodology, learning some critically important information, assessing the educational level of peers, and sharing an experience with colleagues.

KNOWLEDGE CONSTRUCTION ACTIVITY 4.5:
PRENATAL CARE AROUND THE WORLD

In a group of four or five students, study the varied ways that pregnant women receive prenatal care. Select a county and use library resources to find the answers to the following questions.

1. What kind of prenatal care do women receive and who delivers that care?

2. Where do women give birth?

3. Who usually attends a birth?

4. Are there any religious rituals that are typical for childbirth?

5. Are there any social rituals that accompany birth? Describe them

6. Do most women breastfeed or bottle feed their babies?

7. Do poor women have the same kind of access to prenatal and birthing care that wealthy women do?

8. Are there any particularly interesting or unique features to prenatal care in the country you have chosen?

9. When you have the answers to your questions, make a presentation to the class. Include a description of the health care options available to pregnant women in their chosen country.

Your instructor will use the information of each group to create a summary table on an overhead transparency or chalkboard. When all of the information is presented, have a class discussion of the differences between countries.

7. RESOURCES FOR INSTRUCTORS

Books and Journal Articles

Brown, J. (1983). *Nutrition for your pregnancy: The University of Minnesota guide.* Minneapolis: University of Minnesota Press.

David, H. P., Dytryck, Z., Matejcek, Z., & Schuller, V. (1988). *Born unwanted: Developmental effects of denied abortion.* New York: Springer.

Frank, D. A., Zuckerman, B. S., Amaro, H., et al. (1988). Cocaine use during pregnancy: Prevalence and correlates. *Pediatrics, 82,* 888-895.

Moore, M. L.(1983). *Realities in childbearing,* 2d ed. Philadelphia: Saunders.

Nilsson, L., Furuhjelm, M., Ingelman-Sundberg, A., & Wirsen, C. (1977). *A child is born,* 2d ed. New York: Delacorte Press.

Rothman, B. K. (1987). *The tentative pregnancy: Prenatal diagnosis and the future of motherhood.* New York: Penguin.

Sluder,L.C., Kinnison, L.R., & Cates, D. (1998). Prenatal drug exposure: Meeting the challenge. Article 5 in *Annual Editions Human Development 1998/1999* (pp. 33-36). Guilford, CT: Dushkin/McGraw-Hill.

Video resources

The development of the human brain (FFHS, 1994, video, 40 min.). This program follows the physiological development of the human brain from conception through the growth of the neurological system in utero to the moment of birth.

Developmental phases before and after birth (FFHS, 1994, video, 30 min.). This program examines the development of the fetus in utero and the child during the first year.

Fetal rights (FFHS, 1994, video, 28 min.). An examination of the obligations of the mother to her unborn child and her rights to privacy and control over her own body.

Genetic counseling I and II: Heredity and birth defects and amniocentesis (MF, 11 min. each). Presents basic genetic principles, human inheritance, and genetic counseling techniques.

The miracle of life (NOVA, 1986, video, 60 min.). Excellent coverage of the development of life from conception until birth.

Pregnancy and birth: Caring and preparing for the life within (MS, 1996, video, 26 min.). Presentation of current birth processes including medical monitoring during pregnancy, labor, and delivery.

Prenatal development: A life in the making (MS, 1996, video, 26 min.). Coverage of life from conception until birth including maternal, paternal, and environmental factors.

The process of birth (FFHS, 1994, video, 30 min.). This program shows how different cultures and different individuals within the same culture respond to questions concerning the birth process.

Psychological development before birth (FFHS, 1994, video, 30 min.). The development of the individual can be followed in utero.

Siamese twins (NOVA, date unknown, video, 60 min.). Coverage of plans and operations that allow two girls to be separated at the pelvis.

5 *BIRTH AND THE NEWBORN BABY*

HOW CHILDBIRTH HAS CHANGED

THE BIRTH PROCESS
Stages of Childbirth
Methods of Delivery
Settings and Attendants for Childbirth

THE NEWBORN BABY
Size and Appearance
Body Systems

IS THE BABY HEALTHY?
Medical and Behavioral Assessment
Complications of Childbirth
Can a Supportive Environment Overcome Effects of Birth Complications?

NEWBORNS AND THEIR PARENTS
Childbirth and Bonding
Getting to Know the Baby: States of Arousal and Activity Levels
How Parenthood Affects a Marriage

In This Chapter of Your Instructor's Manual You Will Find:
1. Total Teaching Package Outline
2. Expanded Outline (transparency-ready)
3. Guideposts for Study
4. Learning Objectives
5. Key Terms
6. Teaching and Learning Activities
     Lecture Topics
     Discussion Topics
     Independent Studies
     Choosing Sides
     Knowledge Construction Activities
7. Resources for Instructors

1. TOTAL TEACHING PACKAGE OUTLINE

Chapter 5: Birth and the Newborn Baby

The birth process	
Stages of childbirth	**Guidepost for study 5.1, 5.2** **Learning objective 5.2** **Lecture topic 5.1**
Methods of delivery	**Learning objectives 5.3, 5.4** **Knowledge construction activity 5.4** **Choosing sides 5.1**
Settings and attendants for childbirth	**Guidepost for study 5.3** **Learning objectives 5.1, 5.5** **Knowledge construction activity 5.2** **Independent study 5.1**
The newborn baby	
Size and appearance	**Learning objective 5.6**
Body systems	**Guidepost for study 5.4** **Learning objective 5.7** **Lecture topic 5.3**
Is the baby healthy?	
Medical and behavioral assessment	**Guidepost for study 5.5** **Learning objective 5.8** **Lecture topic 5.2** **Knowledge construction activity 5.6**
Complications of childbirth	**Guidepost for study 5.6** **Learning objectives 5.9, 5.9**
Can a supportive environment overcome effects of birth complications?	**Guidepost for study 5.6** **Learning objective 5.12** **Independent study 5.2**
Newborns and their parents	
Childbirth and bonding	**Guidepost for study 5.7** **Learning objective 5.13** **Discussion topic 5.1** **Knowledge construction activity 5.7**
Getting to know the baby: States of arousal and activity levels	**Guidepost for study 5.7** **Learning objectives 5.14, 5.15** **Knowledge construction activity 5.5**
How parenthood affects a marriage	**Guidepost for study 5.8** **Learning objective 5.11** **Knowledge construction activity 5.3**

Please check out the online learning center located at www.mhhe.com/papaliacw9 for further information on these and other topics. There you can also access downloadable PowerPoint slides tailored to each chapter of the text and containing useful teaching notes as well as images and tables from the text itself.

2. EXPANDED OUTLINE (TRANSPARENCY READY)

I. The Birth Process
   A. Parturition
   B. Four stages of childbirth
      1. Dilation of the cervix
      2. Descent and emergence of the baby
      3. Expulsion of the umbilical cord and placenta
      4. Contraction of the uterus, recovery of the mother
   C. Electronic fetal monitoring

II. Methods of Delivery
   A. Cesarean
   B. Natural childbirth
   C. Prepared Childbirth
      1. Lamaze

III. Settings and Attendants for Childbirth
   A. Hospital settings
   B. Nurse midwives
   C. Medicated and unmedicated delivery

IV. The Newborn Baby
   A. Neonatal period
   B. Size and appearance
      1. Fontanels
      2. Lanugo
      3. Vernix caseosa
      4. Anoxia
      5. Meconium
      6. Neonatal jaundice

V. Medical and Behavioral Assessment
   A. Apgar scale
   B. Brazelton Neonatal Behavioral Assessment Scale
   C. Birth trauma

VI. Complications of Childbirth
   A. Low birthweight
   B. Preterm infants
   C. Small-for-gestational-age infants
   D. Postmature infants
   E. Protective factors

VII. Newborns and Their Parents
   A. Childbirth and bonding
      1. Imprinting
   B. Marital transition to parenthood

3. GUIDEPOSTS FOR STUDY

5.1 How have customs surrounding birth changed?
5.2 How does labor begin, and what happens during each of the four stages of childbirth?
5.3 What alternative methods and settings of delivery are available today?
5.4 How do newborn infants adjust to life outside the womb?
5.5 How can we tell whether a new baby is healthy and is developing normally?
5.6 What complications of childbirth can endanger newborn babies and what can be done to enhance the chances of a positive outcome?
5.7 How do parents bond with their baby and respond to the baby's patterns of sleep and activity?
5.8 How does parenthood change the parents' relationship with one another?

4. LEARNING OBJECTIVES

After completing the study of this chapter, the student should be able to:
5.1 Describe at least three changes in birth customs, identifying reasons for the reduction in the risks of childbirth.
5.2 Describe the four stages of vaginal childbirth.
5.3 Discuss the uses and disadvantages of cesarean births and electronic fetal monitoring.
5.4 Compare medicated delivery, natural childbirth, and prepared childbirth.
5.5 Weigh the comparative advantages of various types of settings and attendants for childbirth.
5.6 Describe the normal size and appearance of a newborn baby.
5.7 Compare the fetal and neonatal systems of circulation, respiration, digestion and excretion, and temperature regulation.
5.8 Discuss the uses of the Apgar scale and the Brazelton scale.
5.9 Discuss the risk factors, treatment, and outcomes for low-birthweight babies.
5.10 Explain the risks of postmaturity.
5.11 Discuss the coping responses of parents who have experienced stillbirth.
5.12 Discuss the effectiveness of the home environment and of intervention programs in overcoming effects of low birthweight and other birth complications.
5.13 Summarize the current status of research on bonding.
5.14 Describe typical patterns of sleep and arousal during the first few months.
5.15 Identify at least two ways in which a neonate may show the beginnings of temperament and the bidirectionality of effects between infant and parents.

5. KEY TERMS

Parturition	Neonatal period
Electronic fetal monitoring	Fontanels
Cesarean delivery	Lanugo
Natural childbirth	Vernix caseosa
Prepared childbirth	Anoxia
Neonate	Meconium

Neonatal jaundice	Low birthweight
State of arousal	Preterm (premature) infants
Apgar scale	Small-for-date (small-for-gestational-age)
Brazelton Neonatal Behavioral	infants
Assessment Scale	Postmature infants
Birth trauma	Protective factors

6. TEACHING AND LEARNING ACTIVITIES

LECTURE TOPICS

LECTURE TOPIC 5.1: PARTURITION

Parturition, the actual process of childbirth, is outlined in the textbook. Depending on their background and experiences, students may or may not have had exposure to what actually occurs during the birth of a baby. If students are not knowledgeable in this area, they are often quite interested in discussing the birth process.

Childbirth occurs in three stages. The onset of the first stage of labor can be recognized by any one of three signs. One sign is the expulsion of the mucous plug from the base of the uterus. This mucous tissue, usually flecked with blood, acts as a barrier between the vagina and the uterus to seal out bacteria or any other undesirable matter. Labor may begin soon after the loss of the mucous plug, but not necessarily. Another sign may be the rupturing of the amniotic membrane, which releases a clear, waterlike fluid from the vagina. Labor may begin within 24 hours of that time. If contractions have begun, rupturing of the amniotic membrane usually causes contractions to speed up, last longer, and be more regular. The third sign of the onset of labor is the actual occurrence of regular contractions. These muscle contractions may feel like a tightening on the sides that works around to a peak in the front and then subsides. They may resemble menstrual cramps, diarrhea, or sometimes even a backache in the lower back. In the earliest stages of labor, contractions are approximately 30 seconds long and anywhere from 5 to 30 minutes apart. As labor progresses, contractions generally become longer and closer together.

These powerful muscle contractions are working to dilate or open the cervix, which is the opening from the uterus to the vagina. Before dilation can actually occur, the neck of the uterus (cervix) must be thinned out. This process is called *effacement*. Effacement often occurs without the knowledge of the mother during the last weeks of pregnancy, or it may occur during early labor. Once effacement is accomplished, dilation begins. The cervix is normally about 2 1/8 inch in diameter. Full dilation (usually measured in centimeters) is 10 centimeters (about 4 inches). This process lasts from 8 to 12 hours for the first baby and from 4 to 8 hours for subsequent babies. These figures are, of course, general estimates. Labor can last as long as 24 hours, or even longer. Approximately two-thirds of this time is spent dilating up to 5 centimeters. Only one-third of the total labor time is taken to dilate from 5 to 10 centimeters. Each contraction pushes the baby's head downward against the cervix with force estimated at 25 or 30 pounds of pressure during hard labor.

Transition is the period from 8 to 10 centimeters dilation when the baby's head begins to move into the 4- to 5-inch-long vagina. This is a difficult part of labor, but it is generally very short. Some symptoms of transition may include irritability, discouragement, perspiration, sleepiness, shaking limbs, slight amnesia, nausea, vomiting, panic, dizziness, and loss of time perception.

The second stage of labor is the actual birth of the baby. Contractions have become longer and more frequent until they are approximately 60 to 90 seconds long and 1 to 2 minutes apart. During this second stage of labor, the contractions slow down somewhat to about 2 to 4 minutes apart. In most cases, the mother has a strong urge to push with each contraction. As the head of the fetus pushes outward, a great deal of stretching must occur in the tissues surrounding the opening of the vagina. If the skin is not sufficiently elastic, it will tear as the baby's head emerges. The obstetrician sometimes performs an episiotomy, cutting this tissue with scissors to enlarge the opening. A straight cut is simple to repair and heals much more rapidly than a tear.

After the baby's head emerges, it turns automatically to the right or left depending on the orientation of the shoulders. After the expulsion of the head and shoulders, the remainder of the birth is relatively simple because the trunk and limbs are quite small by comparison. As the head emerges, the doctor syringes out any blood, amniotic fluid, or mucus present in the infant's mouth and nose to facilitate breathing. With the infant's first breath, tremendous changes occur in the circulatory and respiratory processes. The temperature and pressure changes that forced the baby to breathe create a vacuum in the chest cavity. This forces blood to flow toward the pulmonary artery and lungs. As the blood flow changes, there is no further need for the opening that was present between the two auricles of the heart, and a flap of tissue closes the opening. During the few moments that it takes for this process to occur, the baby is rather bluish in color. As circulation through the pulmonary system becomes established, the baby's color changes to pink. At this point, the umbilical cord is clamped and cut.

From 5 to 15 minutes after the baby's birth, the placenta is expelled. This is the third stage of labor. The muscle contractions that shrink the uterus act to detach the placenta from the uterine wall. This process may also be hastened by nursing the baby immediately after birth. Nursing causes a natural hormone to be released in the mother's system that stimulates the uterine muscle to contract.

If an episiotomy was performed, it is now repaired and parturition is completed.

References

Bean, C. A. (1990). *Methods of childbirth.* New York: William Morrow.
Bradley, R. A. (1965). *Husband-coached childbirth.* New York: Harper & Row.
Roulier, M. (1972). *Childbirth without pain: Education League student manual.* Childbirth Without Pain Education League.
Vellay, P. (1959). *Childbirth without pain.* New York: Dutton.

LECTURE TOPIC 5.2: BRAZELTON NEONATAL BEHAVIORAL ASSESSMENT SCALE

As a pediatrician, Dr. Berry Brazelton was aware that techniques of infant assessment were inadequate. Focusing on reflexes, skin tones, vigor, biochemical characteristics, and so on, gave incomplete pictures of the total individual and interactive functioning of the child. An experienced nurse could give better diagnosis of an infant's recovery chances than many pediatricians. Based on pediatrics and advances in descriptive and experimental research with at-risk and thriving infants, Brazelton published in 1973 his Neonatal Behavioral Assessment Scale. The newness and unique qualities of the scale have made it popular among pediatricians and researchers, although it has not escaped criticism.

The scale is a good example of the applied benefits of basic developmental research. Brazelton assumes (supported by research since the 1960s) that the perceptual system of competent infants is highly developed and that the central nervous system can sensitively control infant behavior. The examiner is required to probe the infant's response abilities during the various states of alertness (from sleep through crying). Taking into account the natural adult-infant interaction found by ethologists, it is possible to assess the infant's general physiological responding, as well as its social responding. Brazelton recognizes that infant health is a function of body functioning and of care-taking responsiveness (attachment). The examiner must be skilled at interpreting medical signs as well as behavior elicited in the normal parent-infant situation.

The 30-minute exam is usually given on day 3 or 4 after birth and again on day 9 or 10. Infant response and recovery to increasing amounts of stimulation are assessed. A standard test of neurological intactness is gained by testing 20 basic reflexes (for example, Babinski, placing, rooting, sucking, and automatic walking). In addition, the examiner gives impressions about the child's need for stimulation in order to show the baby's overall organization. The main part of the exam assesses the newborn's interaction repertoire on 27 behavioral items. According to Brazelton, there are four major dimensions to these latter behaviors: (1) Interactive behaviors show ability to attend to and process simple environmental events. (2) Motor capacities are demonstrations of coordination and control of fingers, hand, thumb in mouth, and so on. (3) Organization of state control indicates systematic, controlled responding to stimulation. (4) Organizational capacities show physiological responses to stress (for example, does stimulation easily overwhelm the infant?). To be qualified to administer the test, the examiner must have attained criteria levels at certain training centers in the United States. This rigid control of the exam may be necessary for proper implementation, but it has been criticized as being too restrictive of scientific inquiry. Critics say all who want to use the test should be allowed to use it as they wish. It does not predict problem areas which benefit from early corrections.

References

Brazelton, T. B. (1984). *Neonatal behavior assessment scale*. Philadelphia: Lippincott.
Sameroff, A. J. (ed.) (1978). Organization and stability of newborn behavior: A commentary on the Brazelton Neonatal Behavioral Assessment Scale. *Monographs of the Society for Research in Child Developmental*, *43*(177), 5-6.

LECTURE TOPIC 5.3: CRY ANALYSIS

In the 1960s, Finnish doctor Wasz-Hockert studied crying patterns of brain-damaged infants with a symptom called *cri du chat* ("the cry of the cat"). These infants have an unusual high-pitched cry. When recorded on a sound spectrograph, a normal infant's crying pattern graphs as a smooth curve with a quick rising between 200 and 600 cycles per second, followed by a plateau, and then a dropping off. The brain-damaged child's cry graphs as a straight line around 800 cycles. Using computer analysis Lester did important research in the area of cry analysis in the 1970s. He published his findings on crying and medical diagnosis in *Child Development* in 1976, but only recently have doctors started using these techniques.

Signals from crying may warn of disabilities before they show up in the baby's behavior. This early detection might allow successful treatment while the brain and nervous system are most malleable. For example, some doctors believe that SIDS (Sudden Infant Death Syndrome) is associated with a low-pitched cry. Suspected infants can be closely monitored and saved. There is also a need to find a central nervous system (CNS) disorder that causes both the low-pitched cry and the respiratory problems that characterize SIDS. Infants who were exposed to marijuana prenatally also have a unique cry.

During his research, Lester looked at the crying pattern of malnourished babies; their crying tends to be high-pitched, arrhythmic, low in intensity, and long in duration, but with extended pauses. He suggests several correlations between crying style and physiological damage. For example, an unusually high pitch suggests damage in the part of the brain controlling the larynx muscles. On the other hand, wide fluctuations in pitch are more likely to be due to the CNS being unable to control larynx muscle spasms. Quiet and short cries may indicate that the lungs are not properly developed. A monotone sound suggests problems with the muscles and nerves of the upper air passages.

Analysis of crying may also be a technique for measuring the pace at which the brains of healthy children are developing. In the neonate, crying is reflexivelike and designed to regulate physiological homeostasis. There is a hunger cry and a pain cry (the pain cry has a more rapid rise, an increase in pitch, and initially a longer phonation). Within a couple of months there is more voluntary control and therefore more differentiated crying. Crying is now done for affective expression as well, and the child has added an angry cry and a cry for attention. From 7 to 9 months of age, more cognitive aspects have developed and there is now crying for fear and for stranger anxiety. Before the second year the child also learns a frustration cry and a fear-of-failure cry.

Studies of crying also tell us more about how language develops. It seems that the way the human baby gives emotional signals (cries) is shared with many species. Researchers have found many similarities between the structure of a baby's cry and that of a kitten's cry. For example, kittens and human infants have similar isolation cries—the sound patterns the newborn makes when separated from the mother. These sounds originate in the hypothalamus. These findings contradict Chomsky's theory of language development as a uniquely human "language organ." Human speech may not be qualitatively different from animal communication; the differences may be more a matter of complexity.

References

Angier, N. (1984). Medical clues from babies' cries. *Discover*, 49-51.
Lester, B. (1983). There's more to crying than meets the ear. *Child Care Newsletter, 2*, 1-5.
Lester, B. M., Boukydis, C. F. Z., Garcia-Coll, C. T., Hole, W., & Peucker, M. (1992). Infantile colic: Acoustic cry characteristics, maternal perception of cry, and temperament. *Infant Behavior and Development, 15*, 15-26.
Lester, B. M., & Dreher, M. (1989). Effects of marijuana use during pregnancy on newborn cry. *Child Development, 60*, 765-771.

DISCUSSION TOPICS

DISCUSSION TOPIC 5.1: PARENTS OF PREMATURE BABIES

Information from the text indicates that the women who are most likely to give birth to premature babies are those with histories of difficult pregnancies, spontaneous abortion, or stillbirths; teenagers (probably because of poor nutrition and inadequate prenatal care rather than age); women who gain too little weight during pregnancy; smokers, alcoholics, and drug abusers; and women with such chronic medical conditions as diabetes, toxemia, thyroid dysfunction, kidney disorders, congenital heart problems, and respiratory problems. Poll your class for their opinions about which two of these conditions would be easiest to overcome and which two would be most difficult to overcome. Then discuss with the class possible ways to overcome the perceived easier problems (such as better education programs for pregnant women, free and confidential prenatal care for pregnant teenagers, a national ad campaign about the problems associated with smoking and with drug and alcohol abuse). For the two that emerge as the most difficult problems to overcome, discuss with your class the reasons why they perceive these to be so difficult to overcome. This discussion can be guided into a class project wherein some or all of the students devise (and even implement) a plan to locally educate women about one of the risk factors for premature births.

INDEPENDENT STUDIES

INDEPENDENT STUDY 5.1: BIRTH PRACTICES

Study the effects of various birth practices on neonatal adjustment. Within cultures, people have strong emotional attachments to particular birth practices. For example, in the United States there is a strong emphasis on the scientific approach to birth, in which medical professionals attend birthing women in hospitals. How much scientific evidence is there to support this model? Examine other cultural models for childbirth. We can easily understand practices other than our own as being culturally dictated. How much of the American way of birth is dictated by our cultures of science and medicine? What elements are clearly linked to infant health and which are a function of other factors?

Write an essay that contrasts American birth practices with two other cultures'. Clearly show the similarities and differences and explain which practices are influenced by the biological event of birth and which are influenced by culture.

INDEPENDENT STUDY 5.2: BEHAVIORAL TERATOGENS

In the 1990's, there was a great deal of media attention to the behavioral effects of prenatal exposure to harmful substances; for example, there was concern about the effects of prenatal exposure to crack. The original fears of gross abnormalities may have been unfounded. However, there are a variety of more subtle effects that are both substance-specific and dose-specific. What kinds of behaviors are linked to prenatal exposure to teratogens? You might begin with a study of Fetal Alcohol Effects (FAE) and "crack babies" Are these terms really useful? How do individual differences in resilience and the post-natal environment influence the outcomes for babies?

CHOOSING SIDES

CHOOSING SIDES 5.1: NATURAL CHILDBIRTH

Women have given birth without the use of medical intervention for thousands of years. Until the last century, most women did not have any chemical means for coping with the pain of birth. At the present time, most American women give birth in hospitals, and most use drugs. The pharmaceuticals used in birth have changed tremendously in the past fifty years.

Early attempts to medicate included morphine for pain. This had an extremely negative effect on the baby. Later, doctors used the more sophisticated scopolamine cocktail, a combination of painkillers and amnesiac. Either of these resulted in women asleep, sometimes with a general anaesthetic, for the birth. The babies born to mothers under these circumstances were drugged, had trouble breathing, and were often assisted from the birth canal via forceps, because the mothers, being unconscious, could not push the babies out.

The advent of anaesthetic agents for childbirth made a dramatic difference for mothers and babies. These include the spinal and the far more sophisticated epidural anaesthesia. A thin catheter is introduced into the mother's lower back and the drug dripped into the space surrounding her spinal cord. The effect is to numb the lower abdomen so that the pain of contractions is not felt. Women remain awake and capable of a degree of control for pushing during the second stage of labor.

The epidural is used most often in childbirth the United Sates. The medication cannot be given too early in labor or it will slow the progress. The incidence of other medical interventions jumps once the epidural is introduced. For example, mothers with epidural anaesthesia are more likely to have Cesarean births, pitocin augmentation (to speed labor), and forceps used during delivery.

Pro:
1. Women have given birth naturally for thousand of years; women's bodies are meant to give birth naturally.
2. Babies are more interactive with mothers are unmedicated.
3. Breastfeeding can happen earlier when the mother is unmedicated.
4. Women who give birth naturally feel a sense of empowerment.
5. Babies have no ill effects of medication when the mother gives birth naturally.
6. Epidural medication increases the risk of other types of childbirth complications.
7. The pain of labor is manageable with alternative coping strategies.

Con:
1. Women gave birth naturally but babies and women were more likely to die without medical intervention.
2. Epidural medication has minimal systemic effects on the mother; there is very little effect on the baby.
3. Women who are comfortable in labor may bond better with their babies
4. Women who are comfortable in labor will have a more positive birth experience.
5. Other family members can participate with the woman when she is not focused on coping with pain.

Have students research and debate the topic. Some of them may have personal experiences to share.

KNOWLEDGE CONSTRUCTION ACTIVITIES

KNOWLEDGE CONSTRUCTION ACTIVITY 5.1: GENERATIVE TERMS

This activity will use the principles of generative learning as explained in the Introduction to assist students in gaining a better understanding of terms. Divide the class into groups of four or five. Assign each group the task of generating an example for a generative term from this chapter.

The example that each group creates cannot be one that has been used in the class or in the book. They must think of a new application for the term that they are given. Groups are allowed to use their books and notes. By creating their own example of the term, they demonstrate an understanding of the term to the level of application. There are several approaches that can be used in this exercise. Students may be given the entire list at once, but often one group will finish far ahead of the others and topics will get out of sequence. Another strategy is to give all of the groups the same term to create an example and then go around the room to discuss outcomes. This has been very successful, but also takes the most time. A third approach is to give each group a different term and see what examples they can generate.

Listed below are some generative examples for Chapter 5.

Give an example of (a):
Development that takes place in the neonatal period
State of arousal
Birth trauma
Preterm infant
Small-for-date infant
Postmature infant
Protective factor
Something that can be identified by an electronic fetal monitor

KNOWLEDGE CONSTRUCTION ACTIVITY 5.2: TOUR A BIRTHING CENTER

Take your class on a tour of a local hospital or clinic where babies are delivered. What do labor and delivery rooms look like? Are husbands, children, or friends permitted in labor, delivery, and recovery rooms? What is the general hospital procedure for handling the baby at birth? Is the Apgar scale used? Can mother and father hold their infant immediately? Is the mother allowed to breastfeed the baby in the delivery room? What type of equipment is available; for example, ultrasound, fetal monitors, and so on? How do birthing centers differ from regular hospitals?

KNOWLEDGE CONSTRUCTION ACTIVITY 5.3:
HOW EXPENSIVE IS HAVING A BABY?

Ask students to estimate what it costs to have a baby. Make assignments to call a variety of obstetricians, pediatricians, and hospitals. What are the current fees for prenatal care, delivery, hospital room, nursery charges for the baby, pediatric exam, and circumcision? It might also be informative to have some students investigate general costs that might commonly be incurred during the first year after a baby's birth. Some items to price include crib and bedding, diapers (reusable vs. disposable), clothing (covering four or five different sizes from newborn to 12-month size), high chair, stroller, backpack baby carrier, formula, baby food, and toys. Assign one or more items and figure the costs as a class.

KNOWLEDGE CONSTRUCTION ACTIVITY 5.4: NATURAL CHILDBIRTH

Invite a teacher of a local natural childbirth class to explain and demonstrate relaxation and breathing techniques used during labor and delivery. Most communities have such classes in Lamaze techniques. Some parents who have practiced this method of childbirth may be willing to discuss their experience with the class. An alternative might be to obtain a film demonstrating the procedures. Many organizations that teach natural childbirth have available for rent films that show preparation for childbirth as well as the actual delivery. Two examples of such films are *The Story of Eric* (American Society of Psychoprophylaxis in Obstetrics [ASPO]) and *Becoming* (Stanford University Communications Department). Other information, films, and publications could be obtained from one of the following organizations:

International Childbirth Education Association (ICEA)
Publication Distribution Center
P.O. Box 9316, Midtown Plaza
Rochester, NY 14604

Childbirth Without Pain Education League, Inc. (CWPEL)
3940 11th Street
Riverside, CA 92500

Perinatal Association
Perinatal Center
Sutter Memorial Hospital
52 and F Streets
Sacramento, CA 95819

KNOWLEDGE CONSTRUCTION ACTIVITY 5.5: VISIT A NEWBORN NURSERY
Have students go to a hospital during visiting hours and observe babies in the nursery. What behaviors do they observe? What kind of movement are the newborns capable of? What do the babies watch? Compare eye movements when awake and asleep. Watch their breathing. How regular or irregular is it? What is the hospital routine like? How do the nurses handle the babies and how often? How are the babies fed and how often? How many times per day and for how long do the mothers have their infants with them? Are the lights always on in the nursery—even at night? How do parents and visitors respond to the babies? Compare premature babies in isolettes to full-term infants in appearance and behavior.

KNOWLEDGE CONSTRUCTION ACTIVITY 5.6: NEWBORN ASSESSMENT
Have students contact local hospitals and birthing centers and determine what types of neonatal assessment they use. When possible, have the students collect examples of these assessment devices and procedures. Obtain videotapes of several neonates, or, when feasible, produce a videotape for classroom use and have students attempt to rate the infants by using one or more of the tests.

KNOWLEDGE CONSTRUCTION ACTIVITY 5.7: FATHERS' EXPERIENCES

Many fathers who are present at the birth and who help care for their infants in the hospital become fascinated with their newborns. Interview a father who had contact with his baby at birth. Some possible questions might include:

1. Could you recognize your infant among a crowd of newborns?

2. What does the baby feel like?

3. Are you aware of any distinctive characteristics of your infant?

4. How would you rate your baby on a 10-point scale from 0 = ugly to 10 = perfect?

5. How would you rate babies in general?

6. What were your emotions as you saw your baby being born?

7. How do you feel toward your baby?

8. How did the birth make you feel about yourself and your wife?

It might also be interesting to compare these responses to those answers given by a father who was not present to see the birth.

7. RESOURCES FOR INSTRUCTORS

Books and Journal Articles

Anand, K. J. S., & Hickey, P. R. (1987). Pain and its effects in the human neonate and fetus. *The New England Journal of Medicine, 317,* 1321-1329.

Ball, J. A. (1987). *Reactions to motherhood.* New York: Cambridge University Press.

Binkin, N. J., Yip, R., Fleshwood, L., & Trowbridge, F. L. (1988). Birthweight and childhood growth. *Pediatric, 82,* 828-833

Cole, D. (July 1987). It might have been: Mourning the unborn. *Psychology Today,* 64-65.

Entwisle, D. R.; & Alexander, K. L. (1987). Long-term effects of cesarean delivery on parents' beliefs and children's schooling. *Developmental Psychology, 23,* 676-682.

Lagercrantz, H., & Slotkin, T. A. (April 1986). The "stress" of being born. *Scientific American,* 100-107.

Maurer, D., & Aurer, C. (1988). *The world of the newborn.* New York: Basic Books.

Rosenblith, J. F. (1992*). In the beginning: Development in the first two years of life, 2nd ed.* Newbury Park, CA: Sage.

Video resources

AIDS Babies (Cinema Guild, 1990, 58 min.). Documentary examines the plight of babies born with AIDS. Filmed in various countries around the world, film compares the reaction of various governments to the AIDS crisis and speculates on the future consequences of a generation of AIDS babies.

Cross-cultural differences in newborn behavior (PSU, 1980, approximately 10 min.). Shows neonates from varied racial and ethnic groups (Caucasian, Navajo, Aborigine, African) to illustrate behavioral differences.

Mothers, fathers, and babies (FFHS, 1994, video, 30 min.). This program observes the role of breastfeeding in different cultures and its effect on the role of the father.

The postpartum blues (FFHS, 1994, video, 19 min.). Women discuss the physical and psychological demands on them immediately after childbirth; an obstetrician explains the physical and hormonal changes that take place during pregnancy and childbirth.

LINKUPS

Some of the most exciting developmental research during the past quarter-century has been on the period from birth to age 3, the period known as infancy and toddlerhood. By measuring how long infants look at various objects or patterns, or how vigorously they suck on nipples that turn on recordings of their mothers' and other women's voices, researchers have discovered that even newborns can discriminate sights and sounds--and have definite preferences about what they see and hear. By noting babies' reactions to boxes teetering on the edge of tabletops, investigators have found that infants as young as 3 months understand basic principles that govern the physical world. By videotaping babies' facial expressions, researchers have documented when specific early emotions (such as joy, anger, and fear) first appear. Other researchers have analyzed the emotional signals babies send to, and receive from, their caregivers. Still others have described how the complex emotions of pride, shame, and guilt emerge with the cognitive growth that takes place during the second year. All in all, we now know that the world of infants and toddlers is far richer, and their abilities far more impressive, than was previously suspected.

Infancy begins at birth and ends when a child begins walking and stringing words together--two events which typically take place between 12 and 18 months of age. Toddlerhood lasts from about 18 to 36 months, a period when children become more verbal, independent, and able to move about. As we study how neonates become infants and toddlers (and, later, grow into children and adolescents), we see how each of the three aspects of development is bound up with the others. Thus, while we focus on the physical development of infants and toddlers in Chapter 5, on their cognitive development in Chapter 6, and on their psychosocial development in Chapter 7, we will see many examples of how these aspects of development intertwine.

Linkups to Look For:

o	The physical growth of the brain before and after birth makes possible a great burst of cognitive and emotional development. Fetuses whose ears and brains have developed enough to hear sounds from the outside world seem to retain a memory of these sounds after birth.

o	An infant's earliest smiles arise from central nervous system activity and may reflect nothing more than a pleasant physiological state, such as drowsiness and a full stomach. As the infant becomes cognitively aware of the warm responses of caregivers, and as vision becomes sharp enough to recognize a familiar face, the infant's smiles become more emotionally expressive and more socially directed.

o	Infants learn through their physical movements where their bodies end and everything else begins. As they drop toys, splash water, and hurl sand, their minds grasp how their bodies can change their world, and their sense of self begins to flourish.

o	Without the vocal structures and motor coordination to form sounds, babies would not be able to speak. Physical gestures precede and often accompany early attempts to form words. The acquisition of language dramatically advances cognitive understanding and social communication.

6 PHYSICAL DEVELOPMENT AND HEALTH DURING THE FIRST THREE YEARS

GROWTH AND NUTRITION
Patterns of Growth
Influences on Growth
Nourishment

THE BRAIN AND REFLEX BEHAVIOR
Building the Brain
Early Reflexes
Molding the Brain: The Role of Experience

EARLY SENSORY CAPACITIES
Touch and Pain
Smell and Taste
Hearing
Sight

MOTOR DEVELOPMENT
Milestones of Motor Development
How Motor Development Occurs:
    Maturation in Context
Motor Development and Perception
Cultural Influence on Motor Development
Training Motor Skills Experimentally

HEALTH
Reducing Infant Mortality
Immunization for Better Health

In This Chapter of Your Instructor's Manual You Will Find :
1. Total Teaching Package Outline
2. Expanded Outline (transparency-ready)
3. Guideposts for Study
4. Learning Objectives
5. Key Terms
6. Teaching and Learning Activities
    Lecture Topics
    Discussion Topics
    Independent Studies
    Choosing Sides
    Knowledge Construction Activities
7. Resources for Instructors

1. TOTAL TEACHING PACKAGE OUTLINE

CHAPTER 6: Physical Development And Health During The First Three Years

Growth and nutrition	**Guidepost for study 6.1**
Patterns of growth	**Learning objective 6.1**
Influences on growth	**Learning objective 6.2**
Nourishment	**Guidepost for study 6.1** **Learning objective 6.3** **Lecture topic 6.1** **Choosing sides 6.1** **Knowledge construction activity 6.2**
The brain and reflex behavior	**Guidepost for study 6.3, 6.4** **Lecture topics 6.2, 6.3**
Building the brain	**Learning objective 6.5**
Early reflexes	**Learning objective 6.6**
Molding the brain: The role of experience	**Learning objective 6.6**
Early sensory capacities	**Guidepost for study 6.4**
Touch and pain	**Learning objective 6.8**
Smell and taste	**Learning objective 6.7** **Lecture topic 6.4**
Hearing	**Learning objective 6.10**
Sight	**Learning objective 6.11**
Motor development	**Guidepost for study 6.5**
Milestones of motor development	**Learning objective 6.12** **Box 6.1 (textbook p. 156)**
How motor development occurs: Maturation in context	**Learning objective 6.13** **Knowledge construction activity 6.3**
Motor development and perception	**Lecture topic 6.5** **Discussion topic 6.4**
Cultural influence on motor development	**Box 6.2, (textbook p.140)**
Training motor skills experimentally	**Discussion topic 6.3**
Health	**Independent study 6.1**
Reducing infant mortality	**Learning objectives 6.14, 6.15, 6.16** **Discussion topic 6.2**

Please check out the online learning center located at www.mhhe.com/papaliacw9 for further information on these and other topics. There you can also access downloadable PowerPoint slides tailored to each chapter of the text and containing useful teaching notes as well as images and tables from the text itself.

2. EXPANDED OUTLINE (TRANSPARENCY READY)

I. Growth and Nutrition
    A. Breastfeeding
        1. Colostrum
    B. Formulas
    C. Cow's milk, solid foods, and juice
    D. Obesity
    E. Cholesterol
        1. Atherosclerosis

II. The Brain and Reflex Behavior
    A. Central nervous system
    B. Brain growth spurts
    C. Lateralization
    D. Neurons
        1. Myelination
        2. Integration
        3. Differentiation
        4. Cell death
    E. Reflex behaviors
    F. Plasticity

III. Early Sensory Capacities
    A. Touch and pain
    B. Smell and taste
    C. Hearing
    D. Sight
        1. Depth perception
        2. Visual cliff

IV. Motor Development
  A. Systems of action
  B. Denver Developmental Screening Test
    1. Gross motor skills
    2. Fine motor skills
  C. Head control, hand control, locomotion

V. Health
  A. Infant mortality rate
  B. Sudden infant death syndrome

3. GUIDEPOSTS FOR STUDY

6.1 How do babies grow and what influences their growth?

6.2 How and what should infants be fed?

6.3 How does the brain develop and how do environmental factors affect its early growth?

6.4 How do the senses develop during infancy?

6.5 What are some early milestones in motor development?

6.6 What are some influences on motor development?

6.7 How can we enhance babies' chances of survival and health?

4. LEARNING OBJECTIVES

After completing the study of this chapter, the student should be able to:

6.1 Summarize typical patterns of growth during the first 3 years.

6.2 Identify several factors that affect growth.

6.3 Summarize pediatric recommendations regarding early feeding.

6.4 Cite factors that contribute to obesity and cardiac problems later in life.

6.5 Describe the most important features of brain development before and after birth.

6.6 Explain the functions of inborn reflex behaviors and why some of these reflexes drop out during the early months of life while others remain.

6.7 Discuss the role of early experience in brain growth and development.

6.8 Give evidence for the early development of a sense of touch.

6.9 Describe the newborn's sense of smell and taste.

6.10 Describe how auditory discrimination in newborns is related to fetal hearing.

6.11 List three ways in which newborns' vision is underdeveloped.

6.12 Trace a typical infant's progress in head control, hand control, and locomotion.

6.13 Discuss how maturation, perception, environmental influence, and training relate to early motor development.

6.14 Summarize trends in infant mortality.

6.15 Discuss risk factors, causes, and prevention of sudden infant death syndrome.

6.16 Explain why full immunization of all infants and preschoolers is important.

5. KEY TERMS

Central nervous system
Brain growth spurts
Lateralization
Neurons
Integration

Differentiation
Cell death
Myelination
Reflex behaviors
Systems of action

Denver Developmental Screening Test   Depth perception
Gross motor skills   Infant mortality rate
Fine motor skills   Sudden infant death syndrome
Visual cliff

6. TEACHING AND LEARNING ACTIVITIES

LECTURE TOPICS

LECTURE TOPIC 6.1: WHY MOTHERS SHOULD BREASTFEED: HISTORICAL PERSPECTIVE

As pointed out by Kessen in his book *The Child*, certain child-rearing practices continually resurface and are rediscovered. Breastfeeding is a good example of a continuing child-care topic. For the last 2000 years, philosophers, doctors, and child-care specialists (mostly men, of course) have emphasized that mothers should take care of their own children and breastfeed them. According to historical records, a large percentage of women have preferred to have governesses and wet nurses. The following quotes from Kessen demonstrate the persistence of the "problem." Read each of the following quotes to the class and discuss them in light of such issues as nature-nurture, scientific reasoning, medical advances, human nature, and current arguments for and against breastfeeding. (Quotes are from Kessen, W. (1965). *The Child*. New York: Wiley.)

Plutarch

The affection of wet nurses and governesses is spurious and constrained, for they love for hire. Nature itself makes it plain that mothers should themselves nurture and sustain what they have brought forth: for every animal which brings forth nature has provided a supply of milk. (p. 2)

Heinrich von Louffenburg (1429, German poet)

Therefore the child should delight in taking its mother's breast. On that it subsists better and without harm than on that of any other woman, because it became accustomed to it in the mother's womb. . . (p. 2)

John Comenius (1633)

If they suckle from their real mother rather than another, children might approach nearer to the disposition and virtues of their parents than generally happens. The philosopher Favorinus shows that the milk of animals, by some occult virtue, possesses the power of fashioning the body and mind like the form of its original . . . Who then, unless he be blind, does not see that babies imbibe, along with the alien milk of the foster mother, morals different from those of their parents? (p. 3)

Rousseau (1762, French philosopher)

When mothers' nurse their own children . . . natural feeling will revive in every heart; there will be no lack of citizens for the state; this first step by itself will restore mutual affection. (p. 3)

J. B. Davis (1817, English physician)

The mother's breast is an infant's birthright and suckling a sacred duty, to neglect which is prejudicial to the mother and fatal to the child.

LECTURE TOPIC 6.2: EARLY SENSORY CAPACITIES AND MOTOR DEVELOPMENT

Infants have immature but remarkably effective sensory capacities. They are able to see, hear, taste, smell, and feel pain—though not to the extent that they will as the senses mature. The neonate can distinguish color, and even very young babies seem to have some idea of depth perception, as demonstrated by their reaction to the visual cliff. Babies apparently have some visual preference, which tells us that the neonate's world is far from chaotic. The human auditory system, functioning before birth, continues to develop after birth. Infants' hearing has been studied through habituation. Infants as young as 3 days old were found to discriminate between sounds. Infants have a better-developed pain response than previously thought.

Wide variations exist in the ages at which children develop certain physical skills. Nonetheless some general developmental trends are evident. During the first 3 years babies grow markedly in size and exhibit great changes in body proportion. Several factors, including genetics, home environment, and prolonged illness, can influence physical growth. Motor development, the increasing ability of the child to do things with his or her body, is very orderly. It is differentiating and integrative; it proceeds from the simple to the complex. Reflex behavior is replaced by increasing mastery of voluntary movements as the infant's nervous system shifts from subcortical to cortical control. Reflexes that are protective (such as sneezing, coughing, and yawning) remain, but mastery of the voluntary movements is marked by such milestones as rolling over, sitting, crawling, standing, and walking. Environmental influences (repetitive processes, lack of support, cross-cultural influences) may play a part in motor development, but the process itself appears to be programmed through progressive stages. A healthy, caring atmosphere where the caregiver responds to the baby's needs, talks to the baby, is patient, and gives the baby freedom to explore safely is the best environment in which to develop.

LECTURE TOPIC 6.3: INSIGHTS FROM THE VISUAL CLIFF

The visual cliff is a classic experimental technique for testing depth perception in human infants and the young of other species. In the early research, 6-month-old infants who could crawl were coaxed by their mothers, who stood on the opposite side of the apparatus, to crawl across a space with illusionary depth. As pointed out in the text, more recent research has used younger infants and measures of their heart rates as indicators of whether they react to the illusionary perception of depth. The results have provided mixed evidence about whether depth perception is present at birth.

A more recent study has evaluated the effects of emotional signaling by the mothers' facial expressions on the crawling infants' responses. The researchers used the visual cliff (visual illusion of depth in the presence of tactile contact with a surface) to test infants' responses to their mothers' facial expressions of joy, fear, interest, anger, and sadness. Additionally, the study evaluated whether the infants' reactions to the facial expressions were the result of their need for more information in an uncertain situation or the result of the unexpectedness or discrepancy of the expressions.

The findings of the study indicate that infants use their mothers' facial expressions to help clarify the ambiguous situation of the visual cliff. When the mothers' expressions were of joy, the infants ignored the illusion of depth and crossed over to their mothers. However, when the mothers' facial expressions were of fear or anger, few of the infants would venture out onto the "deep" side. When the illusion of depth was removed (the situation was no longer ambiguous), few infants looked at their mothers. When infants did look at their mothers in this situation, facial expressions of fear caused the infants to hesitate but did not keep them from crossing to their mothers.

The researchers concluded that emotional signaling through maternal facial expressions was a source of information to help infants regulate their behaviors in uncertain situations. This is demonstrated in the videotape, *Life's First Feelings*.

References

Gibson, E. J., & Walk, R. D. (1960). The "visual cliff." *Scientific American, 202*, 64-71.
Grunwald, L. (July 1993). The amazing minds of infants, *Life*.
Sorce, J. F., Emde, R. N., Campos, J. J., & Klinnert, M. D. (1985). Maternal emotional signaling: Its effect on the visual cliff behavior of one-year-olds. *Developmental Psychology, 21*, 195-200.

LECTURE TOPIC 6.4: FAMILY COMMON SCENTS

Although psychologists have looked at primate and other animal olfactory communication, until recently most psychologists believed that humans' sense of smell was too weak and underused to help in identification. Over the last decade, however, several studies have suggested that individuals within families share smells and are identifiable by these smells. Here are a few of the recent research findings:

1. By the time they are 6 days old, infants can distinguish the smell of breast pads their mothers wore from that of breast pads that had been worn by other nursing females.
2. Six hours after birth, 61 percent of the mothers correctly picked their own infant out of three infants on the basis of odor alone.
3. Breastfed babies, but not bottle-fed babies, were able to detect and prefer underarm pads worn by their mothers over those worn by nursing strangers or nonmothers. These infants could not indicate a preference for their own fathers' underarm pads.
4. Children wore T-shirts for three nights. Seventeen out of 18 mothers were able to pick out their own children's T-shirts over other children's T-shirts.
5. Sixteen of 18 parents were able to correctly match the T-shirts worn by one of their offspring when compared to T-shirts worn by two others of their offspring.
6. With just 2 hours of exposure to their babies, 13 of 17 mothers were able to sniff out their babies' clothing. After 24 hours of exposure, 16 of 20 mothers did this task successfully.

7. Strangers were fairly successful at matching mother and offspring T-shirts. Mothers and their children may share similar detectable odors.

8. Strangers could not match T-shirts of spouses, who, of course, do not share the same genetic background.

Research in this area of olfactory communication is called *chemical-signature research*. More studies need to be conducted, especially to determine whether smell plays a major role in the mother-infant attachment process.

References

McCarthy, P. (July 1986). Scent: The tie that binds. *Psychology Today, 6.*
Rovee-Collier, C. (1993). The capacity for long-term memory in infancy. *Current Directions in Psychological Science, 2,* 130-135.

LECTURE TOPIC 6.5: TRAINING FOR IMPROVED MOTOR SKILLS

An abiding controversy in medical and psychological circles centers on the significance of reflexes in newborns. Some authorities believe that reflexes are vestigial responses from the ancestral past; others believe that reflexes demonstrate innate capabilities of the infant and a readiness to usefully respond to the environment. Traditionally, neonatal tests have relied heavily on the eliciting of reflexes to demonstrate neural integration, maturation, and even mental capacity. It is currently believed that reflexes do indeed indicate neural processes and maturation but are not related to later intellectual ability. The interactive effect of these reflexes with environmental encouragement and the effect of exercising these reflexes are not known. Do these reflexes make it easier for a child to grasp items, walk, swim, cling, smile, search for the source of tactile stimulation, and so on? There are reflexes similar to each of these behaviors. Normally, these behaviors lose their reflexive nature or disappear after a few months. Few studies have systematically investigated the progression from reflexive patterns to the enduring instrumental behaviors that seem to replace them.

Interesting studies were reported by Zelazo and his colleagues. Using appropriate control groups, the experimenters investigated the stepping response of infants at 1 week of age and the subsequent effect of exercising that reflex. The experimental group received 12 minutes of stepping exercise each day for 7 weeks. A second group was given passive exercise 12 minutes a day for 7 weeks, during which the babies' arms and legs were pumped and exercised. These first two groups and a third group that received no systematic exercise were all tested at each 1-week interval. A fourth group was only tested when the infants were 8 weeks old. At the end of 8 weeks, the experimental group gave an average of 30 walking responses per minute. The passive-exercise and the no-exercise (but frequently tested) groups averaged about 3 steps per minute when 8 weeks old. All three of these groups had averaged about 6 steps per minute at 1 week of age. The fourth group, tested only at 8 weeks of age, produced hardly any stepping responses. This experiment showed a rather smooth transition from a reflexive behavior to an instrumentally controlled and learned response. Obviously, the training affected the continuance and increase in a behavior that was once purely reflexive. A follow-up study showed that early training did accelerate specific behaviors but did not generalize. Contrary to previous assumptions, reflexes apparently do not just disappear. (This would have been the conclusion if only 1-week-old and 8-week-old infants had been tested.) Similar results were obtained when infants were given "walking" exercise for 6 weeks but starting at 2, 6, and 10 weeks of age for different groups. All groups increased their stepping 70 percent or more. It is significant that the researchers did not teach the stepping response but only allowed the children to exercise an already existing tendency. This shows a nice interaction between nature and nurture. However, it should not be assumed that precocious development of motor milestones such as walking can thus be taught. Classic studies by Dennis with Hopi Indians and by McGraw with twins showed relatively little influence of training on such behaviors.

References
Lipsitt, L. P. (ed.) (1976). *Developmental psychobiology: The significance of infancy*. Hillsdale, NJ: Lawrence Erlbaum Associates.
Zelazo, N. A. et al. (1993). Specificity of practice effects on elementary neuromotor patterns. *Development Psychology, 29*, 686-691.

LECTURE TOPIC 6.6: BABY BRAIN DEVELOPMENT
The topic of critical periods in the development of the infant brain has become popularized by media reports and a White House conference on the subject. It is widely believed that babies must have certain experiences in the first months or years to enable them to develop optimally. The research does not completely support this idea, however.

High-quality nutrition is essential to optimal brain development, at least in part because of the formation of the myelin sheath on axons, which is incomplete at birth. In addition, the environment provides essential experiences that foster development through proliferation of dendrites, pruning of unneeded synapses, and strengthening of frequently used neural pathways, such as the visual pathway. What is not supported is the idea that infants need special environments, special toys, or special activities other than those that are typically provided by a nurturing caregiver during everyday activities.

DISCUSSION TOPICS
DISCUSSION TOPIC 6.1: EARLY INTERVENTION
The research cited in this chapter reflects how much more we know than we used to know about the early sensory capacities of infants. Yet to date, the sensory capacities of very few infants have been closely observed. Possibly, with much greater screening (or certainly with mandatory testing), not only would we know more about infants' early development but many more infants with deficits would be detected and intervention measures could be undertaken to lessen the behavioral and cognitive impact of the deficit. Explore with your class the attitudes of class members toward societal intervention in children's lives. Should parents be fined for not having their children tested and for not taking the remedial measures recommended? How much say should society have in how parents raise their children? Should society be able to intervene for medical reasons but not for other reasons?

This area has lost much of its funding during the last decade. Would you rather your tax dollars be used for early intervention or other programs later? Have students talk to politicians about this.

DISCUSSION TOPIC 6.2: AMERICAN CHILD-REARING PRACTICES AND SIDS

The infant-mortality rate in the United States is the lowest in history; however, infant mortality is still over twice as high for black babies as for white babies. The overall improvement in infant survival can be attributed to a variety of factors, such as regional health centers, early recognition of high-risk pregnancies, and increased use of contraceptives. Unfortunately, some deaths still do occur. Sudden infant death syndrome (SIDS), or "crib death," is still a puzzle. Many causes have been explored, but all we have really learned is what does *not* cause this tragedy. New theories proposed include virus, respiratory dysfunction (many of the babies experienced apnea), and neurological dysfunction or abnormality in brain chemistry. There has been a push to have up-to-date immunizations, which has lagged in the United States.

What relationships exist between American child-rearing practices and its high rate of SIDS? Have students investigate and discuss possible connections. (One connection is that most babies no longer sleep in the same bed as their parents. The suggestion has been made that babies miss getting signals from their parents' breathing that help regulate and sustain the babies' breathing.)

DISCUSSION TOPIC 6.3: INFANT EQUIPMENT

Manufacturers are creating more and more equipment for parents to buy for their children. This equipment includes such items as car safety seats (essential to safety), playpens, walkers (essentially unsafe), baby gyms, baby monitors. These items vary in terms of how useful they are and how necessary they are. Equipment manufacturers would have parents believe that all equipment is both necessary and useful. Have students discuss whether pieces of equipment fill a need for infants or a desire for parents.

DISCUSSION TOPIC 6.4: INFANT PERCEPTUAL DEVELOPMENT

Have students discuss the following question: Do you believe that William James' statement conceptualizing the world of the infant as a "great blooming, buzzing, confusion" is correct? Why or why not? Students will incorporate information from the text to discuss the infant's experience of the world.

Our knowledge of the infant's sensory capacities indicates that, although most of the senses are operating, their sensitivity increases with age. Furthermore, sensory functioning seems to be organized rather than random. Babies show that they have distinct visual preferences, for example, and look at only small portions of visual targets. They are attracted by motion, light and dark contrasts and some amount of complexity. Neonates can also differentiate distinct sounds, distinctive odors, and various strong-tasting solutions.

INDEPENDENT STUDIES
INDEPENDENT STUDY 6.1

How have the use of early childhood immunizations and the prevalence of major childhood illnesses changed during your lifetime? To find out, first check your own health records to find out (1) which immunizations you had before the ages of 2 to 5 and (2) which major childhood illnesses you had, if any, and the ages at which you had them. If these records are not readily available, use library resources to find out (1) which immunizations were recommended or required when you were 2 to 5 years old and (b) how prevalent such illnesses as measles, mumps, chicken pox, and infantile paralysis were at that time, as well as today. Possible sources of such statistics are official publications of the U.S. Center for Disease Prevention and Control and your state's department of public health or epidemiology. Also use these sources to find out what immunizations are currently recommended for infants and young children in the United States. Then compare the current recommendations with the immunizations that were normally done when you were a child, or with the ones you had. Also compare the prevalence of major childhood illnesses during both periods, or, alternatively, compare the illnesses you had with the chances that a young child will contract these illnesses today.

CHOOSING SIDES

CHOOSING SIDES 6.1: BREASTFEEDING VERSUS BOTTLE-FEEDING

Make available in the form of a handout or overhead transparency the following information about mother's milk for a class discussion on breastfeeding versus bottle-feeding. You could also invite a speaker from LaLeche League or use some of their materials. Some facts about mother's milk (MM):

1. For the first 6 months of life, infants can satisfy all their nutritional needs with MM.
2. MM contains antibodies that destroy viruses, bacteria, and other microorganisms, providing the baby with added immunity.
3. MM promotes the growth of good bifid bacteria in the baby's intestinal tracts. These good bacteria can destroy disease-causing bacteria.
4. MM helps to reduce allergies.
5. MM is easier for a baby to digest than cow's milk.
6. More breastfed than bottle-fed babies survive to age 1.
7. MM is associated with lower rates of childhood diabetes.
8. MM does not increase intelligence scores.
9. Drugs being taken by the mother can show up in MM.
10. Certain foods that the mother eats such as garlic, onion, cabbage, red wine, tomatoes, and seafood can influence the taste of MM and its digestibility.
11. Hormones in oral contraceptives can influence the supply of MM (combination pills—those that have both estrogen and progesterone—tend to reduce MM supply; progesterone-only pills tend to increase MM supply).

References

Newman, J. (December 1995). How breast milk protects newborns. *Scientific American*, 76-79.
Zimmerman, D. R. (April 1985). Fifty fascinating facts about mother's milk. *Good Housekeeping*, 84-89.

KNOWLEDGE CONSTRUCTION ACTIVITIES

KNOWLEDGE CONSTRUCTION ACTIVITY 6.1: GENERATIVE TERMS

This activity will use the principles of generative learning as explained in the Introduction to assist students in gaining a better understanding of terms. Divide the class into groups of four or five. Assign each group the task of generating an example for a generative term from this chapter. The example that each group creates cannot be one that has been used in the class or in the book. They must think of a new application for the term that they are given. Groups are allowed to use their books and notes. By creating their own example of the term, they demonstrate an understanding of the term to the level of application. There are several approaches that can be used in this exercise. Students may be given the entire list at once, but often one group will finish far ahead of the others and topics will get out of sequence. Another strategy is to give all of the groups the same term to create an example and then go around the room to discuss outcomes. This has been very successful, but also takes the most time. A third approach is to give each group a different term and see what examples they can generate.

Some generative terms for Chapter 6 are listed below.

Reflex behaviors	Auditory discrimination
Systems of action	Risk factor
Gross motor skill	Cultural influence on motor development
Fine motor skill	Immunization

KNOWLEDGE CONSTRUCTION ACTIVITY 6.2: INTERVIEW A BREASTFEEDING MOTHER ABOUT WEANING

Divide students into small groups to develop their interview questions. They may want to ask the mother about her responses to weaning, the strategies she used, the baby's responses, and how weaning was perceived by other family members. Have each member of the group conduct an interview, remembering that the prospective interviewees include mothers of infants but also their own mothers, grandmothers, or any women who have had this experience. Have the groups get back together to discuss the similarities and differences among their respondents. Each group will compile results and present a summary to the class. This process will enable comparisons across many individuals. What differences do students see that could be attributed to cohort? To the age or stage of development of the infant at weaning? To the age or stage of development of the mother?

KNOWLEDGE CONSTRUCTION ACTIVITY 6.3: INFANT CAREGIVING ACROSS CULTURES

Divide the class into small groups to do research on different cultural practices in child rearing. Groups each choose a different culture to study. This project would be a good way to explore library and/or Internet resources. Students are responsible for discovering how infants are cared for in their assigned country/culture. Include diapering, feeding, weaning, dress, toilet training, who provides primary care, toys, health practices, and any other practice of interest. Each group presents a brief overview to the class. The instructor compiles a summary table of information across areas so that students can make comparisons among cultures.

KNOWLEDGE CONSTRUCTION ACTIVITY 6.4: OBSERVING IN A DAY CARE CENTER

This activity will both help you obtain practical experience with developmental needs and issues of infants as well as expose you to a day care environment.

Identify a day care facility that has an infant program. Call to make an appointment to observe infant care. Be polite and courteous on the phone. It is also important to be honest that this observation is a class assignment. Observing for one full day or half-day would be the most valuable. Be sure to take notes on your observations.

Watch closely to see how well the infants are cared for:

Are diapers changed when needed?
Are babies fed at appropriate times?
Are babies fed in an appropriate way?
Do teachers pay attention to outbursts of crying?
How much physical contact is there between adults and babies?
What kinds of records do teachers keep for each infant?

Look at the room where the infants are kept:

Is it clean?
Are the necessary supplies available?
Are the cribs adequate?
What is the level of stimulation? Are there things for babies to look at, play with, listen to? Are there quiet places for babies and caregivers?

Observe the infant teachers:

Are they trained?
Do they seem comfortable with the babies?
Are they patient?
How many teachers per infant are there?

Record these observations and any others you feel are significant. Write a paper giving your observations and your reactions. The paper:

1. Should be 3 to 5 pages long
2. Should be typed, double spaced, and have 1-inch margins
3. Should include a cover sheet that includes your name, the title of your paper, your ID #, the course name, the course section number, and the date

7. RESOURCES FOR INSTRUCTORS

Books and Journal Articles

Aslin, R. N., & Smith, L. B. (1988). Perceptual development. *Annual Review of Psychology, 39,* 435-473.

Barrett, D. E., & Frank, D. A. (1987). *The effects of undernutrition on children's behavior.* New York: Gordon & Breach Science Publishers.

Bloom, K. (ed.) (1981). *Prospective issues in infancy research.* Hillsdale, NJ: Lawrence Erlbaum Associates.

Bower, T. G. R. (1977). *A primer of infant development.* San Francisco: Freeman.

Cohen, L., & Salapatek, P. (1975). *Infant perception: From sensation to cognition,* vols. 1 and 2. New York: Academic Press.

Eiger, M. S., & Olds, S. W. (1987). *The complete book of breastfeeding.* New York: Workman.

Haith, M. M. (1980). *Rules that newborn babies look by.* Hillsdale, NJ: Lawrence Erlbaum Associates.

Kempe, C. H., Silver, H. K., O'Brien, D., & Fulginiti, V. A. (eds.) (1987). *Current pediatric diagnosis and treatment.* Norwalk, CT: Appleton.

Osofsky, J. D. (ed.) (1980). *Handbook of infant development.* New York: Wiley.

Richards, M. (1979). *Infancy: World of the newborn.* New York: Harper & Row.

Rickert, V. I., & Johnson, M. (1988). Reducing nocturnal awakening and crying episodes in infants and young children: A comparison between scheduled awakenings and systematic ignoring. *Pediatrics, 81,* 203-212.

Rosenblith, J. F., & Sims-Knight, J. E. (1985). *In the beginning: Development in the first two years of life.* Monterey, CA: Brooks/Cole.

Walk, R. D. (1981). *Perceptual development.* Monterey, CA: Brooks/Cole.

Weggemann, T., Brown, J. K., Fulford, G. E., & Minns, R. A. (1987). A study of normal baby movements. *Child: Care, Health, and Development, 13,* 41-58.

Video resources

Life's first feelings (Coronet, 1986, 60 min.) This film shows perceptual and emotional development in the first three years.

The first ten months of life: Part 1 (CRM, 27 min.). The film depicts and discusses common problems of premature infants.

The first 365 days in the life of a child (FFHS, 1994, video, 13-part series, 28 min. each). This 13-part series shows the normal development of an average healthy child during the first year of its life.

7 COGNITIVE DEVELOPMENT DURING THE FIRST THREE YEARS

STUDYING COGNITIVE DEVELOPMENT:
CLASSIC APPROACHES
Behaviorist Approach: Basic Mechanics of Learning
Psychometric Approach: Developmental and Intelligence Testing
Piagetian Approach: The Sensorimotor Stage

STUDYING COGNITIVE DEVELOPMENT:
NEWER APPROACHES
Information-Processing Approach: Perceptions and Representations
Cognitive Neuroscience Approach: The Brain's Cognitive Structures
Social-Contextual Approach: Learning from Interactions with Caregivers

LANGUAGE DEVELOPMENT
Sequence of Early Language Development
Characteristics of Early Speech
Classic Theories of Language Acquisition: The Nature-Nurture Debate
Influences on Language Development
Preparing for Literacy: The Benefits of Reading Aloud

In This Chapter of Your Instructor's Manual You Will Find:
1. Total Teaching Package Outline
2.   Expanded Outline (transparency-ready)
3. Guideposts for Study
4. Learning Objectives
5. Key Terms
6. Teaching and Learning Activities
    Lecture Topics
    Discussion Topics
    Independent Study
    Choosing Sides
    Knowledge Construction Activities
7. Resources for Instructors

1. TOTAL TEACHING PACKAGE OUTLINE

Chapter 7: Cognitive Development In The First Three Years

Studying cognitive development: **Classic approaches**	**Learning objective 7.1** **Knowledge construction activity 7.1**
Behaviorist approach: Basic mechanics of learning	**Guidepost for study 7.1** **Learning objectives 7.2, 7.3** **Lecture topic 7.3**
Psychometric approach: Developmental and intelligence testing	**Guidepost for study 7.2** **Learning objectives 7.4, 7.5**
Piagetian approach: The sensorimotor stage	**Guidepost for study 7.3** **Learning objectives 7.6 7.7, 7.8, 7.9** **Lecture topic 7.2** **Knowledge construction activity 7.2** **Box 7.1, (textbook p. 156)**
Studying cognitive development: **Newer approaches**	**Knowledge construction activity 7.1**
Information-processing approach: Perceptions and representations	**Guidepost for study 7.4, 7.5** **Learning objectives 7.10, 7.11, 7.12** **Lecture topic 7.1**
Cognitive neuroscience approach: The brain's cognitive structures	**Guidepost for study 7.6** **Learning objective 7.13** **Discussion topic 7.1**
Social-contextual approach: Learning from interactions with caregivers	**Guidepost for study 7.7** **Learning objective 7.15** **Choosing sides 7.1** **Knowledge construction activity 7.5** **Box 7.2, (textbook p. 169)**
Language development	**Guidepost for study 7.8** **Knowledge construction activity 7.1**
Sequence of early language development	**Learning objective 7.16** **Knowledge construction activities 7.3, 7.8** **Independent study 7.1**

Characteristics of early speech	**Learning objective 7.17** **Knowledge construction activities 7.4, 7.6**
Classic theories of language acquisition: The nature-nurture debate	**Guidepost for study 7.9** **Learning objectives 7.18, 7.19,7.20**
Influences on language development	**Learning objectives 7.21, 7.22, 7.23** **Lecture topics 7.4, 7.5** **Discussion topic 7.2**
Preparing for literacy: The benefits of reading aloud	**Learning objective 7.24** **Knowledge construction activity 7.7**

Please check out the online learning center located at www.mhhe.com/papaliacw9 for further information on these and other topics. There you can also access downloadable PowerPoint slides tailored to each chapter of the text and containing useful teaching notes as well as images and tables from the text itself.

2. EXPANDED OUTLINE (TRANSPARENCY READY)

I. Cognitive Development
  A. Intelligent behavior
    1. Goal-oriented
    2. Adaptive
  B. Classic approaches
    1. Behaviorist approach
      a. Classical conditioning
      b. Operant conditioning
    2. Psychometric approach
      a. IQ—Intelligence quotient tests
      b. Standardized norms
      c. Test validity
      d. Test reliability
    3. Piagetian approach
      a. Sensorimotor stage
        i. Schemes
        ii. Circular reactions
        iii. Object permanence
  C. Newer approaches
    1. Information processing
      a. Perception, learning, memory, problem solving
        i. Habituation
        ii. Visual preference
        iii. Visual recognition memory
    2. Cognitive neuroscience
      a. Brain structure
      b. Neurology
    3. Social-contextual
      a. Environmental aspects
        i. Guided participation

II. Language Development
- A. Language
    1. Literacy
- B. Sequence of early language development
    1. Prelinguistic speech
    2. Linguistic speech
- C. Characteristics of speech
    1. Holophrase
    2. Telegraphic speech
    3. Syntax
- D. Classic theories of language acquisition
    1. Nativism
        a. Language acquisition device (LAD)
    2. Learning theorists
- E. Influences on language development
    1. Preparing for literacy
    2. Benefits of reading aloud

3. GUIDEPOSTS FOR STUDY

7.1 How do infants learn and how long can they remember?

7.2 Can infants' and toddlers' intelligence be measured and how can it be improved?

7.3 How did Piaget describe infants' and toddlers' cognitive development and how have his claims stood up under later scrutiny?

7.4 How can we measure infants' ability to process information and how does this ability relate to future intelligence?

7.5 When do babies begin to think about characteristics of the physical world?

7.6 What can brain research reveal about the development of cognitive skills?

7.7 How does social interaction with adults advance cognitive competence?

7.8 How do babies develop language?

7.9 What influences contribute to linguistic progress?

4. LEARNING OBJECTIVES

After completing this chapter, the student should be able to:

7.1 Distinguish among the goals of the behaviorist, psychometric, and Piagetian approaches to the study of cognitive development.

7.2 Identify conditions under which newborns can be classically or operantly conditioned.

7.3 Summarize the findings of research on operant conditioning and long-term memory in infants.

7.4 Explain why developmental tests may be used with infants and toddlers and why they are unreliable in predicting later IQ.

7.5 Articulate the relationships among socioeconomic status, parenting practices, and cognitive development.

7.6 Summarize the major development during the six substages of Piaget's sensorimotor stage.

7.7 Explain how circular reactions work, and distinguish among primary, secondary, and tertiary circular reactions.

7.8 Tell why the development of representational ability is important.

7.9 Summarize Piaget's views on the development of object permanence and spatial knowledge.

7.10 Explain why Piaget may have underestimated some of infants' cognitive abilities.

7.11 Explain the violations-of-expectations method, tell how and why it is used, and identify some criticisms of it.

7.12 Explain how the violations-of- expectations research seems to contradict Piaget's account of development.

7.13 Identify the brain structures apparently involved in implicit, preexplicit, explicit, and working memory; give an example of a task made possible by each type of memory.

7.14 Describe how brain research helps to explain Piagetian developments and information-processing skills.

7.15 Compare two cultural patterns of guided participation in toddlers' learning.

7.16 Trace the typical milestones in early language development.

7.17 Describe five ways in which early speech differs from adult speech.

7.18 Summarize how nativism and learning theory seek to explain language acquisition, pointing out strengths and weaknesses of each.

7.19 Name two important areas of the brain involved in the use of language.

7.20 Give evidence for plasticity in the brain's linguistic area.

7.21 Explain the importance of social interaction to language development; give three examples of how parents or caregivers help babies learn to talk.

7.22 Tell how socioeconomic status and other family characteristics may influence language development.

7.23 Compare the arguments for and against child-directed speech.

7.24 Tell why reading aloud to children at an early age is beneficial and describe an effective way of reading aloud to infants and toddlers.

4. KEY TERMS

Intelligent behavior
Behaviorist approach
Psychometric approach
Piagetian approach
Classical conditioning
Operant conditioning
IQ (intelligent quotient) tests
Standardized norms
Validity
Reliability
Bayley Scales of Infant Development
Home Observation for Measurement of the Environment (HOME)
Developmental priming mechanisms
Early intervention
Sensorimotor stage
Schemes
Circular reaction
Representational ability
Deferred imitation
Object permanence
A, not B, error
Invisible imitation
Visible imitation
Information-processing approach

Cognitive neuroscience approach
Social-contextual approach
Habituation
Dishabituation
Visual preference
Cross-modal transfer
Visual-recognition memory
Violation-of-expectations
Explicit memory
Implicit memory
Working memory
Guided participation
Language
Literacy
Prelinguistic speech
Linguistic speech
Holophrase
Telegraphic speech
Syntax
Nativism
Language acquisition device (LAD)
Code mixing
Code switching
Child-directed speech

6. TEACHING AND LEARNING ACTIVITIES
LECTURE TOPICS
LECTURE TOPIC 7.1: CONTINUITY IN INFANT MENTAL DEVELOPMENT

Many psychologists believe that cognitive development during infancy is a discontinuous process, and they can cite numerous research studies that suggest little relationship between measures of infant intelligence and intelligence scores during childhood. Typical of this research are the correlational studies comparing results of the Bayley Scales of Infant Development and standard IQ scores during the school years. The correlations are very low until after the age of 5; at age 5, the correlation between child scores and adult scores is about 0.60, and the correlation between scores at ages 11 and 18 is about 0.90. The researchers often concluded that intelligence in infancy is very different from intelligence as people age.

However, some psychologists believe that mental development is continuous throughout the life span and that studies fail to show this continuity merely because of the type of measurements used during infancy. Most infant scales tap sensory and motor capacities, whereas later childhood scales feature verbal and qualitative abilities. According to these psychologists, new measures of infant mental capacity are needed—and they suggest that these measures should emphasize attention.

Two aspects of infant attention may be correlated to later intelligence: (1) *Decrement of attention* refers to *habituation* and the turning away of attention from familiar or constant stimuli. Greater decrements are associated with efficient information processing. (2) *Recovery of attention* refers to *novelty preference* and the attending to discrepant stimuli. "Relatively greater amounts of looking at novel stimuli, or reciprocally lesser amounts of looking at familiar stimuli, are generally interpreted as more efficient information processing." Decrement and recovery of attention are likely to be central mental capacities, related to each other, and perhaps predictive of childhood cognitive competence. Six-month-old infants' decrement and recovery of attention correlate with measures of language ability and standardized intelligence tests of children between 2 and 8 years of age.

The following abilities have been shown to be related to efficient decrement and recovery of attention: preference for complexity, advanced sensorimotor development, above-average play sophistication, quicker problem-solving strategies, and better picture-matching scores.

Research findings resulting from the use of decrement and recovery of attention support moderate continuity in early cognitive development. Knowledge about mental continuity will grow as researchers continue to develop better ways of measuring infant responses.

Reference

Bernstein, M., & Sigman, M. (1986). Continuity in mental development from infancy. Child Development, 57, 251-274.

LECTURE TOPIC 7.2: PIAGET'S BIOGRAPHY

Piaget's writings are filled with delightful anecdotes about children's behavior. However, on first reading his theory, one often loses this flavor in a discussion of assimilation, accommodation, schemes, adaptation, equilibrium, disequilibrium, and so on. A biographical look into the life of this genius may help students appreciate his approach.

Jean Piaget was born in 1896 in Neuchatel, Switzerland. He was a child prodigy who studied mollusks and published research papers while still in high school. He was even offered a job as curator of a museum mollusk collection on the basis of his work.

After receiving his doctorate in biological science at the University of Lausanne, he worked in Binet's laboratory during the development of the first IQ tests. He was fascinated by the "wrong" answers children gave. Frustrated by the routine constraints on exactly what and how questions should be asked in this testing situation, Piaget later developed a clinical interview approach that has been criticized as unscientific and nonreplicable. A great quantity of his data also comes from extensively studying his own three children.

The first area of child development investigated by Piaget dealt with the child's spontaneous ideas about the physical world: Where does the sun go at night? Where do dreams come from? The second area of research (1930s) focused on spontaneous cognitive development in infancy, including such ideas as object permanence. About 1940, Piaget began concentrating on older children and adolescents. His theory describes the changes that occur in children's conceptions of reality and their understanding of adult concepts.

Piaget died in 1980 at the age of 80. His life has been described as very disciplined. He arose early and daily wrote several publishable pages. Mornings were spent teaching and attending meetings. In the afternoon he pondered the current issue of his concern on long walks. Then in the evening, he read.

During the summer break in the school year, Piaget took the research data that his assistants had gathered and retired to the Alps. At his retreat, alone in an abandoned farmhouse, he assimilated the new data and wrote. In the fall, he descended from the mountain like a modern-day Moses with new books and articles, the product of his "vacation." He published more than 40 books and hundreds of articles that have drastically changed the fields of developmental psychology and education.

References

Flavell, J. H. (1992). Cognitive development: Past, present, and future. Developmental Psychology, 28, 998-1005.

Ginsburg, H., & Opper, S. (1969). *Piaget's theory of intellectual development: An introduction.* Englewood Cliffs, NJ: Prentice-Hall.

LECTURE TOPIC 7.3: B. F. SKINNER'S "BABY BOX"

Skinner's famous "baby box," about which there are many legends, could provide the basis of an interesting discussion in which to clarify the principles of operant conditioning. The major focus of operant conditioning is the immediate environment. For Skinner's second child, Deborah, he built a controlled environment for the purpose of simplifying baby care.

The crib-sized living space called the "baby tender" had a large picture window and sound-absorbing walls. There was a canvas mattress at the bottom stretched over air filters that warmed and humidified the air. A long strip of sheet could be moved over the canvas so that a clean section was always available. Deborah could live in this environment in only a diaper, regardless of the temperature in the rest of the house. Her movement was unencumbered by clothing or bedding.

In the baby tender, it was possible to introduce sounds systematically, control exposure to infection, systematically control temperature, control light and dark, and so forth. (Such an environment would simplify experimentation with infants, but no experimentation was done with Deborah.) Popular knowledge of the apparatus came from an article Skinner submitted to *Ladies Home Journal* in 1945. In response to this article, several baby tenders were built on a trial basis, and marketability of the device was investigated. General Mills Company turned down the opportunity because it doubted that the item could be patented and there was uncertainty about public reaction. Another company borrowed money and took advances from customers to produce "Heir Conditioners." This firm failed to manufacture the devices, and the owner absconded. Finally, a furniture company produced a working model, but the selling price was over $420 a unit. Several later attempts at building an "air crib" also failed. Meanwhile, Deborah continued to sleep and take naps in the baby tender until she was 2 ½ years old. Rumors of Deborah's psychotic breakdown, her suicide, and her lawsuit against her father are all unfounded. She is currently a successful artist who lives in London with her husband, Dr. Barry Bugan.

Reference

Skinner, B. F. (March 1979). My experience with the baby tender. *Psychology Today*.

LECTURE TOPIC 7.4: LANGUAGE COMPETENCY

The appearance of "motherese" some time shortly after the infant's first birthday as the major form of language interaction between parent and child highlights the fact that parents are more interested in conversing with their children than with *teaching* them language use. In addition to being fairly simple, highly repetitive, higher-pitched, and in the form of questions, parents' conversations with their children at this time are generally restricted to the use of concrete nouns and the present tense and are usually directed to the child's actions or experiences.

Despite the fact that parents are naturally conversational with their infants in a most beneficial way, parents (and a surprising number of nonparent students) are concerned about how best to enhance the development of language competency in children. Results from the Language Indices Project (LIP), which followed the language acquisition of 56 babies, provides information about some of the key factors.

Principal researcher Paula Menyuk and her associates Martin Schultz and Jacqueline Leibergott selected a sample made up half of full-term babies and half of premature babies for their study. The infants came from four socioeconomic groups with two-parent families where the mother did not work outside the home. Major goals of the study were to determine the normal range of language development during the first 3 years and to study the frequency and style of verbal interactions exhibited between the mothers and their children. It is important to note that the study was designed to be a descriptive study, not to teach the mothers how to interact with their children in order to foster language development. Nonetheless, because the study tended to focus the mothers' attention on their children's language development, and because the researchers modeled appropriate language interactions when testing the children, the parents undoubtedly altered their typical "motherese" and practiced with their children between observation sessions.

One of the most important findings was that the mothers interacted with their children in a wide variety of ways that were successful in helping the infants to acquire language. Many individual patterns of development resulted in the children attaining language competency. This finding suggests that parents should be less concerned about the inevitable comparisons that occur between their children's progress and that of others!

A second key finding was that talking to children rather than at them is beneficial but that giving them the opportunity to respond is even more important in successful language mastery. Even very young children benefit from the chance to have their say, even if their "say" is prelinguistic speech. An additional finding was that, at 3 years of age, there was little difference between the children who had been fastest at language mastery and those who achieved mastery more than 6 months later. Likewise, preemies were not at a disadvantage in language development by the time they were 3.

The researchers are currently investigating ways to identify early signs of difficulty with language development. They are also looking for connections between early language development and later school achievement.

References

Robbins, L. (July 1984). Baby talk. *Bostonia*, 26-28.
Snow, C. E. (1977). The development of conversation between mothers and babies. *Journal of Child Language, 4*, 1-22.

LECTURE TOPIC 7.5: LANGUAGE TEACHABILITY

Language acquisition is assumed to be a universal occurrence for humans. However, some children do not acquire language on their own and must be explicitly taught. Failure to acquire language skills will diminish their social worlds, decrease their learning capabilities and chances for later academic success, and ultimately reduce their opportunities to lead independent, self-fulfilling lives.

Mabel Rice, in a review article on language acquisition, points out that the failure to acquire language skills "should not be automatically equated with limited intelligence, sensory handicaps, poor parental skills, or impoverished environmental circumstances." Furthermore, she maintains that teaching language in these special cases requires specialized strategies that meet the needs of individual children.

Rice believes that because these children have not learned language while interacting in ordinary situations, they will not profit from placement in typical preschool situations. Instead, she believes such children will profit from specially designed preschools where efforts are concentrated on incorporating the development of language skills within each of the children's daily activities and setting specific goals for individual children. Specialized individualized teaching may be needed for these children throughout their elementary and secondary schooling.

Three components for the teachability of language have been noted by Rice and Schiefelbusch. First, word meanings, especially those of verbs, are the key elements of language to teach. Second, the training must balance the skills to be learned and techniques to be used with the individual's existing intellectual, perceptual, social, and motor competencies. Third, teaching new language skills requires convergent strategies that match the child's language-learning style with the skills to be learned.

References

Rice, M. L. (1989). Children's language learning. *American Psychologist, 44*, 149-156.
Rice, M. L., & Schiefelbusch, R. L. (eds.) (1989*). Teachability of language*. Baltimore, MD: Brookes.

DISCUSSION TOPICS

DISCUSSION TOPIC 7.1: MRI AND INTELLIGENCE TESTING

With the development of PET scans (positron emission tomography), a new level of observation for biological functions was created. One of the most sophisticated techniques to be derived from this new technology is magnetic resonance imaging (MRI). With this technique, even specific chemicals at work in the brain can be identified. MRI may make possible more reliable measures of differences in intellectual functioning that are based in biological differences. Explore with your students the ramifications of determining to what degree infant intelligence is based on biological factors rather than behavioral factors such as using brain scans for placement in programs.

DISCUSSION TOPIC 7.2: CULTURAL DIFFERENCES IN LANGUAGE DEVELOPMENT

Most people process isolated vowel sounds mainly in the right hemisphere of the brain. However, the Japanese (and Americans and Europeans who are reared in Japan) handle isolated vowel sounds in the left hemisphere. The Japanese language is more heavily dependent on vowel sounds than other languages are. Language is a determinant of brain organization and thinking patterns. Discuss the impact on culture that the English and Japanese languages seem to have.

INDEPENDENT STUDY

INDEPENDENT STUDY 7.1: LANGUAGE LEARNING

Have students research speech and language therapy programs for developmentally delayed infants. Contact the local early intervention center, speech and language clinic, or university speech pathology program to seek information. An Internet search on language development should yield some programs designed for parents to use to support language acquisition.

CHOOSING SIDES

SUPERBABIES - HEREDITY OR ENVIRONMENT

Pro: Parents should expose their infants to as much education as possible so that they will have a head start in cognitive development. Infants are capable of learning a lot more than we give them credit for, and it is up to parents to make use of their baby's potential for learning.

Con: Infants exposed to a fairly interesting environment will naturally learn as their biological system matures. To push learning on infants is to push them into a world where anxiety and competition dominate.

The following list gives arguments which might be advanced to support each side of the debate.

Pro: Early Education the Key to Cognitive Development
1. Infancy is the time when children can be exposed most efficiently to lots of information, because infancy is the greatest learning time in the entire life span.
2. Musical, scientific, and literary geniuses are created by parents who start tapping a child's potential early.
3. If more parents would try to develop "superbabies," our society would benefit by the production of more top-notch scientists, outstanding artists, and better thinkers.
4. Infants have an innate desire to learn and will incorporate lots of information if it is presented in the right way.
5. Infants who are taught early are likely to make learning a lifelong goal and therefore outachieve their peers.
6. The competition for good jobs is getting tougher and tougher. Only children who have been pushed into achievement will be prepared to get the top spots.

Con: Biological Maturation the Key to Cognitive Development
1. There can be too much emphasis on cognitive skills at the expense of emotional adjustment.
2. Some children might become cognitively skilled but stay emotionally overdependent on their parents.
3. Some "superbabies" might come to believe that achievement is everything.
4. Pushing babies educationally may result in negative attitudes toward learning and inability to initiate their own learning activities.
5. Infant education programs teach data but teach little about how to think.
6. There is biologically caused discontinuity in early childhood, so many of the efforts at intense early education are wasted.
7. Some kinds of learning must wait for maturation of the central nervous system; some of the parents' efforts are too much, too soon.

KNOWLEDGE CONSTRUCTION ACTIVITIES
KNOWLEDGE CONSTRUCTION ACTIVITY 7.1: GENERATIVE TERMS

This activity will use the principles of generative learning as explained in the Introduction to assist students in gaining a better understanding of terms. Divide the class into groups of four or five. Assign each group the task of generating an example for a generative term from this chapter. The example that each group creates cannot be one that has been used in the class or in the book. They must think of a new application for the term that they are given. Groups are allowed to use their books and notes. By creating their own example of the term, they demonstrate an understanding of the term to the level of application. There are several approaches that can be used in this exercise. Students may be given the entire list at once, but often one group will finish far ahead of the others and topics will get out of sequence. Another strategy is to give all of the groups the same term to create an example and then go around the room to discuss outcomes. This has been very successful, but also takes the most time. A third approach is to give each group a different term and see what examples they can generate.

Some generative terms for Chapter 7 are listed below.

Qualitative development
Primary circular reaction
Secondary circular reaction
Tertiary circular reaction
Object permanence
Schema
Habituation
Guided participation
Holophrase
Telegraphic speech

KNOWLEDGE CONSTRUCTION ACTIVITY 7.2: OBJECT PERMANENCE

One excellent demonstration involves displaying various stages in the acquisition of the schema of the permanent object. The following object-permanence tasks can be attempted with infants age 4 to 8 months, 8 to 12 months, 12 to 18 months, and 18 to 24 months.

Task 1: Show each infant an interesting object, such as a rattle. Then cover it with a piece of cloth. Note the infant's response. Now move the cloth so that part of the rattle is exposed. What does the infant do?

Task 2: Show the child the rattle again. Now move it so that it disappears behind a screen. Does the infant try to find it? Now try this task again, but this time have the toy go behind one screen and then another one located close by. Again note the child's response.

Task 3: Show the infant the rattle, then cover it with a small box. Move the box behind the screen, let the rattle remain behind the screen, and bring the box back into view. Does the child look behind the screen?

How well do the class's observations agree with Piaget's findings, described in the text?

KNOWLEDGE CONSTRUCTION ACTIVITY 7.3: PREVERBAL COMMUNICATION

Have students observe language and communication patterns of a preverbal child approximately 12 to 18 months old. Here are some interesting things to look for (tape-record the language if possible to analyze as a class):

a.   What sounds is the child capable of producing? Are the sounds limited to those found in English?

b.   What babbling patterns occur, for example, consonant-vowel syllables (da) and syllable repetition (babababa)?

c.   Can you detect English intonation patterns? An example is rising intonation for questions and falling intonation for statements, though the content is entirely babbled syllables.

d. Does the child expect to "carry on a conversation" with whomever is present, and does the child talk while alone? Talking while alone demonstrates the child's need to practice what she is learning. Carrying on a babbled conversation demonstrates the child's limited understanding of the social nature of speech.

KNOWLEDGE CONSTRUCTION 7.4: PARENT TRAINING

Many programs are now being offered to help people become more effective parents and raise more competent children. These programs are available in many formats (print, video, film) and are offered by many different groups (day care centers, schools, churches, social services agencies). Invite students to investigate those programs that are available in your community and to report their findings to the class.

KNOWLEDGE CONSTRUCTION ACTIVITY 7.5: YOUR FIRST WORD—WERE YOU REALLY TALKING?

Have the student identify his or her first word (perhaps a good reason to call home?) and discuss in small groups whether it was a real word or babbling. Have them understand that it was a first word if:
1. It was used only for an object or group of objects.
2. It was used consistently.
3. It occurred at about one year of age.

If it was recorded in the baby book at 6 months of age, it was probably babbling. This is a good time to discuss how information from caregivers is often altered over time, which is a good example of the flaws of retrospective data collection.

KNOWLEDGE CONSTRUCTION ACTIVITY 7.6: CREATE A BROCHURE FOR PARENTS

In small groups, have students write a brochure for parents who want to do the right things to encourage their child to learn to speak clearly and correctly. They can use the information given in the textbook as a starting point, but they will need to consult parenting books and magazines as well. Students should also consult psychological journals for information.

Students will submit the following:
1. A reference page listing the sources of their information.
2. A brochure that could be photocopied and given to parents. The brochure should involve one sheet of typing paper, but they can fold it any way they would like. They can turn the page sideways and fold it once for a booklet style or fold it three times for a trifold. They can type on both sides of the paper, but stick to one sheet of typing paper. The brochure must be typed. You can be creative in terms of the way you present the material (such as with the use of graphics).

KNOWLEDGE CONSTRUCTION ACTIVITY 7.7: OBSERVE DEVELOPMENT OF PREVERBAL VOCALIZATION

The focus of this project is to begin to notice the differences in vocalizations made as children are learning to talk. Your students will need a tape recorder and tape for this project.

Directions: You will need to record approximately 20 minutes of vocalizations made by three children: one 10- to 14-month-old, two 22- to 26-month-old, and three 34- to 38-month-old infants. Check with the caregiver to find out what would be the best time to record vocalizations. There may be a time of day when the child is particularly playful and talkative.

Writing the paper: Summarize your findings in a paper. Use the language vocabulary words listed in Chapter 4 as much as possible. The paper should include introductory and concluding paragraphs and should answer the following questions:

1. How would you categorize the vocalizations of the 10- to 14-month-old? Was there a great variety in the sound the baby could make? Was the baby able to say any words? How clear were the words? About how many different words could the baby say?
2. How would you categorize the vocalizations of the 22- to 26-month-old? Was the baby able to say any words? How clear were the words? About how many different words could the baby say?
3. How would you categorize the vocalizations of the 34- to 38-month-old? Was the baby able to say any words? How clear were the words? About how many different words could the baby say?
4. How great was the difference in ability between each baby?

The paper:
1. Should be 4 to 6 pages long
2. Should be typed, double-spaced, 1-inch margins
3. Should include a cover sheet with your name, the title of your paper, your ID #, your course name, your section number, and the date
4. Should reference all your sources using APA format

You should turn in your cassette tape with the project.

7. RESOURCES FOR INSTRUCTORS

Books and Journal Articles

Baron, N. S. (1992). *Growing up with language: How children learn to talk*. Reading, MA: Addison-Wesley.

Brown, R. (1973). *A first language: The early stages*. Cambridge, MA: Harvard University Press.

Ginsburg, H., & Opper, S. (1979). *Piaget's theory of intellectual development*, 2d ed. Englewood Cliffs, NJ: Prentice Hall.

Piaget, J. (1952). *The origins of intelligence in children*. New York: International Universities Press.

Pinker, S. (1994). *The language instinct: How the mind creates language*. New York: Morrow.

White, B. L. (1985). *The first three years of life* (rev. ed.). Englewood Cliffs, NJ: Prentice Hall.

Wilde, J. A. (1993). *The child's discovery of the mind*. Cambridge, MA: Harvard University Press.

Video resources

Piaget on Piaget (YU, 1977, approx. 40 min.). Includes descriptions of Piaget's classic studies of infant intelligence.

Brandon and Rachel: Patterns of infant development (UCEMC, video, 30 min.). This is an excellent summary of infant development.

The developing child: The crucial early years (FFHS, 1994, video, 26 min.). This program deals with ways in which mental growth can be assisted in infants and young children.

Sex roles: Charting the complexity of development (IM, 1991, video, 60 min.). Beginning with a look at the cultural ramifications of sex roles and the myths associated with them, this program examines three theories of socialization: Freudian, social-learning, and cognitive-developmental.

The infant mind (IM, 1992, video, 30 min.). Jean Piaget's stage theories of object permanence and sensory-motor development are explained and challenged in this new investigation of infant learning.

Baby talk (IM, 1985, video, 60 min.). Beginning with the radical reappraisal of linguistic development that stemmed from the studies of Noam Chomsky, this video investigates the development of language.

First adaptations (IM, 1992, video, 30 min.). This program shows how infants' sleeping patterns contribute to mental organization and later to learning abilities and illustrates how the brain develops as the infant attains higher levels of cognitive processing.

Language and thinking (IM, 1992, video, 30 min.). Examining research on language development, this program investigates the role of the brain in facilitating and processing language during early childhood.

8

PSYCHOSOCIAL DEVELOPMENT DURING THE FIRST THREE YEARS

FOUNDATIONS OF PSYCHOSOCIAL DEVELOPMENT
Emotions
Temperament
Earliest Social Experiences: The Infant in the Family

DEVELOPMENTAL ISSUES IN INFANCY
Developing Trust
Developing Attachments
Emotional Communication with Caregivers: Mutual Regulation
Social Referencing

DEVELOPMENTAL ISSUES IN TODDLERHOOD
The Emerging Sense of Self
Developing Autonomy
Socialization and Internalization: Developing a Conscience

CONTACT WITH OTHER CHILDREN
Siblings
Sociability with Nonsiblings

CHILDREN OF WORKING PARENTS
Effects of Parental Employment
The Impact of Early Child Care

In This Chapter of Your Instructor's Manual You Will Find:
1. Total Teaching Package Outline
2. Expanded Outline (transparency-ready)
3. Guideposts for Study
4. Learning Objectives
5. Key Terms
6. Teaching and Learning Activities
   - Lecture Topics
   - Discussion Topics
   - Independent Studies
   - Choosing Sides
   - Knowledge Construction Activities
7. Resources for Instructors

1. Total Teaching Package Outline
Chapter 8: Psychosocial Development During the First Three Years

Foundations of psychosocial development	**Discussion topic 8.1** **Knowledge construction activity 8.1**
Emotions	**Guidepost for study 8.1** **Learning objectives 8.1, 8.2, 8.3** **Lecture topic 8.3** **Discussion topic 82**
Temperament	**Guidepost for study 8.2** **Learning objectives 8.4, 8.5** **Box 8-1 (textbook p. 186)** **Lecture topic 8.5** **Discussion topic 8.3**
Earliest social experiences: The infant in the family	**Learning objectives 8.6, 8.7**
Developmental issues in infancy	
Developing trust	**Guidepost for study 8.4** **Learning objectives 8.8, 8.12** **Lecture topic 8.1**
Developing attachments	**Guidepost for study 8.3** **Learning objectives 8.9, 8.13, 8.14, 8.15, 8.16** **Lecture topics 8.2, 8.5, 8.6** **Box 8-2 (textbook p. 189)** **Discussion topics 8.5, 8.6** **Knowledge construction activities 8.2,** **Independent study 8.1**
Emotional communication with caregivers: Mutual regulation	**Guidepost for study 8.5** **Learning objectives 8.17, 8.18**
Social referencing	**Learning objective 8.19**
Developmental issues in toddlerhood	
The emerging sense of self	**Guidepost for study 8.6** **Learning objective 8.20**
Developing autonomy	**Guidepost for study 8.7** **Learning objectives 8.21, 8.22**

Socialization and internalization: Developing a conscience	**Learning objectives 8.23, 8.24, 8.25** **Knowledge construction activity 8.4**
Contact with other children	
Siblings	**Guidepost for study 8.8** **Learning objectives 8.26, 8.27** **Knowledge construction activity 8.5**
Sociability with nonsiblings	**Guidepost for study 8.8** **Learning objectives 8.28**
Children of working parents	
Effects of parental employment	**Guidepost for study 8.9** **Discussion topic 8.4** **Knowledge construction activity 8.3** **Choosing sides 8.1**

Please check out the online learning center located at www.mhhe.com/papaliacw9 for further information on these and other topics. There you can also access downloadable PowerPoint slides tailored to each chapter of the text and containing useful teaching notes as well as images and tables from the text itself.

2. EXPANDED OUTLINE (TRANSPARENCY READY)

I. Foundations of Psychosocial Development
- A. Emotions
- B. Self-awareness
- C. Temperament
    1. Easy children
    2. Difficult children
    3. Slow-to-warm-up children
    4. Goodness of fit
- D. Gender
    1. Gender typing

II. Developmental Issues in Infancy
- A. Basic trust versus basic mistrust
- B. Attachment
    1. Strange situation
        a. Secure attachment
        b. Avoidant attachment
        c. Ambivalent (resistant) attachment
        d. Disorganized-disoriented attachment
    2. Stranger anxiety
    3. Separation anxiety
- C. Mutual regulation
- D. Social referencing

III. Developmental Issues in Toddlerhood
- A. Self-concept
- B. Autonomy versus shame and doubt
    1. Negativism
- C. Socialization
    1. Internalization
    2. Self-regulation
    3. Conscience
        a. Committed compliance
        b. Situational compliance
    4. Reciprocity

3. GUIDEPOSTS FOR STUDY

8.1 When and how do emotions develop and how do babies show them?

8.2 How do infants show temperamental differences and how enduring are those differences?

8.3 What roles do mothers and fathers play in early personality development?

8.4 How do infants gain trust in their world and for attachments?

8.5 How do infants and caregivers "read" each other's nonverbal signals?

8.6 When does the sense of self arise and what are three steps in its development?

8.7 How do toddlers develop autonomy and standards for socially acceptable behavior?

8.8 How do infants and toddlers interact with siblings and other children?

8.9 How do parental employment and early childcare affect infant and toddler development?

4. LEARNING OBJECTIVES

After completing the study of this chapter, the student will be able to:

8.1 Cite two important functions of emotions.

8.2 Explain the significance of patterns of crying, smiling, and laughing.

8.3 Trace atypical sequence of emergence of the basic, self-conscious, and evaluative emotions, and explain its connection with cognitive and neurological development.

8.4 List and describe nine aspects and three patterns of temperament identified by the New York Longitudinal Study.

8.5 Assess evidence for the stability of temperament.

8.6 Discuss how temperament can affect social adjustment, and explain the importance of "goodness of fit."

8.7 Give evidence of the cultural differences in temperament and discuss ways of interpreting it.

8.8 Discuss the implications of Harlow's research.

8.9 Compare the roles of fathers and mothers, and describe cultural differences in the ways fathers play with their babies.

8.10 Describe the influences of mothers and fathers on gender-typing, especially during toddlerhood.

8.11 Discuss the changing roles of grandparents.

8.12 Explain the importance of Erikson's crisis of basic trust versus basic mistrust.

8.13 Describe four patterns of attachment.

8.14 Discuss how attachment is established, including the roles of mothers and fathers and of the baby's temperament.

8.15 Discuss factors affecting stranger anxiety and separation anxiety.

8.16 Describe long-term behavioral differences influenced by attachment patterns.

8.17 Describe how mutual regulation works.

8.18 Discuss how a mother's depression can affect her baby.

8.19 Tell what social referencing is and give examples.

8.20 Trace three stages in the development of the sense of self during toddlerhood.

8.21 Describe Erikson's crisis of autonomy versus shame and doubt.
8.22 Explain why the "terrible twos' are a normal developmental phenomenon.
8.23 Tell how and when self-regulation develops and how it contributes to socialization.
8.24 Distinguish between situational and committed compliance in relation to conscience.
8.25 Discuss how temperament and parenting practices affect socialization.
8.26 Discuss factors affecting a child's adjustment to a new baby.
8.27 Describe changes in sibling interaction and sibling conflict during toddlerhood.
8.28 Trace changes in and influences on sociability during the first 3 years.

5. KEY TERMS

Emotions
Self-awareness
Temperament
"Easy" children
"Difficult" children
"Slow-to-warm-up" children
Goodness of fit
Gender
Gender-typing
Basic trust versus basic mistrust
Attachment
Strange Situation
Secure attachment
Avoidant attachment

Ambivalent (resistant) attachment
Disorganized-disoriented attachment
Stranger anxiety
Separation anxiety
Mutual regulation
"Still-face" paradigm
Social referencing
Self-concept
Autonomy versus shame and doubt
Socialization
Internalization
Self-regulation
Conscience
Committed compliance
Situational compliance
Reciprocity

6. TEACHING AND LEARNING ACTIVITIES
LECTURE TOPICS

LECTURE TOPIC 8.1: BIOGRAPHICAL INFORMATION ON ERIK ERIKSON

Erik Erikson is an important thinker who has theorized about the development of infants. Erikson looks to cultural and societal influences. Two of Erikson's eight "crises" occur during infancy. The crisis of basic trust versus basic mistrust rests on the quality of the parent-child relationship and on whether the child experiences the world as basically good and secure. The crisis of autonomy versus shame and doubt follows the resolution of trust versus mistrust, with evolution of the child's own sense of self and the development of independence. The "terrible twos" are a normal manifestation of the need for autonomy that develops during this time. The child learns self-regulation methods to control the negativism that characterizes this stage.

One possible area for expansion on the text materials would be to discuss Erikson the man and his philosophy in somewhat greater detail. This material might also be presented at various times throughout the course when a specific stage of psychosocial development is being discussed.

Erik Erikson was born in Frankfurt, Germany, in 1902, of Danish ancestry. He lost his father at an early age and 3 years later his mother married the family pediatrician, Dr. Theodore Homburger. In spite of his stepfather's desire that he become a physician, Erikson became a portrait artist specializing in portraits of young children. As Erikson put it, "I was an artist then, which in Europe is a euphemism for a young man with some talent and nowhere to go." His own adolescent identity crisis was so severe that he felt he was either a borderline neurotic or an adolescent psychotic. Living in Vienna, Erikson became a tutor for children of friends and patients of Freud. Here, in the late 1920s, Erikson taught at the American School while completing his psychoanalytic training with Freud's daughter Anna. Erikson was also a certified Montessori teacher and, from the beginning, integrated psychoanalysis and education.

Erikson and his wife, Joan Mowat Serson, came to America in 1933, the year the Nazis took over in Germany. He became one of the original child psychoanalysts in the Boston area. Over the next 20 years, Erikson was on the faculties of Harvard, Yale, and Berkeley, though he dropped out of the doctoral program at Harvard without completing his degree. During this time, he was concerned that his focus not be entirely on disturbed children or on children of a single culture. He studied the development of normal children while in San Francisco and also investigated the life of the Sioux Indians of South Dakota and the Yurok Indians of Northern California. It was through working with these Indian tribes that Erikson developed his ideas on "identity confusion." He saw their uprootedness and the lack of continuity between their modern lifestyle and tribal tradition.

Refusing to sign a state loyalty oath, Erikson left Berkeley and moved to Massachusetts. He worked at the Austen Riggs Center, a private residential clinic for disturbed adolescents. After 10 years with this center, he was appointed professor at Harvard in human development and psychiatry. He retired in 1970. One advantage he believed that old people have is that they think like children—with wonder, joy, and playfulness. He observed these qualities in his own later years until his death in 1994.

One of Erikson's major contributions was his work on the role that society or culture plays in development. Several of his books deal with the impact the times have had on major historical figures such as Adolf Hitler, Martin Luther, and Gandhi. His book *Gandhi's Truth* won both a Pulitzer Prize and the National Book Award. Another of his major contributions was to extend development past adolescence and examine changes occurring in adulthood. A third modification of the Freudian approach was to see a positive as well as a negative side to development, thereby designing a more optimistic theory.

References

Hall, E. (June 1983). A conversation with Erik Erikson. *Psychology Today*, 22-30.
Schultz, D. (1976). *Theories of personality.* Belmont, CA: Wadsworth.

LECTURE TOPIC 8.2: FOUNDATIONS OF PSYCHOSOCIAL DEVELOPMENT

The study of infants' emotions has long been controversial. Early researchers believed that infants were born with only one emotion. However, more recent studies suggest that babies may have a fairly wide range of emotions in the first few months of life. Although an inborn biological clock may program the emotions as the brain matures, environment influences development as well. Emotions are complex, and the same emotional response can have different meanings. In addition, there are many individual differences in temperament that affect a child's emotional response to the environment.

Crying is an infant behavior that seems related to emotion. The cry is the way babies can signal to the outside world that they need something. Wolff describes four types of crying: the rhythmic cry, the angry cry, the pain cry, and the cry of frustration. The smile appears early; babies of 1 week of age smile spontaneously and fleetingly when content. Later at about 4 months of age, babies begin to laugh out loud. As they grow older, they laugh at more situations. It is thought that laughter in the first year of life marks an important transaction between infants and their environment.

Babies are born different, and individual differences become even more apparent during development. Temperament, which is largely inborn, is also influenced by the environment. Children seem to fall into three temperamental patterns: the easy child, the difficult child, and the slow-to-warm-up child. Research has determined that children do respond to the way their parents treat them and temper their traits in ways that help them function. Sex difference is another controversial area of research. Some studies indicate a difference in activity levels between the sexes. Yet when the studies were repeated by other investigators, these findings did not hold up. Other studies have focused on the way adults act toward infants. Apparently a baby, even a newborn, is treated differently depending on its gender.

Reference

Wolff, P. H. (1969) The natural history of crying and other vocalizations in early infancy. In B. M. Foss (Ed.) *Determinants of Infant Development* (Vol. 4). London: Methuen

LECTURE TOPIC 8.3: THE SMILE

Few infant behaviors can delight a parent more than a smile. Although frequently observed and studied, an infant's smile is not fully understood. To a parent, any smilelike behavior is delightful, and no doubt nature "intended" smiles to build attachments. Fortunately, parents do not care that research has shown that first smiles present in the newborn (asleep or awake) are mainly reflexive and apparently a result of nervous system discharge. Premature as well as full-term babies exhibit this type of mock smile; it is not a wide, emotion-laden smile. By 6 weeks of age, a different full smile is apparent and again seems to be somewhat biologically determined rather than social; for example, blind babies smile, and premature babies are delayed according to extent of prematurity. Before 6 weeks of age, a squeaky human voice is the most effective elicitor of a smile.

There are a number of hypotheses about the cause of the true social smile. Perceptual research has shown that circles with black dots, black and white patterns, and moving patterns are as effective as, or more effective than, human faces in producing smiling. However, these stimuli later lose their effect, whereas the human face, especially a familiar one, continues to bring forth smiles. Obviously, as pointed out by T. G. R. Bower, infants respond because of social pleasure rather than because they see two black blobs (eyes) in the middle of a face. Some have therefore hypothesized that, through classical conditioning, a smile is associated with pleasant experiences, such as feeding, being picked up, and receiving attention. Indeed, smiling can be increased through reinforcing processes.

Another explanation of social smiles and all later smiles in infants focuses on cognitive development or hypothesis testing by the child. As a by-product of his work in infant perception using operant conditioning procedures, J. S. Watson noticed that at certain crucial times young infants would consistently smile. To Watson, the smile after 3 months of age is an infant's gleeful recognition that his or her own behavior is related to the occurrence of an event. In other words, the child becomes aware of the contingency between his or her behavior and an environmental stimulus. A baby may widen the eyes, flap the arms, coo, or show some other controllable behavior, and in response an adult bobs in front of the child, smiles, bounces baby on the knee, tosses baby in the air, and so on. This is called "The Game" by Watson and is typical of social interactions between parents and babies. Mutual delight repeatedly results, as shown by the myriad of smiles produced in the parent and the infant.

Thus the social smile is possible because of biological reflexes, perceptual-cognitive development, motor control, instrumental learning, and social experience. In order for us to come to understand the social smile fully, studies will need to be longitudinal, begin early, use familiar as well as strange faces, have faces be responsive or unresponsive, employ human and nonhuman voices and visual stimuli, include home-reared and institutional babies, and demonstrate the effect of contingency learning. One study or another has shown each of the above to have an effect. Indeed, smiles, as cute as they may be, are not fully understood.

References

Bower, T. G. R. (1977). *A primer of infant development.* San Francisco: Freeman.

Honig, A. (March 1993). Mental health for babies: What do theory and research teach us? *Young Children.*

MacDonald, N., & Silverman, I. (1978). Smiling and laughter in infants as a function of level of arousal and cognitive evaluation. *Developmental Psychology, 14,* 235-241.

Stone, L., Smith, H., & Murphy, L. (eds.) (1973*). The competent infant: Research and commentary.* New York: Basic Books.

Watson, J. S. (1973). Smiling, cooing, and "The Game." *Merrill-Palmer Quarterly, 18,* 323-339.

LECTURE TOPIC 8.4: TEMPERAMENTAL VARIATION IN INFANTS

Temperamental properties are innate biases toward certain moods and styles of reacting. One popular temperamental classification was proposed by Chess in 1977 and consisted of the three categories: easy to handle, difficult to handle, and slow to warm up to others. A more persistent temperament pattern, however, may be that of inhibited versus uninhibited (or caution versus boldness). This style seems to persist from 1 year old through late childhood. About 10 percent of 2-year-olds are inhibited, and 75 percent of them are still inhibited when 4 years old.

Kagan reports the following characteristics of the inhibited child:

1. Inhibited children rarely approached unfamiliar peers.
2. Inhibited children had more nightmares than uninhibited children.
3. Inhibited children were the most sensitive to parental reprimand, were more obedient, and had closer relationships to their parents.
4. They had the most physiological arousal to challenging situations.
5. As infants, those with an inhibited temperament were more irritable, had more constipation, and had more allergic reactions.
6. These children were described as restrained, watchful, and gentle.
7. Males in this category tended, as adults, to avoid masculine vocations and traditional masculine sexual activities and were more anxious than others in social settings.
8. Inhibited infants had earlier bladder control in toilet training.

Daniel Freedman did a number of studies indicating that there are differences in temperament and behavior of neonates in different ethnic groups. For example, compared to Chinese babies, Caucasian babies cry more; and once they have begun to cry they take longer to stop crying. Caucasian babies also exhibit more response than Navaho babies. The Japanese newborns do not struggle or protest when a cloth covers their noses, but Australian aborigine and Caucasian neonates do. Caucasian and Japanese neonates cannot support their heads, but Australian aborigine newborns can.

References
Freedman, D. G. (January 1979). Ethnic differences in babies. *Human Nature*.
Kagan, J. (1994). *The nature of the child*, 10th anniv. ed. New York: Basic Books.
Kagan, J. (1994). *Galen's prophecy*. New York: Basic Books.

LECTURE TOPIC 8.5: INTERACTIVE AFFECTIVE COMMUNICATION SYSTEMS

In discussing how a mother's depression affects her baby, the authors of the text include information about Gianino and Tronick's mutual regulation model, which depicts how infants regulate their internal emotional states. Included in this lecture topic is more information on this model.

Tronick has reviewed the advances that have been made in understanding the nature of emotional communication between infants and adults. Research has shown that infants display a variety of specific affective expressions appropriate to the contexts in which these expressions occur and that they also have appropriate understanding of the emotional meaning of the affective displays of their caregivers. The mutual regulation model details how the emotional expressions of the infant and the caregiver function to allow them to mutually regulate their interactions.

Tronick and his associates maintain that mutual feedback from the emotional displays of the infant and caregiver is a key element in infants' development of goal-directed, regulatory behaviors.

In terms of goal-directed behaviors, internal emotional states provide feedback that motivates and organizes the infant's behavior. Behavior that furthers reaching a goal yields positive internal emotional states which, in turn, motivate further striving. When the goal is not being attained, different emotional states result, depending on the infant's evaluation of the reachability of the goal. Anger motivates the child to try harder when the infant perceives that the obstacle can be overcome and the goal reached. When the evaluation is that the goal is unreachable, the experience of an internal state of sadness results in the infant's withdrawing from that goal-directed activity.

The caregiver's reading of the infant's emotional displays in goal-directed activities and that caregiver's reactions to the displays have a crucial impact on this process. Coordinated reactions that accurately recognize the infant's emotional state and are followed with appropriate responses affect the child's development positively. Failure to accurately recognize or to appropriately respond to the infant's emotional states, or failure to respond at all to emotional displays, negatively affects the child's development. A particularly important caregiver reaction is to change the situation in such a way that the infant moves from negative to positive effects.

References

Gianino, A., & Tronick, E. Z. (1988). The mutual regulation model: The infant's self and interactive regulation coping and defense. In T. Field, P. McCabe, & N. Schneiderman (eds.), *Stress and coping,* Hillsdale, NJ: Erlbaum.
Tronick, E. Z. (1989). Emotions and emotional communication in infants. *American Psychologist, 44,* 112-119.

LECTURE TOPIC 8.6: FATHERS AND INFANCY

There is little evidence that human mothers have a maternal instinct that makes them exclusively more competent than fathers in infant care and emotional attachment. As mentioned in the text, fathers are just as excited as mothers immediately after a child's birth. In "strange situation" and "separation" experiments, fathers and mothers are generally equally effective attachment figures for their children. However, not all research studies find equality in the responsiveness of the child to the mother versus the father. Today more emphasis is being given to research on child-father interactions and effects. Previously, most research had concentrated on the effects of father absence on children. This was a reflection of concern about divorce, spouse death, or prolonged absence due to occupation. In addition, interactions with mothers are easier to obtain, because fathers are generally away from home at the time when it is most convenient for researchers to visit (researchers like to have their evenings and weekends away from work also).

In our technological and school culture, fathers cannot spend large daily segments of time with their children (this is a rather recent phenomenon in society). Fathers' interactions with their children would be expected to be different from the mothers' and may have a dramatically different impact. In fact, researchers have recently been accumulating evidence to show that maternal behavior fosters attachment systems (child in first 2 years fussing for an adult, seeking proximity, or demanding to be held) and that paternal behaviors seem to affect more the affiliation systems (making-friends behavior such as vocalizing, smiling, and looking). Fathers tend to be less verbal with their children and more physically playful.

Belsky recorded the father-baby verbal interaction in 10 homes. Periodic 24-hour sampling of babies, from 2 weeks to 12 weeks, indicated that the fathers average only 38 seconds a day talking to their babies. The highest verbalizing average was only 10.5 minutes a day. This of course does not indicate the father's total interaction, but mothers definitely are more verbal. Especially as infants grow older, fathers tend to be playing with the infant rather than taking care of it. Of course, this may be a function of the father's perceived role and also of the fact that, in his limited time with the child, he wants a pleasurable experience not afforded by the changing of diapers. Even though most studies indicate that working mothers carry prime responsibility for housework and child care, additional research is needed to show the subtle differences that occur in father-child interaction when both parents work.

In traditional two-parent homes with the father working, it is improper to focus entirely on the father-child or mother-child interactions. Belsky's study can be presented in some detail in class to demonstrate how research on parent-child interaction is performed and also to demonstrate total mother-father-infant interactions. By observing and then recording, during 2-hour observation periods, very specific parent and infant (15 months old) behaviors in alternating 15-second segments, investigators obtained, from naturalistic home environments, results fairly consistent with laboratory and hospital studies. Most importantly, it was noted that maternal and paternal behaviors were more similar than different, though the mother did more caretaking. In general, the amount of interaction with the child decreased as the duration of time with the child increased. There was a slight tendency for parents to interact more with the same-sex child. When one parent was alone with the child, there was more interaction between that parent and the child. Although the child received the same total interaction when the two parents were together, each parent individually interacted less with the child. The infants themselves tended to show objects, offer things, and vocalize to a specific parent more when only one parent was present. With two parents present, the behaviors were as frequent overall but were not specifically directed to the mother more than to the father. In some infant behaviors such as vocalization, there was a slight preference for the father. Apparently this was elicited by the father's more active involvement with the child at those times. The fathers had just come home from work, whereas the mothers had been with the children all day. The observations from this study are important because they appear to validate several of the previously mentioned findings from more controlled laboratory settings.

References

Belsky, J. (1979). Mother-father-infant interaction: A naturalistic observational study. *Developmental Psychology, 15,* 601-607.

Clarke-Stewart, K. A. (1978). And daddy makes three: The father's impact on mother and young child. *Child Development, 49,* 466-478.

Gibbs, N. Bringing up father. *Time,* June 28, 1993.

Lamb, M. (1981). *The role of the father in child development.* New York: Wiley.

Lamb, M., Sternberg, K., & Prodromidis, M. (1992). Nonmaternal care and the security of infant & attachment: A reanalysis of the data. *Infant Behavior and Development, 15,* 71-83.

Roberts, P. (May/June 1996). Father's time. *Psychology Today,* 48-55.

DISCUSSION TOPICS

DISCUSSION TOPIC 8.1: DIFFERING VIEWS OF FREUD

So much has been written about Freud, his psychoanalytic theory, and his personal life that students may harbor a confusing array of attitudes toward and ideas about him. Many times their attitudes are negative as a result of overly critical comments from previous non-Freudian instructors. Even if your views of personality development differ significantly from Freudian psychoanalytic thought, take time to ensure that your students have a balanced view of Freud's contributions. A good way to begin is simply to ask students to tell you what they know or have heard about Freud and his ideas. You can correct inaccurate information and balance the accurate negative views by stressing his major contributions (the concept of unconscious motivation, the systematic development of personality in childhood, the role of biological factors in development, and the influence of the environment through maternal caregiving). You may also take advantage of this opportunity to stress the importance of good writing skills. (One of the reasons why Freud had such great influence was that he was such a good writer.)

DISCUSSION TOPIC 8.2: THE CRY

One of the major difficulties in studying infants is correctly interpreting their reactions. They cannot tell us what they are thinking, if anything, or what the meaning of their actions is. To help students more fully comprehend this problem, pose the following question for class discussion: "Why do babies cry when their diapers are wet?" An obvious response is that they cry because wet diapers are uncomfortable or painful. At least this answer often seems obvious from the adult perspective. We would be uncomfortable if we were wearing a wet diaper! Actually the question is a set-up, as some of your more thoughtful or more experienced students will realize. Not all babies cry when wet. In fact, most newborns are relatively unresponsive to the state of their diapers. So why, then, do more babies later on in development cry when wet? Explore with your students the possibility that the adult caregivers condition this response in babies. Discuss the position that crying may be initially devoid of meaning for the baby except as a reaction to change in the baby's physical state. Do the adults impose their meanings on the baby's cries?

DISCUSSION TOPIC 8.3: WHO WOULD WANT A "DIFFICULT" BABY?

Thomas and Chess's choice of the labels "easy," "difficult," and "slow to warm up" to describe temperament differences in infants is heavily laden with connotations for parents. Our societal stereotype of the "Gerber Baby" implies that all babies should be "easy." Who, if they had the choice, would choose to have a "difficult" baby? And it sounds as though there is something dreadfully wrong with a "slow-to-warm-up" baby. The labels "less reactive," "more reactive," and "cautious" have very different connotations. Students can become more aware of these implicit connotations by discussing the advantages and disadvantages of being each of the three types of babies. For example, who gets held more often, an easy or a difficult baby? Do parents learn to be more precise and slower-paced with slow-to-warm-up babies, or do such babies produce hesitant and less-secure parents? Which baby is most likely to be ignored? What temperament is at greatest risk for abuse?

DISCUSSION TOPIC 8.4: THE FAMILY AND PERSONALITY DEVELOPMENT - RELATIONSHIPS WITH OTHER CHILDREN/THE IMPACT OF DAY CARE

The environmental influence continues in terms of the family. The socialization of the child is greatly influenced by the different members of the family—not only by the mother, as earlier studies suggested. Studies with animals have shown the importance of imprinting and contact comfort by surrogate mothers in forming parent-offspring bonds. It is questionable whether we can transfer these findings to humans. Attachment is an active, affectionate, reciprocal relationship between two individuals. Ainsworth characterized three main patterns of attachment as securely attached, avoidant, and ambivalent. Studies have shown that children who were securely attached at 1 year of age are most likely to be independent as 4- or 5-year-olds. Children who were anxiously attached earlier are more likely to be very dependent. Early studies have shown that the critical time for attachment and bonding is immediately after birth. However, later studies have shown that events occurring throughout childhood can change the nature of attachment. A normal aspect of development and a signal that attachment has occurred is stranger anxiety. Separation anxiety, on the other hand, is not so severe for those who have developed a trusting relationship with their parent as for those who have not. Even so, a child's temperament can influence the extent of these anxieties.

The father's attachment to the infant has become the subject of research. The findings from such research underscore the importance of the father. Many fathers form close attachments to their babies soon after birth, and then they go on to exert a strong influence on their children's social, emotional, and cognitive development. Studies generally show that fathers play with their babies, whereas mothers care for them. However, in a study in which the fathers were the primary caretakers, the fathers behaved more like mothers than like secondary caretakers. Apparently societal expectations influence maternal and paternal styles of child care.

Siblings and birth order are important influences in social development. Singleton (only) children tend be bright and successful, not unlike firstborn children. Interaction of siblings is prosocial, and it is imitative as well as agonistic. One way to help encourage a positive sibling relationship is to prepare the child for the arrival of the new baby and to minimize any feelings of displacement.

The impact of day care varies, depending upon the quality of care, the type of facility, and the child's emotional, physical, and social make-up. Cognitive development may be enhanced, especially for children from stressed and low-income families. Children who attended day care tended to be more comfortable with new situations, but also could be more demanding and disobedient than other children. Attachment and emotional development depends upon the quality of the child care and the timing of being left.

DISCUSSION TOPIC 8.5: THE INFANT-PARENT INTERACTION

The complex reciprocal interactive nature of the attachment process is often a confusing topic for students. An interesting issue for discussion, which may help students to grasp some of this complexity, is whether there are parallels between Thomas and Chess's labels of "easy," "difficult," and "slow to warm up" and Ainsworth's descriptors: "securely attached," "avoidant," and "ambivalent." Ask students to speculate about possible matches between the two sets of labels. For example, are easy babies more likely to become securely attached and difficult ones avoidant? Then ask students to suggest research designs to test these hypotheses. It should quickly become apparent that the caregiver is an important variable in the process and a very difficult variable to control.

Some of Ainsworth's research cited in the text suggests that over time, avoidant and ambivalent mothers produce avoidant and ambivalent children. Discuss with the class whether there is similar evidence with regard to difficult and slow-to-warm-up babies.

DISCUSSION TOPIC 8.6: THEORETICAL EXPLANATIONS OF ATTACHMENT

Attachment is a major concept in this chapter. Ask students to apply their understanding of various theoretical positions to the concept of attachment. How do the theories of Freud, Erikson, Mahler, the behaviorists, and the social learning theorists explain the appearance of attachment? Some obvious starters for discussion are the roles of oral gratification, consistent caregiving, tension reduction, and reinforcement in producing this phenomenon. Help students recognize that all the positions are focusing on the same events and behaviors but employ different emphases and terminology. Pursue the issue by asking for examples of relevant research. The Harlow research on feeding versus contact comfort is useful here. It offers evidence that Erikson's emphasis on the quality of caregiving is a better explanation of attachment than Freud's use of oral gratification. New research suggests attachment styles influence friendships, marriages, and work relationships later in life. Have students speculate about who would be a good friend, partner, and worker.

INDEPENDENT STUDY

INDEPENDENT STUDY 8.1: FATHER-INFANT INTERACTION

Have each student contact a family with a child younger than age 2. Have the parents monitor the interaction between each other and their infant for several days. How much time does each parent spend interacting with the infant each day? Exactly what does each parent do with the child? Some possible behaviors to look for include holding, feeding, talking, singing, changing diapers, reading stories, rough-and-tumble play, smiling, giving instruction, bathing, and dressing. In class, compare what mothers do with their infants and what fathers do with them. How long does each interact with the child each day? Can you see differences in the way parents react to sons as opposed to daughters? Are fathers more physical? Do mothers read more stories or play more with toys? Can you see evidence of father attachment?

CHOOSING SIDES

CHOOSING SIDES 8.1: DAY CARE

With ever-increasing numbers of women in the workforce, there has been growing pressure to provide adequate child-care arrangements for the children of working mothers. This has sparked a debate on the quality of day care available and its effects on young children. The emphasis that psychologists, sociologists, and anthropologists place on the early mother-child relationship has certainly contributed to a general negative attitude toward day care. However, the numbers of mothers taking jobs to beat inflation, the high standard of living that many people expect, higher educational goals, the women's movement, and the focus on fathers and their relationship with children have forced a reassessment of the mother-child bond. Today many people support day care as being beneficial to children and providing children with learning experiences they could not have encountered at home. Students may want to debate the following statement:

> *Full-time day care centers are detrimental to a child. Parents should not enroll a child full time in a day care center.*

Pro: Mothers who enroll their children in day care centers are neglecting their responsibility as mothers and contributing to the destruction of family life in our country today. Day care is a waste of money. Mothers are returning to the workforce because they are being taught that motherhood is not a valuable career. In their search for themselves and a higher income, they are selling the well-being of their own children. Young children, in particular, need a strong attachment to a caregiver, which day care workers cannot provide as well as a parent.

Con: The effect and quality of day care must be considered in comparison to home care. High-quality day care has been shown to have no detrimental effects and can even be shown to be superior to poor home care. For example, impressive gains in IQ scores have been demonstrated. Group child care has been used effectively in many other societies for many years without detrimental effects. It is better for a child to have a happy working mother than a stifled, resentful, home-bound custodian.

The following lists give arguments that can be used to support each side of the debate.

Pro (Students for Home Care):

1. Supporting day care is an effort to remove a mother's responsibility for raising her own children. It is detrimental to the family structure and the mother's self-esteem.
2. The beneficial effects of day care have been found at very specialized centers on university campuses. This is not the type of day care available to the general public.
3. The high expense of providing day care would require government support, thereby allowing government to have too much control over family life.
4. Continued day care through the preschool years cannot provide the stability needed for child development. There is too much of a possibility of turnover among day care staff to allow for the constancy required by children.
5. Research has shown detrimental effects of day care when the mother is forced into the labor force and prefers to remain at home with her children.

6. It is possible to cite, from students' and mothers' experiences, poor or abusive practices at day care centers.

Con (Students for Day Care):
1. Many societies (for example, Israel and the Soviet Union) have had group day care for years without adverse effects.
2. Interacting with peers in day care centers plays an important role in learning social skills.
3. Day care can be used positively to eliminate some of the differences between deprived children and middle-class, advantaged children before they reach school age.
4. Some mothers are less responsive to a baby's needs than a caregiver because of different priorities, lack of training, and less patience or objectivity.
5. Research shows detrimental effects on the children of a mother who stays at home when she would rather have a career. Mothers who have a satisfying, independent life of their own are better able to care for their children.

References

Booth, A. (ed.) (1992). *Child care in the 1990s: Trends and consequences.* Hillsdale, NJ: Erlbaum.

Belsky, J., & Steinberg, L. D. (1978). The effects of day care, a critical review. *Child Development ,49,* 929-949.

Hewett, S. (1991). *When the bough breaks: The cost of neglecting our children.* New York: Basic Books.

Scarr, S. (1984). *Mother care/other care.* New York: Basic Books.

KNOWLEDGE CONSTRUCTION ACTIVITIES

KNOWLEDGE CONSTRUCTION ACTIVITY 8.1: GENERATIVE TERMS

This activity will use the principles of generative learning as explained in the Introduction to assist students in gaining a better understanding of terms. Divide the class into groups of four or five. Assign each group the task of generating an example for a generative term from this chapter. The example that each group creates cannot be one that has been used in the class or in the book. They must think of a new application for the term that they are given. Groups are allowed to use their books and notes. By creating their own example of the term, they demonstrate an understanding of the term to the level of application. There are several approaches that can be used in this exercise. Students may be given the entire list at once, but often one group will finish far ahead of the others and topics will get out of sequence. Another strategy is to give all of the groups the same term to create an example and then go around the room to discuss outcomes. This has been very successful, but also takes the most time. A third approach is to give each group a different term and see what examples they can generate.

Some generative terms for Chapter 8 are listed below.

Easy children
Difficult children
Slow-to-warm children
Goodness of fit
Trust, mistrust
Stranger anxiety
Separation anxiety
Gender-typing
Mutual regulation
Social referencing
Autonomy, shame and doubt
Internalization
Self-regulation

KNOWLEDGE CONSTRUCTION ACTIVITY 8.2: ATTACHMENT AND SEPARATION DISTRESS

Have several mothers with children 12 to 24 months old attend class. Demonstrate attachment and separation distress by having the mothers leave the room and then return after several minutes. You will need to have several chairs and some toys available in a corner of the room. Have a mother and child come in, sit down, and begin to play with the toys. After several minutes, ask the mother to leave. Try to comfort the child and get him or her to play with the toys again. Then have the mother return. You might also have two mothers and their children enter simultaneously. Have one mother leave, then several minutes later have the second mother leave. Have them return separately also. Throughout this demonstration, have the class observe the behaviors of both mothers and children. Did each mother explain to her child that she was leaving or merely try to slip out unnoticed? Did the mother's style cause more or less distress? What did the children do to exhibit separation distress? How did the children react when their mothers returned? Did you observe signs of secure attachment or insecure attachment? Were there different responses when another child was present than when no other child was present? Can you detect age differences? Was a stranger able to comfort the child?

KNOWLEDGE CONSTRUCTION 8.3: INFANT DAY CARE STANDARDS

Have students report on the legal standards for day care licensing in your state. Criteria might include size of the facility, physical condition of the facility, passage of fire and safety inspection, number of toys available, caretaker-child ratio, provisions for illness, meals provided, and training or education of the teacher. How do the minimum standards for licensing compare with the necessary standards for good intellectual and emotional development elaborated in the text? Day care standards are probably available on your state's regulatory agency website. Another point of contact might be your college's early childhood education department.

KNOWLEDGE CONSTRUCTION ACTIVITY 8.4: OBSERVING TODDLERS

Observe toddlers with familiar people and strangers in a play situation—for example, at a day care center, park, church, preschool, or home. Record their play behavior. Are they afraid of strangers? Are they willing or unwilling to share? Do they grab toys from other children? Do they always want what another child has? Are they aggressive, pushing and biting to get their way? Can you find evidence of sharing on their own initiative without prompting or praise? What types of things do they share and with whom? In general, are they friendly?

KNOWLEDGE CONSTRUCTION 8.5: TEMPERAMENT DIFFERENCES IN SIBLINGS

Ask each student to interview a parent of two or more children about the differences in temperament between their offspring. Students should use the nine aspects of temperament identified in the New York Longitudinal Study and the patterns of "easy," "difficult," and "slow to warm up" as a framework for analyzing the parents' comparisons of their children. How often is one child described as easy and another as difficult? Do parents recognize some children as slow to warm up? How many of the nine features of temperament do the parents regularly use in describing the similarities and differences between their children's temperaments?

KNOWLEDGE CONSTRUCTION 8.6: EXPLORING INFANT EMOTION AND MUTUAL REGULATION

Prepare:

1. Reread the sections of Chapter 8 that discuss research on infant emotions.
2. Gather pictures of infants showing different emotions. These can be gathered from magazines, newspapers, snapshots, or the Internet. Cut the pictures so that the baby's face is the primary focus and contextual cues are at a minimum. For example, if the baby is laughing because someone is tickling him or her, it is easier to guess the emotion if the picture shows the baby being tickled. For this research you want to show primarily the baby's face to see if people can identify the baby's emotions.
3. Arrange the pictures in a notebook or on a series of cards for people to look at. Number the pictures.

Experiment:

Show the pictures to five male and five female college students and ask them to identify the emotion the baby is showing. Write down the emotion given to each picture.

Write Your Results:

You need to write a paper with the following headings:

1. *Introduction:* Give a brief overview of the current research on infant emotions. You can use your textbook and library resources. A handbook of development psychology would be very useful for this.
2. *Participants:* Describe the 10 people who participated in your study. Include age and sex.
3. *Methodology:* Describe how you put your instrument together (the pictures) and how the experiment was administered to the participants.
4. *Results:* What emotions did the participants attribute to the babies in the pictures?
5. *Discussion:* Did you find much agreement among your participants? How confident were the participants in determining the babies' emotions? Is this method of research a good one to determine what emotions an infant is feeling? Include a concluding paragraph in the discussion.

7. RESOURCES FOR INSTRUCTORS

Books and Journal Articles

Ainsworth, M. D. S., Blehar, M. C., Waters, E., & Wall, S. (1979). *Patterns of attachment.* New York: Holsted Press.

Aronoff, J., Rabin, A. I., & Zucker, R. A. (eds.) (1987). *The emergence of personality.* New York: Springer.

Bowlby, J. (1976). *Attachment and separation.* New York: Basic Books.

Dunn, J. (1985). *Sisters and brothers.* Cambridge, MA: Harvard University Press.

Eyer, D. D. (1992). *Mother-infant bonding: A scientific fiction.* New Haven, CT: Yale University Press.

Greenspan, S., & Greenspan, N. T. (1985). *First feelings: Milestones in the emotional development of your baby and child.* New York: Viking.

Harlow, F. H., & Mears, C. (1979). *The human model: Primate perspectives.* Washington, DC: V. H. Winston.

Kopp, C. (1994). Baby's steps: The "whys" of your child's behavior in the first two years. New York: W. H. Freeman.

Lamb, M. E., & Campos, J. J. (1993). *Development in infancy: An introduction.* New York: Random House.

Lancaster, J. B., Altmann, J., Rossi, A. S., & Sherrod, L. R. (eds.) (1987). *Parenting across the life span: Biosocial dimensions.* New York: Aldine.

Olds, S. W. (1989). *The working parents' survival guide.* Rocklin, CA: Prima.

Schlein, S. (ed.) (1987). *A way of looking at things: Selected papers from 1930 to 1980. Erik H. Erikson.* New York: Norton.

Stern, D. N. (1990). *Diary of a baby.* New York: Basic Books.

Video resources

Mother love (PSU, 1960, BW, approx. 30 min.). Although this film is quite old, it presents Harlow's classic research on the importance of "contact comfort."

First feelings (IM, 1992, video, 30 min.). This video features interviews with Jerome Kagan, Mary Ainsworth, and Alan Sroufe, who explain their research on infant attachment.

Toddler (IM, 1992, video, 30 min.) . The fine line between a toddler's need for others and need for autonomy is explored in this program. The video contrasts the development of a securely attached toddler with that of a child whose mother is in prison.

In the land of giants (IM, 1991, video, 57 min.). Urie Bronfenbrenner characterizes the family as "the most efficient means for making human beings human." This program examines models of behavior and codes of discipline used to mold children to a culturally desirable social image.

No more secrets (FFHS, 1994, video, 24 min.). This video tells stories of sexually abused children and of adults who were abused as children and shows how children can be encouraged to share their secret.

Child abuse (FFHS, 1994, video, 19 min.). A therapist describes the common characteristics of child abuse offenders, and a clinical social worker discusses the effects of physical and sexual ?

Social services and child abuse (FFHS, 1994, video, 28 min.). This specially adapted Phil Donahue program examines reports of agencies unable or unwilling to prevent vicious and sometimes fatal child abuse.

Having a mentally handicapped baby: A crack in the crystal (FFHS, 1994, video, 50 min.). The agonies and joys, as well as the endless cycle of questions, that families face when confronted by mental handicap in their child are explored.

Prodigies: Great expectations (FFHS, 1994, video, 52 min.). The problems and privileges of brilliant children are examined.

Life's first feelings (NOVA, video, 1 hr.). Provides an excellent depiction of the work of Izard, Kagan, Greenspan, Lewis, and others as well as classic footage from Rene Spitz's work with deprivation.

Pediatric neuroscience: Rage of innocents (FFHS, 1999, video, 47 min.). Discusses how emotional neglect alters brain chemistry and therefore alters behaviors.

Early socialization: From birth to age two (FFHS, 1999, video, 22 min.). Follows two children during their first two years to examine how they learn to interact with others.

Attachment (IM, 1996, video, 24 min.). Reviews research on bonding and attachment.

LINKUPS

During the years from 3 to 6, often called the preschool years, children make the transition from toddlerhood to childhood. Their bodies become slimmer, their motor and mental abilities sharper, and their personalities and relationships more complex.

The 3-year-old is no longer a baby, but a sturdy adventurer, at home in the world and eager to explore its possibilities as well as the developing capabilities of his or her own body and mind. A child of this age has come through a relatively dangerous time of life--the years of infancy and toddlerhood--to enter a healthier, less threatening phase.

Growth and change are less rapid in early childhood than in infancy and toddlerhood, but, as we see in Chapters 9, 10, and 11, all aspects of development--physical, cognitive, emotional, and social--continue to intertwine.

Linkups to Look For:
o   As muscles come under more conscious control, children can tend to more of their own personal needs, such as dressing and toileting, and thus gain a greater sense of competence and independence.
o   Eating and sleep patterns are influenced by cultural attitudes.
o   Even the common cold can have emotional and cognitive implications. Occasional minor illnesses not only build immunity; they help children learn to cope with physical distress and understand its causes.
o   Social interaction plays a major role in the development of preliteracy skills, memory, and measured intelligence.
o   Cognitive awareness of gender has far-reaching psychosocial implications, affecting children's sense of self and their attitudes toward the roles the two sexes play in their society.
o   Environmental influences, including the parents' life circumstances, affect health and safety. The link between developmental realms is especially evident in the tragic results of child abuse and neglect; although the most obvious effects may be physical; these conditions can stunt cognitive growth and can leave lasting emotional scars.

9
PHYSICAL DEVELOPMENT AND HEALTH IN EARLY CHILDHOOD

ASPECTS OF PHYSIOLOGICAL DEVELOPMENT
Bodily Growth and Change
Nutrition
Oral Health
Sleep Patterns and Problems

MOTOR DEVELOPMENT
Gross Motor Skills
Fine Motor Skills and Artistic Development
Handedness

HEALTH AND SAFETY
Minor Illnesses
Accidental Injuries
Health in Context: Environmental Influences

MALTREATMENT: ABUSE AND NEGLECT
Maltreatment: Facts and Figures
Contributing Factors: An Ecological View
Effects of Maltreatment
Helping Families in Trouble or at Risk

In This Chapter of Your Instructor's Manual You Will Find:
1. Total Teaching Package Outline
2. Expanded Outline (transparency-ready)
3. Guideposts for Study
4. Learning Objectives
5. Key Terms
6. Teaching and Learning Activities
   Lecture Topics
   Discussion Topics
   Independent Study
   Choosing Sides
   Knowledge Construction Activities
7. Resources for Instructors

1. TOTAL TEACHING PACKAGE OUTLINE

Chapter 9: Physical Development And Health In Early Childhood

Aspects of physiological development	Guidepost for study 9.1 Knowledge construction activity 9.1
Bodily growth and change	Learning objective 9.1
Nutrition	Guidepost for study 9.2 Learning objective 9.2 Lecture topics 9.1, 9.2 Knowledge construction activity 9.2
Oral health	Guidepost for study 9.2 Learning objectives 9.3, 9.4 Knowledge construction activity 9.3
Sleep patterns and problems	Guidepost for study 9.2 Knowledge construction activity 9.6 Box 9.1 (textbook p. 214)
Gross motor development	Guidepost for study 9.3 Independent study 9.2
Gross motor skills	Discussion topics 9.1, 9.2 Knowledge construction activity 9.5
Handedness	Knowledge construction activity 9.7
Artistic development and fine motor skills	Knowledge construction activities 9.6, 9.8 Discussion topic 9.5 Independent study 9.1
Health and safety	Guidepost for study 9.4 Knowledge construction activity 9.4 Discussion topic 9.3
Minor illnesses	Learning objective 9.4
Accidental injuries	Learning objective 9.5
Health in context: Environmental influences	Learning objective 9.6 Choosing sides 9.1 Box 9.2 (textbook p. 224)

Maltreatment: Abuse and neglect	**Guidepost for study 9.5** **Lecture topics 9.3, 9.4**
Maltreatment: Facts and figures	**Learning objectives 9.7, 9.8** **Discussion topic 9.4**
Contributing factors: An ecological view	**Learning objective 9.9**
Long-term effects	**Learning objective 9.10**
Helping families in trouble or at risk	**Learning objective 9.11**

Please check out the online learning center located at www.mhhe.com/papaliacw9 for further information on these and other topics. There you can also access downloadable PowerPoint slides tailored to each chapter of the text and containing useful teaching notes as well as images and tables from the text itself.

2. EXPANDED OUTLINE (TRANSPARENCY READY)

I. Aspects of Physiological Development
    A. Physical Growth
    B. Nutrition
    C. Sleep patterns
        1. Nightmares
        2. Sleep terrors
        3. Enuresis

II. Motor Development
    A. Gross motor skills
    B. Fine motor skills
    C. Handedness

III. Health and Safety
    A. Illness
    B. Accidents
    C. Environmental factors
        1. Stress

IV. Maltreatment: Abuse and Neglect
    A. Physical abuse
    B. Neglect
    C. Sexual abuse
    D. Emotional maltreatment

3. GUIDEPOSTS FOR STUDY

9.1 How do children's bodies change between ages 3 and 6 and what are their nutritional and dental needs?

9.2 What sleep patterns and problems tend to develop during early childhood?

9.3 What are the main motor achievements of early childhood and how does artwork done by children show their physical and cognitive maturation?

9.4 What are the major health and safety risks for children?

9.5 What are the causes and consequences of child abuse and neglect and what can be done about it?

4. LEARNING OBJECTIVES

After completing the study of this chapter, the student will be able to:

9.1 Describe typical physiological changes around the age of 3.

9.2 Summarize preschoolers' dietary needs and explain why obesity and tooth decay can become concerns at this age.

9.3 Discuss how and when thumb-sucking should be treated.

9.4 Identify two benefits of minor illnesses.

9.5 Tell where and how young children are most likely to be injured and list ways in which injuries can be avoided.

9.6 Discuss several environmental influences that endanger children's health and development.

9.7 Define four types of child abuse and neglect.

9.8 Discuss the incidence of maltreatment and explain why it is hard to measure.

9.9 Identify contributing factors having to do with the child, the family, the neighborhood, and the wider society.

9.10 Give several examples of child abuse and neglect.

9.11 Describe ways to prevent or stop maltreatment and help its victims.

5. KEY TERMS

Enuresis
Gross motor skills
Fine motor skills
Handedness
Physical abuse
Neglect
Sexual abuse
Emotional maltreatment

6. TEACHING AND LEARNING ACTIVITIES
LECTURE TOPICS

LECTURE TOPIC 9.1: TASTE DISGUSTS

Would you eat or drink any of the following?

> A washed, dead grasshopper
> A piece of chocolate in the shape of feces
> A glass of milk after the removal of a dead, sterilized fly
> A glass of punch that contains a plastic cockroach
> Spaghetti served in a thoroughly washed dog dish
> A bowl of soup that has been stirred by a clean, never-used fly swatter
> A glass of water that contains some of your own saliva

If you would try several of these items, you are braver than the average person. Three categories of potential foods are usually rejected as disgusting. First, people reject foods that contain items they have learned to think of as disgusting. Even if the food is properly prepared, most people don't want to try worms on their pizza or eat chocolate-covered cockroaches. Second, people reject foods that they believe will taste bad, even though they have never tasted them. Many people are reluctant to try sushi (includes raw fish) or escargot (snails). Third, we tend to reject foods that are offensive in appearance or odor.

Disgust at foods tends to develop between the ages of 3 and 6. The first area of food rejection to develop tends to be based on sensory characteristics, such as taste and texture. Next people learn to avoid harmful foods. Finally, people learn to reject food on the basis of what it is (such as snake or insect) and where it comes from (such as tongue or stomach). For adults, especially, a critical psychological feature is contamination. That is, a food becomes inedible if it is even associated with something offensive. The opening examples involve the contamination feature.

One explanation for food rejection is that people use the laws of sympathetic magic in determining what foods to reject. One law is the law of contagion, which states that when two objects come into contact, they leave permanent traces in each other. This law may explain why the majority of people would reject a glass of milk even after the removal of a dead, sterilized fly. A second law is the law of similarity, which states that objects that look similar share fundamental properties. This law may play a role when a person refuses to eat a piece of candy formed in the shape of feces.

References

Fallon, A. E., & Rozin, P. (1985). Sex differences in perceptions of desirable body shape. *Journal of Abnormal Psychology, 94,* 102-105.

Fallon, A. E., & Rozin, P. (1984). The child's conception of food: The development of food rejections with special reference to disgust and contamination sensitivity. *Child Development, 55,* 566-575.

Rozin, P., & Fallon, A. (July 1985). That's disgusting. *Psychology Today,* 60-63.

Rozin, P., Fallon, A., & Mandell, R. (1984). Family resemblance in attitudes to foods. *Developmental Psychology, 20,* 309-314.

LECTURE TOPIC 9.2: UNDERNUTRITION

The problem of severe malnutrition, a condition that may affect 3 to 7 percent of the world's children, has received widespread media attention. Even so, the problem of undernutrition, a condition that may affect 40 to 60 percent of the world's children, is less widely understood. Protein-energy undernutrition is one type of undernutrition that has long-term developmental effects, and supplemental treatment does not appear to overcome all of the different types.

Galler conducted a large-sample longitudinal study in Barbados comparing the behavior and development of school-aged children who suffered from severe protein-energy undernutrition during their first year of life with those of classmates who had no history of undernutrition. The first year of life is a critical period for brain development, which depends on adequate protein resources for normal development. The two groups were carefully screened so that the only significantly different factor in their development was protein-energy undernutrition during the first year of life.

Although they initially lagged behind in growth, the undernourished children eventually caught up in physical growth to the children in the control group. However, the undernourished children continued to exhibit cognitive and behavioral deficits, compared to their counterparts in the study. The IQ scores of children in the early-undernutrition group were, on the average, 12 points lower than those of the children in the control group. The early-undernutrition group exhibited a fourfold increase in symptoms of attention deficit disorder. The attention deficit disorder syndrome appeared in 60 percent of the early undernutrition group. The attention deficits persisted through testing at age 18 and were associated with poor school performance and school dropout rates.

The mechanisms by which undernutrition produces these deficits are not well understood. Barrett has proposed a model in which the deficits result from "functional isolation." During periods of undernutrition the infant becomes listless and inactive—behaviors that conserve energy but functionally isolate the child from the stimulation and experiences necessary for optimal development. Because such infants appear apathetic and withdrawn, caregivers interact less with them, regardless of the caregiver's prior interactional style. Undernourished infants also spend less time exploring their physical and social environments. This model suggests that the behavior of undernourished children leads to their experiencing less cognitive and social stimulation.

Intensive intervention programs can remove many of the deficits, but promoting programs that prevent early protein-energy undernutrition from occurring in the first place appears to be a better policy to pursue.

References

Barrett, D. E. (1986). Nutrition and social behavior. In H. E. Fitzgerald, B. M. Lester, & M. W. Yogman (eds.), *Theory and research in behavioral pediatrics* (vol. 3, pp. 147-198). New York: Plenum.

Galler, J. R. (ed.) (1984). *Human nutrition: A comprehensive treatise. Vol. 5. Nutrition and behavior.* New York: Plenum.

Grantham-McGregor, S., Schofield, W., & Powell, C. (1987). Development of severely malnourished children who received psychosocial stimulation: Six-year follow-up. *Pediatrics, 79*, 247-254.

LECTURE TOPIC 9.3: THE CHILDREN OF ALCOHOLICS

At least 28 million Americans are children of alcoholics, and 7 million of them are under the age of 18. These children must deal with the alcohol drinking itself and with a wide range of associated problems such as unemployment, isolation from peers, divorce, physical and emotional abuse, neglect, and added responsibilities in the home. Anyone who plans to work with children should become aware of characteristics associated with children coming from alcoholic homes and be familiar with ways to help these children. (Of course, the characteristics suggested here may also be seen in children without an alcoholic parent, and some offspring of alcoholics do not exhibit these characteristics.)

Alcoholic parents may force children into more extreme roles within the family than are typical. One child, usually the oldest, may be in the hero role and may very maturely assume adult roles and responsibilities. This child, in effect, surrenders his or her childhood to try to keep the family functioning. Another child may serve as *scapegoat* and take undeserved blame for family problems and crises. Another possible role is that of the lost child, often an ignored middle child. The youngest child is most likely to get the *mascot* role; this child is protected and is isolated from most of the family problems. Having strong roles helps to add some consistency to an inconsistent, dysfunctional family atmosphere.

Children of alcoholics often have several of the following characteristics:

1. May seek approval at all costs, including giving up their individual identities.
2. May isolate themselves from others out of fear of authority figures.
3. May overreact to personal criticism or to hearing anger in someone's voice.
4. May become "super-helpers" who seek out "victims" to help and save.
5. May have a sense of over-responsibility.
6. May have trouble separating love and pity.
7. May judge themselves severely due to low self-esteem.
8. May overuse the defense mechanisms of regression, repression, sublimation, and projection as ways to escape their feelings. May be viewed as burying feelings.
9. May be terrified of being abandoned. The need for security is unfulfilled.
10. May become an alcoholic, have an intimate relationship with an alcoholic, or have a relationship with a compulsive personality. Fifty percent of the children of alcoholics become alcoholics.

What can help a child of an alcoholic? First, anyone who wants to help must be aware of such a child's personality development. It is likely that this child did not develop a sense of trust during infancy, and, during toddlerhood, autonomy may have been thwarted by overprotection by the nonalcoholic parent or by criticism by the alcoholic parent. The child probably feels a sense of inferiority because his or her achievements have been overlooked by parents. The child may be in a chaotic family situation and may experience erratic and inconsistent punishment and praise.

154

The child may fight a lot with his or her peers, exhibit learning problems in school, have a high rate of absenteeism in school, and have few friends. Many of these children are dependent, socially aggressive, and emotionally detached in their elementary school years. The better-adjusted children of alcoholics may come off as "super-copers."

The following characteristics are typical of children of alcoholics between the ages of 10 and 16:

1. They feel responsible for their parents' drinking.
2. They equate their parents' drinking with not being loved; if the parents "really loved them," they wouldn't drink.
3. They may be most angry at the nonalcoholic parent for not being able to change the situation and because this parent may not have protected them from abusive situations.
4. They may be afraid of alcoholic parents getting hurt or sick because of their drinking.
5. They may be confused by the differences in their alcoholic parents' personalities moods when intoxicated versus when sober.
6. They may avoid friendships so that peers will not know about their home life.
7. They may feel abandoned or be ashamed of the stigma of alcoholism.

Considering the foregoing information, you can see the difficulties one may encounter when intervening in the situation. You may really want to help, but the children's lack of trust may at first keep them from accepting your help. They may cover up the situation to protect their parents. Questions that you might ask out of concern may appear to be intrusive.

It is good to reach out to help, especially if you do not "demand" an immediate response to your helpful gesture. Instead of asking many questions, give information that can reduce their sense of responsibility for the situation. Help them develop coping mechanisms. The following organizations can provide additional information and local resources.

Alcoholics Anonymous
P.O. Box 459
Grand Central Station
New York, NY 10163

Al-Anon Family Group Headquarters
1372 Broadway
New York, NY 10018

Children of Alcoholics Foundation
540 Madison Avenue
23rd Floor
New York, NY 10022

References

McAndrew, J. (1985). Children of alcoholics: School intervention. *Childhood Education, 61,* 343-345.

Weddle, C., & Wishon, P. (1986). Children of alcoholics: What we should know; How we can help. *Children Today*, 8-12.

LECTURE TOPIC 9.4: SEXUAL ABUSE OF CHILDREN AND CONSEQUENCES

Sexual abuse of children is the secret that has emerged recently. A problem associated with this area of research is the lack of definitions and common language because there is such diverse activity, from presenting pornography to children to repeated sexual intercourse. Most information comes from men in prison and omits the other offenders—women, siblings, and other children.

The consequences for the abused child include emotional problems, sexual relationships, and behavior problems. Emotionally the child may experience guilt, anger, depression, anxiety, low self-esteem, sleep disturbances, nightmares, and somatic complaints. Sexually the child may exhibit either hypersexuality or fear and difficulty in later adult sexual activity. The child's relationships are influenced with greater isolation, withdrawal, and a tendency to enter abusive relationships. The child's behaviors include antisocial acts, self-mutilation, and suicidal tendencies. The child experiences grief due to loss of being like other children, loss of innocence, and loss of a normal childhood. The incidence of posttraumatic stress disorder is very high among sexual abuse victims.

References

Haugaard, J. J., & Reppucci, N. D. (1988). *The sexual abuse of children.* San Francisco: Jossey-Bass.
Kritsberg, W. (1993). *The invisible wound: A new approach to healing childhood sexual trauma.* New York: Bantam Books.
Vanderbilt, H. (1992). Incest: A chilling report. *Lear's,* 49-77.

DISCUSSION TOPICS

DISCUSSION TOPIC 9.1: SEX DIFFERENCES IN MOTOR DEVELOPMENT

Papalia, Olds and Feldman suggest that, although differences in proficiency levels for motor development of boys and girls in early childhood may be a result of skeletal differences, the differences are just as likely to be a reflection of societal attitudes that encourage different activities for boys and girls. Explore with the class whether they perceive changes in contemporary society's encouragement of different activities for young girls and boys. Is the differential the artifact of past societal needs that no longer exist? What advantages are there for our society in encouraging these differences today? Discuss the role of the *tomboy*. Are more or fewer young girls tomboys today?

Does continued use of the term indicate that expectations for different behavior from girls and boys are just as strong as they have always been? Conclude the discussion by focusing on the similarities and the high degree of overlap in proficiency in motor skills between boys and girls at any given age.

DISCUSSION TOPIC 9.2: NORMS

The material in this section provides a good opportunity to reinforce accurate understanding of norms. Ask students to compare their own patterns of growth (or, when appropriate, those of their children) to the norms. Use the discussion to emphasize that norms do not indicate desirable or optimal development, nor do they indicate the wide range of individual differences in height and weight of preschoolers. Emphasize that they indicate only what constitutes typical development.

DISCUSSION TOPIC 9.3: EARLY CHILDHOOD SUICIDE

The idea of early childhood suicide may be difficult for students to accept. The "age of innocence" view of early childhood is widely held. Help students to explore this painful and difficult subject by inquiring about their attitudes and beliefs about childhood innocence. How aware are preschoolers? What do they understand about suicide? This topic is important to discuss because, as the authors of the study cited in the text note, our understanding and awareness of early childhood suicide appears to parallel the "history of the recognition of child abuse."

DISCUSSION TOPIC 9.4: MALTREATMENT OF CHILDREN—CHILD ABUSE AND NEGLECT

Society has become more aware of abused and neglected children in recent years. Abuse involves physical injury, while neglect is the withholding of adequate care. Abusers are often unhappy with themselves for their actions. Often they themselves have been deprived of good parenting, do not know how to stop the child from crying, and may lose control. Neglecters, on the other hand, are likely to be personally irresponsible and apathetic and to ignore their children. Abused children tend to be hyperactive, mentally retarded, or physically handicapped. The environmental climate can also affect the interaction of the individuals involved. Education and awareness programs, as well as hot lines for potential abusers, are ways to help prevent child abuse. Abused children need shelter, education, and therapy.

DISCUSSION TOPIC 9.5: ARTISTIC DEVELOPMENT

Collect drawings made by children or encourage your students to add to your collection. These can be easily made into overhead transparencies to demonstrate the developmental progression of children's art as discussed in the text. In addition, students may be interested in the psychological evaluation of children's drawings (rather than just developmental). Goodenow's Draw-A-Person inventory will be interesting, as well as discussion of the projective uses of drawings. Remind students that drawings are not diagnostic, they represent both children's thinking and their perceptual-motor skills, and they are a very limited piece of information. However, students seem to enjoy applying their knowledge of Kellogg's stages and speculating about the symbolic meanings of elements in the drawings.

157

INDEPENDENT STUDIES

INDEPENDENT STUDY 9.1: ASSESSMENT OF KINDERGARTEN READINESS

In many communities, four- and five-year-olds must pass a kindergarten screening test in order to enter school. As kindergarten curricula become increasingly academic, school systems depend on screening measures to help identify children who might benefit from another year of development before entering kindergarten. One such test is the Gesell. These tests assume that children may be developmentally ready for the kindergarten experience as a result of maturation. What kinds of things do kindergarten screening measures look for? How useful is this kind of assessment? Do some research using a database such as ERIC to discover how reliable and valid preschool screening tools are and whether they accurately predict which children are "ready" for kindergarten.

INDEPENDENT STUDY 9.2: CANALIZATION OF MOTOR SKILLS IN EARLY CHILDHOOD

Infant motor development is highly canalized; that is, the range of ages at which a particular development occurs is fairly narrow. For example, babies are expected to roll over for the first time sometime between 2 months and 5.5 months of age. Does this narrow range of expectations persist when we consider children of 3 to 5 years? Research the development of motor skills that we usually associate with older children, for example riding a bicycle. What factors influence the age at which children acquire these more sophisticated skills? What does the research suggest about the impact of family support and experience in contrast to biologically-influenced "natural ability?"

Use a database such as ERIC or the journal *Perceptual and Motor Skills* to help you find answers to these questions.

CHOOSING SIDES

CHOOSING SIDES 9.1: THE WAR ON POVERTY

The authors of the textbook point out that poverty is a major correlate of childhood illness in U.S. society. If you are inclined to use some class time discussing social issues, this is a fruitful topic for classroom debate.

Should we eliminate the poverty in any way we can, or should we work to correct the social factors that lead to poverty in our society? What should be government's role in either of those approaches?

Obviously, this issue will bring out strongly held political views. In order for this to be a useful discussion, it will be important for you to set some ground rules to ensure that all opinions and ideas are approached with respect and impartiality. Advocates on both sides of the issue can be encouraged to do further research on the earlier "war on poverty" and on current governmental programs addressing poverty and to report their findings to the class. An interesting side topic is whether society should have the right to intervene on the behalf of children when their parents refuse, on the grounds of religious beliefs, to provide proper health care for their children. Include the current welfare reforms and how such reforms would affect children.

KNOWLEDGE CONSTRUCTION ACTIVITIES

KNOWLEDGE CONSTRUCTION ACTIVITY 9.1: GENERATIVE TERMS

This activity will use the principles of generative learning as explained in the Introduction to assist students in gaining a better understanding of terms. Divide the class into groups of four or five. Assign each group the task of generating an example for a generative term from this chapter. The example that each group creates cannot be one that has been used in the class or in the book. They must think of a new application for the term that they are given. Groups are allowed to use their books and notes. By creating their own example of the term, they demonstrate an understanding of the term to the level of application. There are several approaches that can be used in this exercise. Students may be given the entire list at once, but often one group will finish far ahead of the others and topics will get out of sequence. Another strategy is to give all of the groups the same term to create an example and then go around the room to discuss outcomes. This has been very successful, but also takes the most time. A third approach is to give each group a different term and see what examples they can generate.

Some generative terms for Chapter 9 are listed below.

Nightmare
Sleep terror
Family characteristics of enuresis
Gross motor skill
Fine motor skill
Left-hand disadvantages in a right-handed world
Physical abuse
Neglect
Emotional maltreatment

KNOWLEDGE CONSTRUCTION ACTIVITY 9.2: NUTRITION AND ADVERTISING TO CHILDREN

Videotape one hour of children's television from Saturday morning. Have students count the advertisements for food and analyze how many of these foods are healthy in terms of fat, salt, and sugar content. How do these advertisements appeal to children? How do they appeal to parents? Discuss how television influences children's eating habits.

KNOWLEDGE CONSTRUCTION ACTIVITY 9.3: CHILDREN IN HOSPITALS

Interview pediatric nurses from a local children's hospital. Discover the major causes of childhood hospitalization. What are some common reactions to being left in a hospital? What attempts are made to help children overcome fears and uncertainty about hospitals?

What is the average duration of a hospital stay? What are some common recovery problems once a child has returned home? Are there any long-range effects of hospitalization? Has the length of stay changed due to increased managed care?

KNOWLEDGE CONSTRUCTION ACTIVITY 9.4: PERCEPTUAL MOTOR DEVELOPMENT ON THE PLAYGROUND

Have students observe 3- to 5-year-old children on a playground or at a park. How sophisticated is their perceptual motor development? For example, how smoothly can they run? Can they walk backwards? Can they walk a straight line or circle drawn on the pavement? Jumping—how far, how high, over barriers, jumping down from a height? How well can a preschooler hop, skip, climb jungle gyms, climb ladders, throw and catch balls (various sizes), dribble, and so on?

KNOWLEDGE CONSTRUCTION ACTIVITY 9.5: INTERVIEW A PRESCHOOLER

Assign students to interview preschoolers of different ages (3-year-olds, 4-year-olds, and 5-year olds). The students should question the preschoolers about their knowledge of the role of nutrition in health. The students may need to be creative in their questioning in order to elicit what the children know. For example, many preschoolers do not know about the basic four food groups but freely respond to questions about whether they should drink milk every day. The students will undoubtedly encounter many humorous replies to their questions. A composite of the more humorous answers would make an enjoyable class project. (You might consider having the results published in the student newspaper or other publication.)

KNOWLEDGE CONSTRUCTION ACTIVITY 9.6: EXPLORING HANDEDNESS

Locate several pairs of left-handed scissors, a left-handed desk, a left-handed baseball glove, and any other artifacts created for lefties. Encourage your right-handed students to try them out and discuss the difficulties encountered by lefties in a right-handed world.

Have students write their names with their preferred hand. On the same sheet of paper, write with the non-preferred hand. Compare their results to classmates'. Are there any students who found it nearly as easy to write with the non-preferred hand as the preferred hand? What other activities do these students do with either hand?

Your students might like to explore their own dominance patterns further. Ask them to fold their arms and observe which arm is on top. Next, try to fold arms the other way. Do the same thing with folding hands and observing which thumb is on the top. Imagine that you are kicking a ball; which foot do you use? Each of these activities can provide insight into the processes involved in right-, left-, and mixed-dominance.

KNOWLEDGE CONSTRUCTION ACTIVITY 9.7: TRACING CHILDREN'S ARTISTIC DEVELOPMENT

Form a working group
  Get together with four other students to do this project. Your task is to create a gallery - like display of children's art that showcases the sequence of development described in your textbook.

Collect children's art
  Divide among group members the responsibility of collecting drawings made by children of different ages. Students will have access to children of varied ages in their homes, workplaces, or neighborhoods.

Ask each child to create a drawing that you will be keeping. Offer children a variety of media, including crayons, markers, chalk, etc., as appropriate. Encourage children to write their own captions, but try not to influence their art. For example, do not suggest what to draw, how to draw, or draw a model for the child.

On each drawing, write the child's age in years and months and the date collected. If the child wishes to dictate a caption or a story that goes with the drawing, write it down.

Inspect your data
Put all of the drawings collected by your group together. Place them in the order of the ages of the children and inspect them sequentially. Do you see age-related changes in children's art? Come to consensus within your group about the stages of development of each of the artists. Label each drawing with the stage it represents.

Create a display
  Assemble the drawings on a large poster board or project board . Use your project board to present your findings to the class. Did the children's art that you collected reflect Kellogg's stages of artistic development? Why or why not?

What did you learn from this activity?

7. RESOURCES FOR INSTRUCTORS

Books and Journal Articles

Kempe, C. H., Silver, H. K., O'Brien, D., & Fulginiti, V. A. (eds.) (1987). *Current pediatric diagnosis and treatment*. Norwalk, CT: Appleton.

Miller, A. (1986). *Thou shalt not be aware*. New York: New American Library.

Rozin, P., & Fallon, A. (July 1985). That's disgusting. *Psychology Today*, 60-63.

Wolfe, D. A. (1987*). Child abuse: Implications for child development and psychopathology*. Newbury Park, IL: Sage.

Video resources

Preschool physical development (IM, 1994, video, 30 min.). This program examines the child's physical development during the preschool ages of 3 to 6—a period of rapid growth in physical skills.

10 COGNITIVE DEVELOPMENT IN EARLY CHILDHOOD

PIAGETIAN APPROACH: THE PREOPERATIONAL CHILD
Advances of Preoperational Thought
Immature Aspects of Preoperational Thought
Do Young Children Have Theories of Mind?

LANGUAGE DEVELOPMENT
Vocabulary
Grammar and Syntax
Pragmatics and Social Speech
Private Speech
Delayed Language Development
Social Interaction and Preparation for Literacy

INFORMATION-PROCESSING APPROACH: MEMORY DEVELOPMENT
Recognition and Recall

Forming Childhood Memories
Influences on Autobiographical Memory
Implicit Memory

INTELLIGENCE: PSYCHOMETRIC AND VYGOTSKIAN APPROACHES
Traditional Psychometric Measures
Influences on Measured Intelligence
Testing and Teaching Based on Vygotsky's "Zone of Proximal Development"

EARLY CHILDHOOD EDUCATION
Goals and Types of Preschools: A Cross-Cultural View
Compensatory Preschool Programs
The Transition to Kindergarten

In This Chapter of Your Instructor's Manual You Will Find:
1. Total Teaching Package Outline
2. Expanded Outline
3. Guideposts for Study
4. Learning Objectives
5. Key Terms
6. Teaching and Learning Activities
    Discussion Topics
    Independent Studies
    Choosing Sides
    Knowledge Construction Activities
7. Resources for Instructors

1. TOTAL TEACHING PACKAGE OUTLINE

Chapter 10: Cognitive Development In Early Childhood

Piagetian approach: The preoperational child	**Guidepost for study 10.1**
Advances of preoperational thought	**Learning objective 10.1** **Lecture topic 10.1**
Immature aspects of preoperational thought	**Learning objectives 10.2, 10.3** **Knowledge construction activities 10.2, 10.4**
Do young children have theories of mind?	**Lecture topics 10.2, 10.3**
Language development	**Guidepost for study 10.2** **Discussion topic 10.4** **Knowledge construction activity 10.1**
Vocabulary	**Learning objective 10.5**
Grammar and syntax	**Learning objective 10.5** **Lecture topic 10.5**
Pragmatics and social speech	**Learning objective 10.5**
Private speech	**Learning objective 10.6**
Delayed language development	**Learning objective 10.7**
Social interaction and preparation for literacy	**Learning objective 10.8** **Lecture topic 10.4** **Discussion topic 10.3** **Box 10.1 (text p. 238)**
Information-processing approach: Memory development	**Guidepost for study 10.3** **Knowledge construction activity 10.1**
Recognition and recall	**Learning objective 10.9** **Knowledge construction activity 10.4**
Forming childhood memories	**Learning objective 10.10**
Influences on autobiographical memory	**Learning objective 10.11** **Box 10.2 (text p. 245)**
Implicit memory	**Knowledge construction activity 10.4**
Intelligence: Psychometric and Vygotskian approaches	**Guidepost for study 10.4** **Generative learning activity 10.1**
Traditional psychometric measures	**Learning objective 10.12** **Discussion topic 10.1**
Influences on measured intelligence	**Learning objective 10.13**

Testing and teaching based on Vygotsky's "zone of proximal development"	**Learning objectives 10.14-10.18** **Discussion topic 10.2**
Early childhood education	**Guidepost for study 10.5**
Goals and types of preschools: A cross-cultural view	**Knowledge construction activities 10.6** **Independent study 10.1**
Compensatory preschool programs	**Choosing sides**
The transition to kindergarten	**Knowledge construction activity 10.5**

Please check out the online learning center located at www.mhhe.com/papaliacw9 for further information on these and other topics. There you can also access downloadable PowerPoint slides tailored to each chapter of the text and containing useful teaching notes as well as images and tables from the text itself.

2. EXPANDED OUTLINE (TRANSPARENCY READY)

I. Piagetian Approach: The Preoperational Child
    A. Preoperational stage
        1. Symbolic function
        2. Dual representation hypothesis
        3. Transduction
        4. Animism
        5. Centration
           a. Decenter
        6. Conservation
        7. Irreversibility
        8. Egocentrism
        9. Theory of mind
      10. Social cognition
      11. Empathy

II. Language Development
    A. Fast mapping
    B. Pragmatics
    C. Social speech
    D. Private speech
    E. Emergent literacy

III. Information-Processing Approach: Memory Development
    A. Recognition
    B. Recall
    C. Generic memory
    D. Script
    E. Episodic memory
    F. Autobiographical memory
    G. Social interaction model

IV. Intelligence: Psychometric and Vygotskian Approaches
    A. Stanford-Binet Intelligence Scale
    B. Wechsler Preschool and Primary Scale of Intelligence

3. GUIDEPOSTS FOR STUDY

10.1 What are typical cognitive advances and immature aspects of preschool children's thinking?

10.2 How does language improve, and what happens when its development is delayed?

10.3 What memory abilities expand in early childhood?

10.4 How is preschoolers' intelligence measured and what factors influence it?

10.5 What purposes does early childhood education serve and how do children make the transition to kindergarten?

4. LEARNING OBJECTIVES

After completing the study of this chapter, the student will be able to:

10.1. Summarize findings about preschool children's understanding of symbols, space, causality, identities, categories, and numbers.

10.2. Tell how centration limits preoperational thought.

10.3. Give several reasons why preoperational children have difficulty with conservation.

10.4. Discuss research that challenges Piaget's views on egocentrism in early childhood.

10.5. Trace normal progress in 3- to 6-year-olds' vocabulary, grammar, syntax, and conversational abilities.

10.6. Give reasons why children of various ages use private speech.

10.7. Discuss possible causes, consequences, and treatment of delayed language development.

10.8. Identify factors in preparation for literacy.

10.9. Compare preschoolers' recognition and recall ability.

10.10. Explain how language development may contribute to the onset of autobiographical memory.

10.11. Identify factors that affect how well a preschool child will remember an event.

10.12. Describe two commonly used individual intelligence tests for preschoolers.

10.13. Discuss several influences on measured intelligence.

10.14. Explain why an intelligence test score using the ZPD might be significantly different from a traditional psychometric test score.

10.15. Compare goals of varying types of preschool programs in the United States and Japan.

10.16. Summarize findings on the short- and long-term effects of academic and child-centered preschool programs.

10.17 Assess the benefits of compensatory preschool education.

10.18 Discuss factors that affect adjustment to kindergarten.

5. KEY TERMS

Preoperational stage
Symbolic function
Dual representation hypothesis
Transduction
Animism
Centration
Decenter
Conservation
Irreversibility
Egocentrism
Theory of mind
Social cognition
Empathy
Fast mapping

Pragmatics
Social speech
Private speech
Emergent literacy
Recognition
Recall
Generic memory
Script
Episodic memory
Autobiographical memory
Social interaction model
Stanford-Binet Intelligence Scale
Wechsler Preschool and Primary Scale of
    Intelligence, Revised (WPPSI-R)

6. TEACHING AND LEARNING ACTIVITIES
Lecture Topics

LECTURE TOPIC 10.1: WHAT PRESCHOOLERS CAN DO

There is persistent controversy over the intellectual capabilities of a child. Determination of a child's competence guides developmental research as well as educational and parenting practices. If research demonstrates, for example, that a child is egocentric until a certain stage of cognitive development, then efforts at teaching the child to respect the rights of others should be fruitless. However, if the child is not egocentric but only limited in cognitive strategies, it should be possible to train a child to perform quite complex tasks previously thought impossible.

Much research in cognitive and language development has been designed to show how "incompetent" the preschooler is compared to older children and adults. Once differences have been found, American researchers, in particular, like to see whether these differences can be modified or changed. Piaget has frequently criticized the American penchant for trying to make children bigger, brighter, healthier, and better rather than letting them develop naturally. In turn, current assumptions of natural cognitive processes in Piaget's and other maturational theories are strongly criticized for underestimating the remarkably complex abilities of the 2- to 5-year old.

There has been a great deal of literature characterizing the preschooler as unable to classify objects and events, communicate empathically, handle number concepts, remember accurately, or determine causal relationships. Part of the problem in this controversy revolves around the competence of the child versus his performance. Many experiments have been designed to show that a preschooler has the competence to conserve number, carry on a reciprocal conversation and show use of cause-and-effect relationships. In other words, children have competence.

However, anyone who has interacted with preschoolers knows that, even if the child has the competence, it does not mean he or she will show the appropriate performance. For example, a baby has competent depth perception but still crawls straight off high places like beds. Or, a daughter was hiding a doll from her dad. She held the doll behind her back even after she walked

168

past her dad who then could quite easily see the doll. These examples may not reflect theoretical competence, but they certainly are observable realistic performances.

Neither Piaget's theory nor any other theory of child development adequately handles the competence-performance factors satisfactorily. Theories must be constantly challenged and changed as their explanatory power is weakened by new data. Efforts should be made by instructors, experimenters, and theoreticians to determine how children really *are* rather than how they *should be*. Indeed, preschoolers think and act differently from older individuals, but this does not mean they are necessarily incapable of performing similarly.

In many respects, researchers are simply unable to ask questions of preschoolers in the right way. It has, for example, been well documented that if you put two rows of five jelly beans each in front of a 3-year-old and then spread one of the rows out wider than the other, the child will typically say there are *more* beans in the wider pile. This supposedly shows that a child cannot focus on *number* and is mislead by width or length. Thus, the child does not conserve number.

Should a preschool educator therefore not try to teach numbers to a child? Rochel Gelman has repeatedly shown that the child has difficulty with the traditional conservation task but that this is not simply a matter of number confusion. Gelman has designed a "magic task." After the initial viewing, she covers the two rows of objects, makes a transformation such as spreading one row out, shows the child the new rows, and then asks the child which row is the winner and which is the loser. The child automatically tends to say that the row with the greater number is the winner. If there are the same number in each row, no matter how spread out or altered, children have consistently "conserved number." These same children would flunk the traditional number conservation task. Obviously, how you ask the questions has a tremendous effect on the children.

Is the Piagetian or the Gelman technique more realistic in its portrayal of preschoolers' cognitive abilities? This is a more complex question than many students and researchers realize.

References

Flavell, J. (1992). Cognitive development: Past, present, and future. *Developmental Psychology, 28*, 998-1005.
Gelman, R. (1979). Preschool thought. *American Psychologist, 34*, 900-905.
Melmed, M. (July 1997). Parents speak. *Young Children.*

LECTURE TOPIC 10.2: NEW THINKING ON THINKING

The three traditional approaches to discussing intellectual development presented in the text (Piagetian, psychometric, and information-processing) are currently being augmented by active discussion and research in the area of thinking skills. The thinking skills approach addresses aspects of intellectual development emphasized in each of the three traditional areas.

James Greeno has suggested three assumptions that he believes must be made in order for research on general thinking abilities to progress more rapidly and for us "to make significant headway toward an adequate understanding of thinking and creativity."

First, Greeno advocates viewing thinking as occurring in specific physical and social contexts. He terms this "situated cognition." Rather than considering thinking to be an event or activity that occurs in an individual's mind, Greeno proposes that thinking be considered an interaction between an individual and a physical and social situation. In this light, thinking becomes a constructive process of interaction between individuals and the situations in which they find themselves.

Second, Greeno proposes an assumption of "personal and social epistemologies." He suggests that thinking occurs within the context of beliefs and understandings about thinking that are both personal and social in nature. Such beliefs and understandings differ from individual to individual and from one social group to another. These implicit and socially defined theories of intelligence, knowing, and learning influence the fundamental ways in which any individual thinks about the world and comes to understand it. For example, if you believe that intelligence is a fixed commodity, then you will also believe that you have little control over how much you are capable of learning and will react within that limit.

Third, in "conceptual competence" Greeno assumes that children have tremendous potential for cognitive growth, which makes possible very complex and subtle ways of thinking. He believes that "thinking, learning, and cognitive growth are activities in which children elaborate and reorganize their knowledge and understanding." This is in contrast to a more traditional view that depicts thinking, learning, and cognitive growth as the result of acquiring and applying cognitive structures and procedures.

If widely adopted, Greeno's reformulation of the assumptions underlying research about thinking will lead to our asking questions differently about cognition and will, undoubtedly, lead to new insights about thinking.

Reference

Greeno, J. G. (1989). A perspective on thinking. *American Psychologist, 44,* 134-141.

LECTURE TOPIC 10.3: EXPLORATORY BEHAVIOR IN CHILDREN

Exploratory behavior consists of curiosity arousal and responding to discrepant and novel stimuli. Psychologists are interested in individual differences in exploratory behavior, the factors that modify exploratory behavior, and how exploratory strategies change with age. Researchers in the area suggest that exploratory behavior can be measured in four fairly independent dimensions:

1. Exploration is associated with preferences for complex visual and auditory stimuli over less-complex stimuli.
2. Exploration is associated with a preference for novelty and the unknown.
3. Exploration can be measured by looking at breadth of examination of objects (Does the child briefly examine a wide range of objects?) or by looking at depth of examination of objects (Does the child examine in a detailed fashion a few objects?).
4. Exploration is associated with asking questions, especially in young children.

Researchers use a variety of materials and tasks to measure exploratory behavior. In some research, children are asked to point out their preferences for visual figures that vary in complexity. In other research, a preference for the unknown is measured by giving children a toy and then asking whether they wish to trade the toy for a toy hidden behind a screen. A third type of task involves giving children a number of objects to explore and noting their questions and comments about the objects, how many objects are examined, and the median time of examination per object.

As children get older, they are more likely to exhibit exploratory behaviors in the presence of a peer, develop a strategy of briefly examining all objects and then choosing one item to explore in detail, choose an unknown object over a given object, and do more systematic, nonredundant, comprehensive exploratory searches in new environments.

References

Gunnar, M. R., Senior, K., & Hartup, W. W. (1984). Peer presence and the exploratory behavior of eighteen- and thirty-month-old children. *Child Development, 55,* 1103-1109.

Henderson, B. B. (1984). Parents and exploration: The effect of context on individual differences in exploratory behavior. *Child Development, 55,* 1237-1245.

Vandenberg, B. (1984). Developmental features of exploration. *Developmental Psychology, 20,* 3-8.

Wellman, H. M., Somerville, S. C., Revelle, G. L., Haake, R. J., & Sophian, C. (1984). The development of comprehensive search skills. *Child Development, 55,* 472-481.

LECTURE TOPIC 10.4: GETTING CHILDREN READY TO READ

Parents can get their children prepared to read by doing the following activities:

1. Surround children with many kinds of reading materials and a variety of ways in which to create stories. Parents should provide a variety of books, either by ownership or by frequent visits to a public library. In addition, children can create stories using old magazines and catalogs; dictate stories to parents, who copy these stories down and then let the children illustrate them; and practice letters on chalkboards or with magnetic letters attached to the refrigerator. Parents should provide lots of paper and writing instruments for experimentation.

2. Use good literature. Children should be exposed to high-quality children's books and should also be taught to think about the stories by being asked questions (What do you think will happen next? What would *you* have done?) throughout the story.

3. Connect the book's tale with actual experiences. This can be done through asking questions that relate the story to something the child has done—or, even better, that connect stories with field trips.

4. Develop children's oral language ability. A positive relationship exists between language development and reading achievement.

5. Help children understand the relationship between spoken and written language. Writing down the children's own stories helps children see the connection between speaking on the one hand and writing and reading on the other. Let the child draw a picture and tell a story about the picture. The adult writes the story for the child.

6. Help children understand how books work. Assist them in learning what an individual word looks like, that reading goes from left to right, when a page gets turned, and what the beginning and the end of the book are.

7. Stimulate children's thinking. Play in general does this, as does asking creative, imaginative questions about characters in books.

Reference

Carver, N. K. (March/April 1986). Reading readiness: Aspects overlooked in structured readiness programs and workbooks. *Childhood Education, 62,* 256-259.

LECTURE TOPIC 10.5: A CHILD'S RULES FOR LEARNING LANGUAGE

As pointed out in the text, language acquisition is not merely a matter of acquiring a larger vocabulary and making longer sentences. The complexity of language learning is readily apparent to any adult who has attempted to learn a new language. Slobin outlined some basic rules that children in all countries seem to follow when learning language. Adults must learn the same strategies when learning a new language..

1. *Look for systematic modifications in the forms of words.* According to Nelson, it takes most children almost 2 years (average of 20 months) before they have produced more than 50 different words. These first words are quite simple utterances and fulfill multiple purposes (holophrases). Although there is controversy on the topic, a common occurrence with these first words is overextension (Fremgen & Fay, 1980) in which "da" or "duck" may mean a reference to a chicken, penguin, or any other bird. While these semantic overextensions are being mastered, the child also must learn that subtle changes in these words have dramatic effects. This will be seen in possessives and pluralization of nouns and pronouns and also in tenses of verbs

2. *Look for grammatical markers that indicate underlying, semantic distinctions clearly and that make sense.*

3. *Avoid exceptions.*

4. *Pay attention to the ends of words.* Nouns and sometimes pronouns are usually changed in meaning to plural and possessive by adding some form of "s" to the end of the word. Initially, children appear to memorize the correct forms but then go through a period in which interesting errors are made (overregularization). Thus you will hear a child saying count-noun plurals for mass nouns; for example, *sugars, milks, deers, sheeps,* and so on, or double possessives on pronouns such as *mines, hers's,* and *Dicks'es.* The same sort of period of incorrect responses occurs with tenses and with regular versus irregular verbs. The third-person singular verb form *he says* may be transferred to the third person plural form *they says.* The irregular verbs will be made past tense by adding "ed," so a child says *comed, runned, goed, doed,* and so forth. For good measure, the child can be heard saying *camed* or *dided.* Even adults have difficulty with words such as *dive* (*dived* or *dove?*) and *thrive* (*thrived* or *throve?*). It is important to point out that children are learning rules of meaning and grammar and apparently try to apply these rules systematically, without exception. They have probably never heard adults make these errors.

5. *Pay attention to the order of words, prefixes, and suffixes.* Interestingly, in English, children seldom place the noun before the preposition or add a suffix to the beginning of a word. Thus, they do not say, "The box is table on" or "nessgood gracious!"

6. *Avoid interruption or rearrangement of linguistic unit.* Children acquire relative-clause usage rather late. Rather than saying "The boy who was watching *Bambi* was crying," the child is more likely to say, "The boy watching *Bambi.* He crying."

These simple and somewhat overlapping principles are important because they represent systematic, semantic, and syntactic development in most children learning language.

References

Fremgen, A., & Fay, D. (1980). Overextensions in production and comprehension: A methodological clarification. *Journal of Child Language, 7,* 205-211.

Nelson, K (1977). Facilitating children's syntax acquisition. *Developmental Psychology, 13,* 101–107.

Pinker, S. (1994). *The language instinct: How the mind creates language.* New York: William Morrow.

Shore, C. (1995). *Individual differences in language development.* Thousands Oaks, CA: Sage.

Slobin, D. (1972, July). Children and language: They learn the same all around the world. *Psychology Today, 26,* 731-737.

DISCUSSION TOPICS

DISCUSSION TOPIC 10.1: THE IQ DILEMMA

Not mentioned in the textbook presentation of intelligence testing are the typical uses of this type of assessment in early childhood. Three- to five-year-olds are not routinely tested with intelligence tests. More often an intelligence test is given only when retarded intellectual development is suspected. Screening such individuals allows for more precise assessment of their deficits and for appropriate remediation, if possible. Propose to the class that all 3-year-olds should be routinely screened with standardized intelligence tests such as the WPPSI. Explore with the class the advantages accrued to society and the problems that could arise with such a program. A discussion of self-fulfilling prophecies would be appropriate here. On the far side of this issue, would it be possible to fine parents if they failed to have their child tested or failed to take remedial action if it were called for? In a society that pushes for superbabies, will intelligence testing of 3-year-olds become more commonplace?

DISCUSSION TOPIC 10.2: EARLY CHILDHOOD EDUCATION

How well a child scores on an intelligence test is determined by a number of variables. Emotional and social functioning, temperament, parental child-rearing practices, and viewing specialized television programs have all been identified as variables that can enhance performance on intelligence tests. A curious child within a sensitive, warm environment who encourages exploration and creativity responds well in school.

Public and private nursery schools and day care centers continue to flourish. Being in preschool helps children grow in many ways—physically, intellectually, socially, and emotionally. Different schools and preschools may emphasize different areas of development. The Montessori schools have a strong cognitive bent. Project Head Start was used as a tool to provide health care, intellectual enrichment, and a supportive environment to improve social competence. Home Start was implemented to improve the learning experience. The latest research suggests that preschool education works in terms of the child's performance and has wider societal ramifications. In many ways, kindergarten is an extension of preschool, except that kindergarten in many areas is provided by the state. The value of kindergarten appears to be well accepted by both educators and the public. Not attending kindergarten can have negative effects.

DISCUSSION TOPIC 10.3: ACCELERATING DEVELOPMENT

The lecture topic on promoting reading readiness in children provides a good opportunity to discuss the idea of accelerating development for preschoolers. Must parents and educators wait until children are ready, or can children be made ready for certain types of learning at earlier ages? What are the advantages and disadvantages of attempting to accelerate development? Ask students to relate their own personal experiences as well as what they have read about the topic.

DISCUSSION TOPIC 10.4: TV'S CHILDREN

We now live in an age where the average 18-year-olds come to college having spent as much time watching TV as attending school. In fact, some of these students' school hours were spent watching TV! It is a rare individual under 25 years of age who did not grow up with at least one TV in the household. It is important for your "under 25" students to understand how television changed their childhood. Did they learn from TV? What did they learn? Ask the class to generate a list of benefits they derived from being part of a television generation. Ask them to then make a list of things earlier generations of children did but they did *not* do because they spent their time watching TV. What differences are there between the radio generation and the TV generations? This is a good opportunity to review normative history-graded influences on development.

INDEPENDENT STUDY

INDEPENDENT STUDY 10.1:DAY CARE LICENSING

Have students report on the legal standards for day care licensing in your state. Criteria might include size of the facility, physical condition of the facility, passing fire and safety inspection, number of toys available, caretaker-child ratio, provisions for illness, meals provided, and training or education of teacher. How do the minimum standards for licensing compare with the necessary standards for good intellectual and emotional development elaborated in the text?

CHOOSING SIDES

CHOOSING SIDES 10.1: MANDATORY COMPENSATORY EDUCATION

For the last three decades, there has been a general state of ferment in early childhood education. The spirit in the early 1960s was one of naive optimism. A 3- to 12-month-long program was provided for disadvantaged and culturally deprived children to give them a "head start" in elementary school. The evaluation studies of the mid-1960s caused a national debate on compensatory education. Some felt that the "failure" of Head Start was inevitable because of the genetic nature of intelligence. Others emphasized that gains were not maintained because the program ended when school began. Still other researchers have found evidence of success and have singled out situations wherein long-term benefits did exist. In the 10 years that followed, research focused more precisely on specific preschool programs to determine exactly what effects, if any, they could have. Intervention programs throughout the country have reported witnessing gains in IQ ranging from 5 to 30 points. Some ethical questions still remain, however, on exactly how to identify a disadvantaged or culturally deprived child to single out for compensatory education. Our society may be moving toward mandatory preschool education. Would such a move discriminate against any person who varied from a white, middle-class standard forcing him or her to assume specified morals and standards of conduct in government-sponsored education? See what emerges when students debate the following proposition:

> *Mandatory compensatory education is unethical and infringes on the rights and individual freedom that our country stands for.*

Pro: Attempting to identify a segment of our population as disadvantaged would lead to discrimination against any who are not in a majority in our society. Forced education could be used as an attempt to control and modify minority groups. Labeling differences as inferior smacks of Nazism. This type of labeling is detrimental to the self-esteem of preschool children and detrimental to society in general.

Con: If the disadvantaged in our society were provided with opportunities to gain readiness prior to elementary school, they could more easily adapt to the education system and experience academic success. This increase of educational and occupational opportunities could alter the poverty cycle, thereby improving the standard of living for individuals and society as a whole. Intervention programs such as the Milwaukee Project have been effective in raising IQ scores from a mentally retarded range (80) to slightly above average (105).

The following lists give arguments that might be used to support each side of the debate.

Pro: Against Forced Education

1. Mandatory preschool education would be an attempt to homogenize our society and would not allow for cultural differences.
2. The reason why minority groups perform poorly in school is not because of deprivation but rather because our schools are inflexible and do not admit cultural diversity.
3. IQ tests have been used as the standard for determining deficiencies and gains. When testing members of minority groups (anyone other than a white, middle-class child), IQ scores are neither a reliable nor a valid measure of social competence.
4. Preschool is a time for play, freedom, and the learning of social skills, not a time for rigid education. Starting early will just make teenagers tired of school and increase the dropout rate.
5. Singling out certain children as needing compensatory education will brand them with a label of "inferior" that could become a self-fulfilling prophecy.
6. There are many alternative models of early education, each of which has a different effect on various groups of children. We don't yet know enough about the impact or the side effects of different preschool programs to establish mandatory compensatory education.
7. The type of extensive intervention programs needed (for example, from 6 weeks of age until the children enters school) are too expensive and disruptive of family life.

Con: Mandatory Preschool Education

1. Disadvantaged children could experience academic success if provided with appropriate readiness education prior to starting school.
2. Increasing educational and occupational opportunities could alter the poverty cycle and improve the standard of living.

3. Intervention programs have been designed that can increase IQ scores up to 30 points and maintain this gain.

4. Preschool programs can reflect the culture from which the child comes as well as teach those cultural values needed to succeed in our society. This would maintain cultural diversity and yet provide children with societal values that their parents cannot teach them.

5. The expense of mandatory compulsory education is minimal when compared to the cost of a deprived segment of society that has lower income, possibly contributes to the level of crime in a community, may be on welfare, and may occasionally be institutionalized due to mental retardation.

6. Education is the foundation of our society. Compulsory education is a strong tradition in our country and has as one of its goals the eventual betterment of humankind.

7. The many early childhood education programs available make it possible to tailor a classroom or curriculum to the needs of specific communities, thereby remaining sensitive to individual and cultural differences.

References

Baratz, S., & Baratz, J. (1971). Early-childhood intervention: The social science base of institutional racism. In S. Chess & A. Thomas (eds.), *Annual Progress in Child Psychiatry and Child Development*. In the same volume, see M. Blank, Implicit assumptions underlying preschool intervention programs.

Brown, B. (1985). Head Start: How research changed public policy. *Young Children*, 9-13.

Hernandez, D. (1995). Changing demographics: Past and future demands for early childhood programs. *The Future of Children*, 145-160.

KNOWLEDGE CONSTRUCTION ACTIVITIES

KNOWLEDGE CONSTRUCTION ACTIVITY 10.1: GENERATIVE TERMS

This activity will use the principles of generative learning as explained in the Introduction to assist students in gaining a better understanding of terms. Divide the class into groups of four or five. Assign each group the task of generating an example for a generative term from this chapter. The example that each group creates cannot be one that has been used in the class or in the book. They must think of a new application for the term that they are given. Groups are allowed to use their books and notes. By creating their own example of the term, they demonstrate an understanding of the term to the level of application. There are several approaches that can be used in this exercise. Students may be given the entire list at once, but often one group will finish far ahead of the others and topics will get out of sequence. Another strategy is to give all of the groups the same term to create an example and then go around the room to discuss outcomes. This has been very successful, but also takes the most time. A third approach is to give each group a different term and see what examples they can generate.

Some generative terms for Chapter 10 are listed below.

Symbolic function	Egocentrism
Centration	Fast mapping
Irreversibility	

Pragmatics
Private speech
Generic memory

Episodic memory
Autobiographical memory

KNOWLEDGE CONSTRUCTION ACTIVITY 10.2: PIAGET'S QUESTIONS FOR YOUNG CHILDREN

Some of Piaget's most entertaining discussions deal with the questions he asked children about the physical world and about their own mental processes. Arrange for several preschool children (3 to 5 years old) to be at class (or, if children would be reluctant to respond in your class setting, individually tape-record several interviews). Many times a student will have a sibling or relative in this age group and will be willing to make a tape of the child's responses. A list of possible questions might include:

Where does the sun go at night?
Why is the grass green?
Why do we have snow?
Why do birds sing?
How do flies walk on the ceiling?
Why do you have freckles?
How did you learn to talk?
Why do you have a belly button?
Why are you ticklish?
Why do the stars shine?
Where do babies come from?

Discuss how the child's answers reflect egocentrism. Can you find evidence of animism and artificialism?

KNOWLEDGE CONSTRUCTION ACTIVITY 10.3: PRESCHOOL EGOCENTRISM

One way to demonstrate egocentrism and the inability to see things from someone else's perspective is to ask a preschool child to give some type of directions. Ask the child's parent for some familiar location that the child can get to easily. Ask the child to tell you how to get to this familiar location. How was egocentrism demonstrated? What type of information did the child omit? What did the child assume on your part (for example, that you knew whether to turn right or left, or that you knew what "Mary's house" looked like)?

177

KNOWLEDGE CONSTRUCTION ACTIVITY 10.4: PRESCHOOLER'S MEMORY

Test a preschool child's memory span. One traditional test of memory is a digit-span memory test. Explain to the child that you are going to say some numbers. Ask the child to listen and, when you are through, to say the same numbers. Start with two- or three-digit strings of numbers to ensure that the child understands (e.g., 3-8-6). Increase the string by one number each time. If the child makes a mistake, give a second chance with another string of similar length. Discontinue the test when two mistakes have been made on the same-length digit string.

Now test the child's ability to recall objects. Bring 10 small objects to class. Be sure to have the child identify each one to ensure that he or she has a label for each object. After verbally labeling all the objects and putting them out on the table, cover the display and ask the child to tell you what was there.

To observe the implicit memory of the preschooler, begin with a question such as how to get from the front door of the child's house to his or her bedroom. Another topic may be how to play a favorite game.

Also include some test of long-term memory. What did the child receive for Christmas last year or for his or her last birthday? Can the child tell you about the events surrounding the birth of his or her younger sibling? By talking to the parent find an event that occurred at least 1 year ago.

Discuss with the class which of these measures is a good test of the child's memory. Is the first task too abstract? Are the children really remembering the actual event in the long-term memory test? Are they remembering pictures or conversations about the event that have helped them to remember?

KNOWLEDGE CONSTRUCTION ACTIVITY 10.5: KINDERGARTEN SCREENING

Often children will have to take a screening test before they enter kindergarten. For an out-of-class activity, have students arrange to interview a kindergarten teacher or an elementary school administrator regarding the test. What does the test assess? What is the educator's experience with starting children early or late in kindergarten? Are parents obligated to abide by test results in deciding when their child should enter kindergarten?

KNOWLEDGE CONSTRUCTION ACTIVITY 10.6: PRESCHOOL OBSERVATION

Objectives: Preschool programs can vary depending on the achievement level of the students and the goals of the program. For example, some preschools are designed to help students prepare for first grade, some are for gifted and excelled students, and some programs may emphasize social or religious values. Some are full-day programs and some meet for half a day. For this assignment you can observe at any type of preschool program.

Directions: Call to make an appointment to observe at a preschool. Be polite and courteous on the phone. It is also important to be honest by telling the person in charge that this observation is a class assignment. Observing for one full day or half-day would be the most valuable.

Observation: Watch the children specifically for:

1. Whether they prefer to play alone or with someone else
2. The types of toys they prefer
3. Their ability to follow rules
4. Their willingness to share
5. Whether they have formed friendships
6. How they respond to discipline
7. How well they are speaking and communicating

Record these observations and any others you feel are significant.

Writing the paper: Write a paper giving your observations and your reactions. You should have an introduction section that tells about the assignment and how you carried it out. The body of the paper should contain three sections that summarize your observations. The conclusion should highlight the main findings of your observations.

The paper:

1. Should be 5 to 7 pages long
2. Should be typed, double spaced, and have 1-inch margins
3. Should include a cover sheet giving your name, the title of your paper, your ID #, your course name, your section number, and the date.

7. RESOURCES FOR INSTRUCTORS

Books and Journal Articles

Anthony, E. J., & Cohler, B. J. (eds.) (1987). *The invulnerable child.* New York: Guilford.

Boden, M. A. (1980). *Jean Piaget.* New York: Viking.

Brainerd, C. J., & Pressley, M. (ed.) (1985). *Basic processes in memory development: Process in cognitive development research.* New York: Springer.

Clark, M. M. (1988). *Children under five: Educational research and evidence.* New York: Gordon & Breach Science Publishers.

Flavell, J. H. (1987). The development of children's knowledge about the appearance-reality distinction. *American Psychologist, 41,* 418-426

Goleman, D. (1995). *Emotional intelligence.* New York: Bantam.

Howes, C. (1988). Relations between early child care and schooling. *Developmental Psychology, 24,* 53-57.

Kagan, J. (1978). *The growth of the child: Reflections on human development.* New York: Norton.

Piaget, J. (1987). *Possibility and necessity*, trans. Helga Feider. Minneapolis: University of Minnesota Press.

Vygotsky, L. S. (1978). *The Mind in Society.* Cambridge, MA: Harvard University Press.

Vygotsky, L. S. (1994). *Thought and Language.* Cambridge, MA: MIT Press.

Video resources
Culture and education of young children (IM, 1985, video, 16 min.). This discussion with Carol Phillips focuses on how programs for young children can be designed to show respect for cultural diversity, thereby enhancing the richness of a child's education.

Play: A Vygotskyian Perspective (Davidson 1996). A video in which Leung and Bodrova discuss how Vygotsky's theory of cognitive development is demonstrated through preschool children's play activities. There are clear explanations of scaffolding and the zone of proximal development, as well as examples of developing self-regulation through play.

11 PSYCHOSOCIAL DEVELOPMENT IN EARLY CHILDHOOD

THE DEVELOPING SELF
The Self-Concept and Cognitive Development
Understanding Emotions
Erikson: Initiative versus Guilt
Self-Esteem

GENDER
Gender differences
Perspectives on Gender Development: Nature and Nurture

PLAY: THE BUSINESS OF EARLY CHILDHOOD
Types of Play
The Social Dimension of Play
How Gender Influences Play
How Culture Influences Play

PARENTING
Forms of Discipline
Parenting Styles
Promoting Altruism and dealing with Aggression and Fearfulness

RELATIONSHIPS WITH OTHER CHILDREN
Siblings – or their Absence
Playmates and Friends

In this Chapter of Your Instructor's Manual You Will Find:
1. Total Teaching Package Outline
2. Expanded outline (transparency-ready)
3. Guideposts for study
4. Learning Objectives
5. Key terms
6. Teaching and Learning Activities
    Lecture Topics
    Discussion
    Choosing Sides
    Independent Studies
    Knowledge Construction Activities
7. Resources for Instructors

1. TOTAL TEACHING PACKAGE OUTLINE

Chapter 11: Psychosocial Development in Early Childhood

The developing self	**Lecture topic 11.1** **Knowledge construction activity 11.1**
The self-concept and cognitive development	**Guidepost for study 11.1** **Learning objective 11.1** **Lecture topic 11.2** **Discussion topic 11.1**
Understanding emotions	**Learning objective 11.2**
Erikson: Initiative versus guilt	**Guidepost for study 11.2** **Learning objective 11.3**
Self-esteem	**Learning objective 11.4**
Gender	**Guidepost for study 11.3** **Lecture topic 11.1** **Knowledge construction activity 11.1**
Gender differences	**Learning objective 11.5**
Perspectives on gender development: Nature and nurture	**Learning objectives 11.6, 11.7, 11.8** **Knowledge construction activities 11.6, 11.7** **Discussion topics 11.2, 11.3** **Choosing sides 11.1**
Play: The business of early childhood	**Guidepost for study 11.4** **Lecture topic 11.1** **Knowledge construction activity 11.1**
Types of play	**Learning objective 11.9** **Discussion topic 11.4**
The social dimension of play	**Learning objective 11.10** **Knowledge construction activity 11.3**
How gender influences play	**Learning objective 11.11**
How culture influences play	
Parenting	**Guidepost for study 11.5** **Lecture topic 11.5, 11.6**
Forms of discipline	**Learning objective 11.12** **Choosing sides 11.2** **Box 11.1 (textbook p. 278)**
Parenting styles	**Learning objective s11.13, 11.14** **Lecture topics 11.3, 11.4** **Knowledge construction activity 11.4**
Promoting altruism and dealing with aggression and fearfulness	**Independent study 11.2**

Relationships with other children	
Siblings—or their absence	**Guidepost for study 11.6** **Learning objectives 11.16, 11.18** **Lecture topic 11.5** **Box 11.2 (textbook p. 286)** **Independent study 11.1**
Playmates and friends	**Guidepost for study 11.7** **Learning objectives 11.19, 11.20** **Knowledge construction activity 11.5**

Please check out the online learning center located at www.mhhe.com/papaliacw9 for further information on these and other topics. There you can also access downloadable PowerPoint slides tailored to each chapter of the text and containing useful teaching notes as well as images and tables from the text itself.

2. EXPANDED OUTLINE (TRANSPARENCY READY)

I. The Developing Self
    A. Self-concept
    B. Self-definition
        1. Single representations
        2. Representational mappings
        3. Real self
        4. Ideal self
    C. Initiative versus guilt
    D. Self-esteem

II. Gender
    A. Gender identity
        1. Gender roles
        2. Gender typing
        3. Gender stereotypes
    B. Gender constancy
    C. Gender-schema theory
    D. Social cognitive theory

III. Play
    A. Functional play
    B. Constructive play
    C. Pretend play

IV. Parenting
    A. Discipline
        1. Corporal punishment
        2. Power assertion
        3. Inductive techniques
        4. Withdrawal of love
    B. Parenting styles
        1. Authoritarian
        2. Permissive
        3. Authoritative

V. Relationships with Other Children
    A. Prosocial behavior
        1. Altruism
    B. Aggression
        1. Instrumental aggression
        2. Overt aggression
        3. Relational aggression

3. GUIDEPOSTS FOR STUDY

11.1 How does the self-concept develop during early childhood and how do children advance in understanding their emotions?

11.2 Ho do young children develop initiative and self-esteem?

11.3 How do boys and girls become aware of the meaning of gender and what are four theoretical explanations for differences in behavior between the sexes?

11.4 How do preschoolers play and how does play contribute to and reflect development?

11.5 What three main forms of discipline and four parenting styles do parents use and how do parenting practices affect development?

11.6 Why do young children help or hurt others and why do they develop fears?

11.7 How do young children get along with (or without) siblings?

11.8 How do young children choose playmates and friends and why are some children more popular than others?

4. LEARNING OBJECTIVES

After completing the study of this chapter, the student will be able to:

11.1 Trace self-concept development between ages 3 and 6.

11.2 Describe the typical progression in understanding (1) emotion directed toward the self and (2) simultaneous emotions.

11.3 Explain the significance of Erikson's third crisis of personality development.

11.4 Tell how young children's self-esteem differs from that of school-age children.

11.5 Summarize the main cognitive and behavioral differences between boys and girls.

11.6 Assess evidence for biological explanations of gender differences.

11.7 Distinguish among four basic approaches to the study of gender development.

11.8 Compare how various theories explain the acquisition of gender roles and assess the support for each theory.

11.9 Describe four cognitive levels of play, according to Piaget, and six categories of social and nonsocial play, according to Parten.

11.10 Explain the connection between the cognitive and social dimensions of play.

11.11 Tell how gender and culture influence the way children play and give an example.

11.12 Compare various forms of discipline and identify factors that influence their effectiveness.

11.13 Describe and evaluate Baumrind's model of parenting styles.

11.14 Discuss how parents' way of resolving conflicts with young children over issues involving autonomy and control can contribute to the success of authoritative child rearing.

11.15 Discuss how parents and other influences contribute to altruism, aggression, and fearfulness.

11.16 Explain how the resolution of sibling disputes contributes to socialization.

11.17 Tell how birth order and gender affect typical patterns of sibling interaction.

11.18 Compare development of only children with that of children with siblings.

11.19 Explain how preschoolers choose playmates and friends, how they behave with friends, and how they benefit from friendships.

11.20 Discuss how relationships at home can influence relationships with peers.

5. KEY TERMS

Self-concept
Self-definition
Single representation
Real self
Ideal self
Representational mappings
Initiative versus guilt
Self-esteem
Gender identity
Gender roles
Gender-typing
Gender stereotypes
Identification
Gender constancy
Gender-schema theory
Social cognitive theory
Functional play

Constructive play
Pretend play
Discipline
Power assertion
Inductive techniques
Withdrawal of love
Corporal punishment
Authoritarian
Permissive
Authoritative
Altruism
Prosocial behavior
Instrumental aggression
Hostile aggression
Overt aggression
Relational aggression
Self-efficacy

6. TEACHING AND LEARNING ACTIVITIES
LECTURE TOPICS

LECTURE TOPIC 11.1: THE DEVELOPING SELF / GENDER / PLAY—AN OVERVIEW

The development of the self-concept includes building one's self-definition which includes the real self and the ideal self. Self-esteem varies from high to low due to parent interaction and feelings of competence. Erikson's third crisis, initiative versus guilt, becomes the focus for the child.

Erikson stressed the importance of identification as a process by which children acquire parental characteristics. Social learning theorists, on the other hand, see identification as the consequence of observing and imitating an adult. According to Jerome Kagan, children want to be like the model, believe they are like the model, experience emotions like those the model is feeling, and act like the model—all of which helps to establish and strengthen identity.

In addition to the obvious biological differences, there are psychological and social differences between boys and girls. While some statistical differences exist between large numbers of boys and girls, there is so much overlap that knowing a child's sex will not predict any individual case with respect to intelligence, strength, leadership, ability, or the like. Cognitive differences don't show up until later childhood, but Maccoby found that boys play more boisterously, fight more, and try to establish dominance over other children. Girls are more likely to set up rules for play and are more apt to be empathic.

Sex typing is the process by which children acquire the behavior and attitudes that their culture regards as characteristically masculine or feminine. The child's awareness of which sex he or she is may be an important aid in establishing gender identity. Two major sources studied by psychologists as possible causes of differences in gender behavior are biological and environmental. The only difference between male and female zygotes at conception is the X versus the Y chromosome until several weeks later, when androgens such as testosterone flood the male embryo. Testosterone has been linked with aggression in the study of animals. Studies in cognitive behavior point out possible differences in brain structures regarding the utilization of different parts of the brain.

In our society, boys and girls and men and women are treated and valued differently. Parents often treat sons and daughters differently, not necessarily consciously, but because of deeply held attitudes that are hard to change. The number of hours one spends watching television also has its impact on sex roles.

Despite the fact that boys and girls are more alike than different, myths persist about important differences and reinforce sex-role stereotypes. Today, conscious of the constricting effects of such stereotypes, many individuals and institutions are making major efforts to overcome the old ideas and beliefs. Bem maintains that the healthiest individual is one whose personality includes a balanced combination of the most positive characteristics of both sexes. An androgynous person may be assertive and self-reliant as well as compassionate and understanding.

Four major theories have evolved to explain the development of gender identity. According to the psychoanalytic theory, children emerge from the phallic period with a strong sense of their maleness or femaleness, and the resolution of the Oedipus or Electra complex determines the normality of adjustment. The social learning theory involves modeling and reward. A child imitates his or her parent(s) and may be encouraged or discouraged in sex-appropriate or sex-inappropriate behavior. Gender identity is linked to cognitive development; according to cognitive theory, a child learns that he or she is a boy or girl and that, because of this, there are certain ways he or she should act. Gender-schema theory proposes that children socialize themselves by developing a concept of male and female. Parents who raise children to be empowered rather than limited by their gender make special efforts to avoid sex-role stereotyping and to help children feel good about themselves as persons.

LECTURE TOPIC 11.2: EFFECTS OF TELEVISION

One current concern of parents and educators is the impact of television viewing on today's children. A major theme that has caused much controversy is violence in TV programming. One viewpoint is that viewing violence has a cathartic effect; that is, it purges the viewer of grief, fear, or anger and makes him or her less likely to be aggressive in the future. The opposing view is the social learning hypothesis, which states that viewing aggression arouses children emotionally and provides aggressive models resulting in increased aggressive behavior.

Correlational research has shown a positive relationship between observing violence and aggressive behavior in children. However, this type of research does not tell us whether watching violence causes aggression or whether aggressive children choose to watch violence. An alternative method is to expose children to violent films, provide them with an opportunity to act aggressively, and measure whether their aggressive behavior then occurs more or less frequently than that in control children.

Several studies of the effects of television deal specifically with preschool children. Stein and Friedrich evaluated 3 ½- to 5 ½-year-old children exposed to television in a summer nursery school. An initial observation of behavior was followed by a 4-week period of exposure to aggressive cartoons (*Batman* and *Power Rangers*), neutral programs (nature and circus shows), or prosocial programs (*Mr. Rogers' Neighborhood* and *Barney*). With less than 6 hours of total viewing over 4 weeks, those who regularly fell in the upper half of their peers on measures of aggressive behavior in the preliminary observation showed a significant increase in aggression toward their peers after viewing aggressive cartoons. Those children who were not previously aggressive were not affected by the programming.

The question has arisen whether parents can modify this effect of television viewing by either condoning or criticizing the behavior observed on the screen. In Grusec's research, 5- and 10-year-old children watched an aggressive film with an adult who was critical, neutral, or approving of the events. Later imitation of the film was observed when the child was alone. The older children were less aggressive when they had viewed the film with a critical adult. However, the 5-year-olds imitated the aggression regardless of the adult's attitude while watching the movie. Moreover, both ages were critical when discussing the behavior that had been rejected by the adult coviewer. That is, the preschoolers appeared to reject the aggressive behavior publicly, but privately they imitated it.

More recent research with television has compared how much attention a child pays with his comprehension; has examined the ethnicity, socioeconomic status, and age of family role models portrayed; and has probed the effect of sex-role stereotyping in network cartoons. These studies also show that the effects of television are mediated by individual differences among children, such as sex, age, and social class.

References

Davidson, E. S., Yasuna, A., & Tower, A. (1979). The effects of television cartoons on sex-role stereotyping in young girls. *Child Development, 50*, 597-600.

Lorch, E. P., Anderson, D. R., & Levin, S. R. (1979). The relationship of visual attention to children's comprehension of television. *Child Development, 50*, 722-727.

Newcomb, A. F., & Collins, W. A. (1979). Children's comprehension of family role portrayals in televised dramas: Effects of socioeconomic status, ethnicity, and age. *Developmental Psychology, 15*, 417-423.

Televised violence and kids: A public health problem? (February 1994). *IRS Newsletter*, University of Michigan.

LECTURE TOPIC 11.3: FAMILY ANTECEDENTS OF LOVE-SHYNESS

Zimbardo found that 42 percent of college students called themselves shy, but only a subgroup of shy people are so severely shy that during their adult years they refrain from all intimate relationships. This subgroup is described as having *love-shyness*. Gilmartin studied the family antecedents of love-shy males.

Gilmartin's control group consisted of 200 nonshy men from the ages of 19 to 24. These single-never-married men were socially successful with women. His other two groups were 200 single-never-married, love-shy men aged 19 to 24 and 100 single-never-married, love-shy men aged 35 to 50 (the younger love-shys and the older love-shys). The love-shy men in both age groups were heterosexual in preference, were virgins, were extremely anxious about even thinking about interacting with women, lacked meaningful female companionship, and had dated fewer than five times in the past year.

The researcher used the Survey of Heterosexual Interactions by Twentyman and McFall to assess the males' love-shyness. In this survey, males read 20 scenarios and ranked themselves from 1 (very shy) to 7 (very non-shy) on their responses. Self-confident college males average 104 on this test (scores can range from 20 to 140). In Gilmartin's sample, the non-shy males averaged 114, the younger love-shy men averaged 48, and the older love-shy men averaged 39.

Gilmartin compared his three samples on nearly 300 questions and found some striking differences between the family backgrounds of nonshy and love-shy males.

1. *The presence of sisters.* Among the nonshy men, 86 percent had grown up with at least one sister (and 51 percent of them with two or more sisters). Only 41 percent of the younger nonshys had a sister (only 6 percent had at least two sisters); only 29 percent of the older nonshys had a sister (just 3 percent had at least two sisters). No difference in male siblings was found among the nonshy and love-shy men. The researcher speculates that growing up with sisters helps males to feel more comfortable with females, enables them to perceive girls as real people, provides learning experience for male-female interactions, and sometimes increases the potential dating pool via friends of sisters.

2. *The family network.* Fewer than 10 percent of the love-shys but 59 percent of the nonshys agreed with the statement, "When I was growing up I always had at least 3 or 4 adult relatives apart from my parents to whom I could turn for help and emotional support." In fact, over 75 percent of the love-shys marked this statement as very untrue (13 percent of the nonshys marked the statement as very untrue). Gilmartin suggests that emotional support networks with relatives teach children how to cope with stress and build competence and self-confidence.

3. *Peer group friendships.* None of the nonshy males, but 65 percent of the younger love-shys and 83 percent of the older love-shys, said they had no close friends their own age as they grew up. Fewer than 10 percent of the love-shys, but 57 percent of the nonshys, said they had three or more close friends while growing up. Gilmartin suggests that the childhood pattern continues through adulthood. Among other effects, lack of close friendships with other males makes it more difficult to date and marry, because most nonshy males meet the majority of their dates through same-sex friendship networks.

4. *Dysfunctional families.* About 89 percent of the nonshys remembered happy childhood family life, compared to 31 percent of the younger love-shys and 19 percent of the older love-shys. (As teenagers the corresponding percentages were 82 percent, 22 percent, and 14 percent.) Twice as many love-shy men than nonshy men remembered frequent parental displays of temper. More of the love-shy individuals felt belittled and subjected to hollering and disparaging labels until they moved from their parents' homes.

5. *Family democracy.* Nonshy males were more likely to come from democratic families—three-quarters of them compared to one-quarter of the love-shy males felt that they participated in their family decision making.

6. *Only children.* Only 7 percent of the nonshy men, but 25 percent of the younger love-shys and 31 percent of the older love-shys, had grown up as only children. Gilmartin felt that being an only child was an added risk for becoming love-shy only when incompetent parenting was involved.

References

Gilmartin, B. G. (1985). Some family antecedents of severe shyness. *Family Relations, 34,* 429-438.

Twentyman, C. T., & McFall, R. M. (1975). Behavioral training of social skills in shy males. *Journal of Consulting and Clinical Psychology, 43,* 384-395.

Zimbardo, P. G. (1977). *Shyness: What it is, what to do about it.* Reading, MA: Addison-Wesley.

LECTURE TOPIC 11.4: PLAY/ PARENTING STYLES AND PRACTICE/ RELATIONSHIP WITH OTHERS

Parents, of course, cannot alter certain genetically based personality traits of their children, but they seem to exert a major influence on the way children express these characteristics. Styles of child rearing vary. Baumrind divides these styles into authoritarian (based on control), permissive (noncontrolling and nondemanding), and authoritative (consistent and respecting). Punishment and reward are a part of parenting. Timing, explaining, and being consistent are important for effectiveness. Benjamin Spock *(Baby and Child Care),* Haim Ginott *(Between Parent and Child)* and Thomas Gordon (parent effectiveness training or PET) all stress the authoritative approach to child rearing. The most important influence on people's lives, however, is apparently how their parents felt about them.

Sibling rivalry is not the dominant pattern between brothers and sisters. Affection, interest, companionship, and influence also exist. The interactions between siblings apparently set the stage for other relationships in life. Friendships and casual interactions with other children are central to children's lives. The most important features of friendship are common activities, affection, support, and propinquity (living nearby).

The years from 2 to 6 seem to harbor the greatest number of new fears. These may be caused by actual events, parental overprotection, anxiety over personal injury, or guilt. With increasing age, fears decrease. Attempts to overcome fears by ridicule, coercion, logic, or an effort to ignore them have no positive effect and may even aggravate the problem. The best way to help children overcome fears is to help children find their own practical methods of dealing with them. Aggression in youngsters surfaces mostly during social play. Limits to aggression occur as dominance hierarchies develop. Also, as a child becomes older, aggression declines and/or is refined. The more successful a child is in getting his or her way through aggression, the more likely the child is to continue to be aggressive. A frustrated child is more likely to act aggressively than a contented one, and a child who has aggressive models is more likely to act aggressively than one who does not.

Prosocial behavior, or altruism, is action intended to benefit other people. Studies on the origins of this behavior suggest that the ability to take the role of another is important. Hence, age and mental ability may influence a child's altruistic behavior. Prosocial or altruistic behavior can be encouraged by modeling and by expecting honesty and helpfulness.

Play consists of many types including social and nonsocial. Cognitive and imaginative play help with the development of thinking. Imaginative play decreases and children begin playing with rules at the end of the stage. Imaginary playmates provide a healthy outlet for wishes and blame.

LECTURE TOPIC 11.5: SOCIALIZATION IN THE FAMILY

Within any complex society, there exists behavior ranging from considerate and cooperative to selfish and cruel. To understand the development of these behavioral characteristics, we must consider a wide range of socializing agents—parents, peers, teachers, mass media, religious authorities, and so on. It is assumed that the parents play the most significant role in this socialization process, because they are the earliest and most significant agents in a child's life. The research in this complex area is not comprehensive but rather consists of separate studies focused on critical variables, such as nurturance, modeling, and physical punishment. With the diversity of research, care must be taken when drawing conclusions on the causality of prosocial behavior.

One type of research deals with modeling, in which children observe a model performing prosocial behavior: for example, the model donating prizes he or she won to some needy children. One finding of this type of research is that modeling does increase a child's helping and sharing behavior. Some studies have shown effects as long as 2 to 4 months later. 1975), and the results appear to generalize to new situations.

One of the most realistic studies was reported by Yarrow, Scott, and Wasler. In this study, a baseline of the child's original tendency to assist others was obtained. The model spent a great deal of time establishing herself as a meaningful adult by caring for the preschool children (3½ to 5½ years of age) and working with each over a 2-week interval. With half of the children she was very nurturant, friendly, empathic, and supportive. With the remainder she was aloof, nonnurturant, and minimally helpful. At the end of 2 weeks, all the children were involved in one of two types of modeling sessions. One type of modeling training included the model acting out and verbalizing helping behavior in staged scenes using dolls and miniature animals. Half of the nurtured and half of the nonnurtured subjects were assigned to these sessions. The remainder of the subjects received similar training but also observed the model actually assisting confederate adults. The children were finally tested on their own helping behavior after 2 days and then after 2 weeks had elapsed. They were taken to a neighboring house to visit a mother and baby. Here they were asked to pick up some toys the baby had dropped out of the crib.

The results showed that modeling with staged scenes produced a smaller increase in helping behavior than the training session that included staged scenes *and* realistic live modeling, especially when the model had been nurturant. Eighty-four percent of these children (staged scenes plus real modeling group) spontaneously helped the mother, though only 24 percent had helped in the pretraining.

These results lead to some practical suggestions for parents. Parents who only explain their values of prosocial behavior to their preschool child may simply teach their children to recite tidy principles. In order for generalized altruism to occur, the parent must not only try to teach the principles but also demonstrate this behavior in everyday life, ideally in a nurturant atmosphere. In addition, the model communicated what she was doing by drawing attention to the distress, making inferences about the victim, and providing labels such as "help." It is assumed that these cognitive aspects aided the child's understanding and acquisition of prosocial behavior.

References

Dunn, J. (1993). *Young children's close relationships*. Newbury Park, CA: Sage.

Mussen, P., & Eisenberg-Berg, N. (1977). *Roots of caring, sharing, and helping: The development of prosocial behavior in children*. San Francisco: Freeman.

Yarrow, M. R., Scott, P., & Waxler, C. Z. (1973). Learning concern for others. *Developmental Psychology, 8,* 240-260.

LECTURE TOPIC 11.6: COMPETENT PARENTS AND COMPETENT PRESCHOOLERS

Competence in a child is based on a number of factors. Parents want their children to be competent. That is, they wish the child to be effective, sociable, nonviolent, empathic, educationally adept, and able to develop any special skills or talents. Early parental treatments have an effect on the development of competence in children. In children a high sense of self, self-esteem, and a feeling of control over their environments (internal locus of control) have been shown to be important. This lecture will show how competent parental behavior can affect such development in the child and how social competence affects a child's interaction with peers.

In a study by Mondell and Tyler, parents interacted with their children in a joint problem-solving/play session. For 30 minutes, the parent (20 mothers, 2 fathers, and 1 grandmother) performed tasks with building blocks and puzzles. The observer rated the degree to which the parent treated the child like a capable problem solver, showed warmth, delighted in the interaction, and was constructively helpful in the tasks. The observers also measured nonverbal interaction (for example, approving and disapproving gestures) and verbal interaction (for example, suggestions, questions, and commands). The parents in this highly educated sample filled out several questionnaires that assessed their own competence. Apparently there may be some bias in these questionnaires, because more highly educated parents (college degree or above) were more likely to be in the high-competence group. These high-competence parents were significantly more internally oriented and more active copers. This tended to be passed on in their child-rearing practices.

The more competent parents treated the child as more capable and resourceful, showed generally warm and positive feelings, and were more helpful with problem solving. The less competent parents were more controlling and less encouraging and gave fewer suggestions and less modeling. Although taking into account that this was a controlled laboratory study, concerning these latter behaviors, Mondell and Tyler suggest: "These behaviors would discourage feelings of self-efficacy and trust and encourage more passive, erratic coping attempts."

There are several ways in which psychologists measure social competence in children—teacher ratings, sociometric measures (the children choose the competent peers), and comments by trained observers of social interaction. The latter two techniques were used by Vaughn and Waters to validate the point that competent children receive more attention from peers than less competent children do. For an entire school year, the researchers observed preschoolers during free play. In addition, they recorded sociometric scores, competitive dominance interactions, play behavior, aggression, and visual attention. The evidence from this study indicated that the amount of time other children directed at certain peers was a good indication of general social competence. Those children who received more visual attention were not so aggressive, disruptive, or dominant as others. It appears that children perceive who is socially competent and pay more attention to those individuals. Perhaps the children learn better from the more competent individuals. In return, the competent children gain even greater self-esteem and acceptance in group situations.

If competent parents foster competent children, and competent children gain even greater competence and positive regard from their peers, the principles engendering this competence should be more widely studied and applied. Many teachers and parents could benefit from increased information and training in ways to instill greater competence and social skills in all children. To date, organized efforts to build competence have been applied only to retarded children and to those who have severe deficits.

References

Gresham, F. M. (1981). Validity of social skills measures for assessing social competence in low-status children: A multivariate investigation. *Developmental Psychology, 17*, 390-398.

Maccoby, E. E. (1980). *Social development: Psychological growth and parent-child relationship*. New York: Harcourt.

Mondell, S., & Tyler, F. B. (1981). Parental competence and styles of problem-solving/play behavior with children. *Developmental Psychology, 17*, 73-78.

Vaughn, B. E., & Waters, E. (1981). Attention structure, sociometric status, and dominance: Interrelations, behavioral correlates, and relationships to social competence. *Developmental Psychology, 17*, 275- 288.

LECTURE TOPIC 11.7: PARENTING AND SOCIOECONOMIC STATUS (SES)

Parental education, income, and occupation have significant effects on the environment of the child. The socioeconomic status of families is not always easy to determine, but it is possible to classify a majority of individuals into higher and lower SES levels. Surprisingly, it is hard to find definitive studies that summarize recent data. However, Maccoby has presented some of the findings that appear more consistently in the literature. In 1970, Hess did a comprehensive review of the SES studies before that time. Extreme caution must be used when presenting these generalizations because: (1) SES levels are not clearly definable (for example, a graduate student's family—high education and little income); (2) there are a large number of familial differences within the groupings; (3) the studies are correlational and cannot prove causation; (4) the long-term effects of child-care practices are not known; and (5) most of the studies were performed by middle-class researchers who have a middle-class bias. The following have been consistent differences between high and low-SES families. According to Maccoby, these few generalizations have been found across races and cultures.

1. Contrary to the stereotype of noncaring, unstructured child-rearing practices among lower-SES parents, studies indicate "that lower-SES parents tend to stress obedience, respect, neatness, cleanliness, and staying out of trouble." In comparison, the higher-SES parents tend to emphasize "happiness, creativity, ambition, independence, curiosity, and self-control."

2. "Lower-SES parents are more controlling, power-assertive, authoritarian, and arbitrary in their discipline, and they are more likely to use physical punishment. Higher-SES parents are more democratic and tend to be either permissive or authoritative (to use Baumrind's terms). They are more likely to use induction—and to be aware of and responsive to their children's perspectives."

3. "Higher-SES parents talk to their children more, reason with them more, and use complex language." (This is especially true with middle-class mothers and daughters.)
4. "Higher-SES parents tend to show more warmth and affection toward children."

We should be careful about making value judgments about these child-rearing differences. These practices may be a result of different stresses, problems, injustices, and situational expectations rather than parental caring or skill. It has been speculated that, given the situations the lower-SES families find themselves in, their child-rearing methods are not only realistic but also preferred. The main concern is that, in our highly technological, education-oriented society where individual success is stressed, certain child-rearing practices limit the children's opportunities and flexibility. Discuss with the students the advantages and disadvantages of the foregoing generalizations about SES.

DISCUSSION TOPICS

DISCUSSION TOPIC 11.1: FREUDIAN THEORY

Freud's theory explains gender development based upon penis envy, castration anxiety, and others factors. Little support exists for this theory, but it still has a strong influence on public opinion. Discuss how much the public is still influenced by this theory in such areas as early sexual trauma, repressed memories, ideas about the causes of homosexuality, and finding mates that are like opposite sex parents. This is a good time to talk about social and cultural differences over the past century.

DISCUSSION TOPIC 11.2: SEX-ROLE EXPECTATIONS AND SOCIOECONOMIC STATUS

Present the following statements to your class for discussion.

1. There is more pressure for children to conform to sex-role stereotypes in lower socioeconomic groups.
2. Lower-class adults offer more stereotyped models of sex-role behavior.
3. Lower-class fathers have traditionally masculine jobs and rarely help around the house or care for children.
4. Lower-class mothers work in traditionally feminine, service-oriented occupations.
5. Middle-class fathers are more likely to shop for groceries, change diapers, or dry dishes.
6. Middle-class mothers are more assertive and more likely to have a nontraditional job.

If you want to continue this discussion over several class periods, send the class or an interested group to the library to look for research support for any of the statements.

DISCUSSION TOPIC 11.3: NAMING THE BABY

Ask everyone in the class to make a list of names they would choose for a baby. Have them list their five favorite names for each sex. Collect the lists and tabulate the data. Either prepare a handout or make a transparency with the compiled list of names and the frequency with which each name was chosen. Analyze the choices with the class. Do the most frequently chosen names reflect a highly traditional sex-role identification or a less traditional view? How many of the names on the list reflect currently popular media names, such as those used in television "soap operas"? Do parents' choices of names for their children reveal anything about the parents' sex-role stereotypes?

DISCUSSION TOPIC 11.4: PLAYTIME

Begin this discussion topic by asking students to play with their pencils. You may have a few uninhibited, creative, or inventive students, but most will simply twirl, tap, or click their pencils and pens. Ask the class to contemplate what preschoolers do when asked to play with a pen or pencil (they will draw, use their imaginations to change the pencil into a plane or a rocket, or create other fanciful uses for the object). Use your students' responses to highlight the social and cognitive functions of play for children.

INDEPENDENT STUDIES

INDEPENDENT STUDY 11.1: SIBLING RIVALRY

Preschool age children often have the experience of becoming siblings. Parents are justifiably concerned about whether their children will get along. Is there such a thing as sibling rivalry? The psychodynamic model suggests that children vie for the attention of their mothers, particularly during the early years when attachment to mom is so important. What is it like for a small child to become a big brother or sister? What can parents do to encourage mutually respectful and supportive relationships between their children? Most important, how do early sibling relationships set a stage for the future? Read research that addresses some of these questions. Look in a database such as PsychInfo under sibling rivalry. Also investigate some Internet resources for parents. Is there congruence between what the research says and the advice "experts" provide for parents?

INDEPENDENT STUDY 11.2: DEATH AND THE PRESCHOOLER

Should preschool children be shielded from death? There is controversy on this question. Americans in general tend to deny death and use euphemistic language (passing away, gone to heaven, etc.) instead of straightforward description. Piaget himself told us that young children cannot understand the permanent nature of death until they get older. However, children will experience death of pets and people. What are recommended practices for parents and caregivers? Research death and dying education for young children.

CHOOSING SIDES

CHOOSING SIDES 11.1: SEX ROLES

Society is currently in a state of flux concerning the appropriateness and even the necessity of sex roles. Affirmative action and Title IX laws represent attempts to change sex-role attitudes and behaviors. To help the class appreciate the significance of the sex-role issue with regard to children, have the class debate or take a stand on the following statement:

Society must maintain distinct male and female sex roles in order to foster optimal social and personality development in children.

Pro: The traditional viewpoint stresses the existence of innate and historical sex differences. These differences would not be there unless they served useful societal purposes. Religious arguments for sex-role differentiation are easily supported by biblical and other religious traditions. Biological differences, though not strong in early childhood, appear in adolescence and must be prepared for in childhood. This is necessary in order to have an adult who can handle the different roles that result from profound sex-related differences such as size, strength, sexual behavior, and childbearing. Recognition that our society has distinct sex-role expectations helps the parent foster behavior appropriate to the child's sex role.

Con: The egalitarian viewpoint stresses that sex roles are mainly learned social behaviors. The imposition of rigid sex roles restricts individual development and imposes severe emotional, physical, social, and economic hardship on individuals or groups of individuals who do not fit into stereotypical molds. Ours is a male-dominated society that handicaps women in particular. Sexism can be seen in all facets of American society: the English language, toys, fairy tales, children's books, television, sex of teachers in elementary grades, parent-child interaction, job aspirations, salaries, and so on. By allowing children to develop according to individual talents and needs irrespective of sex, adults will encourage greater individual achievements and satisfaction. The common good of society will be enhanced because of greater individual satisfaction and reduction in the side effects of sexual stereotyping: violence, sex crimes, and discrimination.

The following lists give arguments that might be used to support each side of the debate.

Pro: Sex-Role Distinctions
1. Early and strong sex-role differentiation is found in preschool children even from homes with egalitarian sex-role attitudes.
2. The weakening of traditional family structures will have deleterious effects on children, as shown by research with father-absent families.
3. Research on both humans and animals indicates the prenatal influence of hormones on masculine and feminine characteristics—for example, aggression, visual-spatial thinking, mating.
4. Sharply defined sex roles have been prevalent in primitive as well as modern societies.
5. There is a general societal rejection of homosexuals; for instance, "sissy" boys, "butch" girls, and so on.
6. The disruptive effects of the equal opportunity laws, Title IX, and other legislation on schools, taxpayers, athletic programs, religious organizations, and other traditions are too great to tolerate.

Con: Egalitarianism
1. Sex differences are determined by socializing experiences, not by biology.
2. Negative effects are produced through differential treatment by parents, peers, and teachers, such as punishing a 3-year-old boy who wants to play with a doll and criticizing females who wish to excel in traditionally male pursuits.
3. Inferior roles for girls and females in general are portrayed in books and mass media.
4. Pressure for dependence and conformity in young girls leads to incompetence in adulthood.

197

5. Androgeny will increase family cohesiveness by enhancing father and mother parenting skills.
6. Sex crimes and exploitation of the female as a sex object are due to sex-role pressures.
7. Sexual harassment is a result of sex-role stereotyping.

References

Doyle, J., & Paludi, M. (1991). *Male and female,* 2d ed. Dubuque, IA: Wm. C. Brown Publishers.

Frieze, I., Parsons, J., Johnson, P., Ruble, D., & Zellman, G. (1978*). Women and sex roles: A social psychology perspective.* New York: Norton.

Golombok, S., & Fivush, R. (1994). *Gender development.* Cambridge, England: Cambridge University Press.

Maccoby, E., & Jacklin, C. (1974). *The psychology of sex differences.* Stanford, CA: Stanford University Press.

Macoby, E. (1990). Gender and relationship: A development account. *American Psychologist, 45,* 513-520.

CHOOSING SIDES 11.2: COMPETENCY TESTING FOR PARENTS

Parenting is a major skill that requires all the competence and love possessed by an adult. Yet there is little formal concern about who become parents. Are there basic ways of improving children's lives by improving their parents? It is now assumed that the genetic *and* environmental endowments of the child are directly or indirectly attributable to parents. Concern for children can be demonstrated by showing concern for those who can parent them. Birth control methods allow for greater choice in making the parenthood decision. As children become a more expensive resource in modern society, the following statement will be the subject of frequent debate:

> *Considering the major genetic and environmental influence a parent has on a child, a person should have a proven level of genetic viability and social competence before being allowed to be a parent.*

Pro: A person must prove a minimal degree of competency in order to qualify to drive a car, graduate from school, or practice a profession. It should not be assumed that individuals will be good parents just because they are human. There are many controllable factors that can be used as screening criteria to prevent the birth of impaired children and to eliminate detrimental home environments. Genetic counseling, parenting classes, medical examinations, and husband-wife planning are now common practices of concerned prospective parents. Licensing parents makes just as much sense as licensing doctors, teachers, or electricians!

Con: The goal of making children healthy and happy is indeed an admirable one. However, this goal cannot be used as an excuse to implement a pernicious, licensing bureaucracy that would sanctify elitism by denying disfavored individuals the right to reproduce. There is no way to establish what minimal competencies should be, let alone enforce the standards. Licensing would not prevent poor parenting any more than licensing prevents poor driving. There are too many other factors to consider. Individuals have the right to decide about their own parenting!

The following are arguments that might be used to support each side of the debate.

Pro: License Parents

1. Children have the right to have good physical bodies and adequate parents.
2. Genetic counseling will prevent the transmission of fatal and handicapping genetic conditions.
3. Prenatal care and a healthy mother can be required in order to prevent handicapped infants—that is, to avoid teratogens.
4. Some states already require tests for syphilis and the mandatory sterilization of certain institutionalized retarded individuals.
5. Adoption agencies already require extensive parenting skills and economic levels.
6. The cost of the necessary bureaucratic mechanism of control is insignificant compared to the gains to be derived by society in the areas of both mental and physical health.

Con: The Right to Parent

1. Parents have the right to choose parenthood and bear its consequences.
2. The minimal standards could be changed capriciously or maliciously to include height, weight, nearsightedness, skin color, education, income, and so on.
3. Who would make the decisions granting or denying permission for parenthood?
4. Scientists are not certain what a good parent is or whether a child has to have a competent parent in order to be emotionally and physically healthy.
5. Some of the world's most competent, creative, and constructive individuals emerged from handicapping conditions.
6. Birth control methods are not always effective or practiced. What happens when an "unlicensed pregnancy" is discovered?

References

American Psychologist (1979). Special issue. Psychology and children: Current research and practice. *34.* See articles by Sroufe, Bronfenbrenner, David and Baldwin, Starr, Schwarz, Kagan, Shore.

Chamberlin, R., Szumowski, E., & Zastowny, T. (1979). An evaluation of efforts to educate mothers about child development in pediatric office practices. *American Journal of Public Health, 69,* 875-886.

KNOWLEDGE CONSTRUCTION ACTIVITIES

KNOWLEDGE CONSTRUCTION ACTIVITY 11.1: GENERATIVE TERMS

This activity will use the principles of generative learning as explained in the Introduction to assist students in gaining a better understanding of terms. Divide the class into groups of four or five. Assign each group the task of generating an example for a generative term from this chapter. The example that each group creates cannot be one that has been used in the class or in the book. They must think of a new application for the term that they are given. Groups are allowed to use their books and notes. By creating their own example of the term, they demonstrate an understanding of the term to the level of application. There are several approaches that can be used in this exercise. Students may be given the entire list at once, but often one group will finish far ahead of the others and topics will get out of sequence. Another strategy is to give all of the groups the same term to create an example and then go around the room to discuss outcomes. This has been very successful, but also takes the most time. A third approach is to give each group a different term and see what examples they can generate.

Some generative terms for Chapter 11 are listed below.

Real self vs. ideal self
Gender role vs. gender stereotype
Functional play
Constructive play
Pretend play
Corporal punishment
Authoritarian parenting
Permissive parenting
Authoritative parenting
Prosocial behavior
Instrumental aggression
Relational aggression

KNOWLEDGE CONSTRUCTION ACTIVITY 11.2: TELEVISION COMPARISONS

Have students watch prime-time television some time during the week previous to this discussion. Assign others to watch Saturday morning programs and children's programs (for example, *Sesame Street, Power Rangers, Barney, Mr. Rogers' Neighborhood*). What is the appropriateness or inappropriateness of television offerings for preschool children? Consider violent acts, abuse, traumatic acts, commercials, and so on. What are the possible effects on children? Compare prime-time programs, children's educational programs, and children's cartoons. What are the themes presented, vocabulary used, age of role models, sex roles, and racial stereotyping on products sold in commercials?

KNOWLEDGE CONSTRUCTION ACTIVITY 11.3: HOME VISITING

Have students visit the homes of families with preschool-age children. What types of toys are available? Do the toys encourage solitary play, interaction and cooperative play with other children, or parental involvement? Where is the child encouraged to play? Where are the toys located? Does the child have easy access to the toys, or must someone assist in getting them out? Observe the preschool child watching television. What does the child pay attention to or respond to? Ask the child to retell the story depicted. Does the child think that television shows are pretend or real? Is the preschooler aware that the purpose of commercials is to sell products? How much time is spent on selling rather than entertaining?

KNOWLEDGE CONSTRUCTION ACTIVITY 11.4: PARENT-CHILD INTERACTION

Have students observe a different parent-child interaction under a variety of circumstances. For example, watch a dialogue for 5 to 10 minutes in a grocery store, restaurant, park, preschool, church, and so on. (It is extremely important that the people not be aware of being observed. Alert the students to the fact that people change their behavior when they know someone is watching. Also warn students that it might arouse the anger of some parents to know that they are being observed.) Is it possible to identify different styles of parenting? How might the location affect the interaction—for example, church or restaurant versus park or playground?

KNOWLEDGE CONSTRUCTION ACTIVITY 11.5: PRESCHOOLERS' FRIENDSHIPS

To illustrate the emerging functions of friendship during early childhood, have students interview both parents and preschoolers (separately) about the preschoolers' friendships. Possible questions include those eliciting information about frequent playmates; opportunities for friendships with babysitters, day care workers, and grandparents; and the need for friends.

KNOWLEDGE CONSTRUCTION ACTIVITY 11.6: GENDER STEREOTYPING IN CHILDREN'S TELEVISION PROGRAMS

Watch two hours of children's television to determine the number of gender stereotyped events. It may be helpful to videotape the 2 hours so you can stop the film while writing.

Preparation: Determine which 2 hours you will watch. Set up the videotape equipment and get paper and a pen. Before you watch the programs think about examples of gender stereotyping. If the characters are stereotyped what would they look like? If the characters play stereotyped roles what would they act like?

Watch the programs: Continually remind yourself to look for gender stereotypes. Sometimes we are so used to seeing such stereotypes that we might miss them. Keep a checklist of the incidents of gender stereotyping you notice.

Your report: Write a paper giving your observations and your reactions. You should have in introduction that tells about the assignment and how you carried it out. Your introduction should define gender stereotyping. The body of the paper should summarize your observations and give many examples. The conclusion should highlight the main findings of your observations and your reactions.

The paper:
1. Should be 2 to 4 pages long
2. Should be typed, double spaced, and have 1-inch margins
3. Should include a cover sheet giving your name, the title of your paper, your ID #, your course name, your section number, and the date

KNOWLEDGE CONSTRUCTION ACTIVITY 11.7: GENDER STEREOTYPING IN THE ADVERTISING FOR CHILDREN'S TOYS

Directions: For this assignment you will need to visit the toy section in a local department store or a toy store in your area. Try to pick a store that carries many types of toys for young children.

Survey: As you walk through the toy section look closely at the packaging. Are there boys or girls or both on the packages? Are the children American? What ethnic groups are represented? If you compare the scene on the package to the toy which is being marketed, are gender stereotypes being encouraged?

Also, consider the task of buying a gender neutral toy. What can you find at the toy store that doesn't encourage gender stereotyping in young children?

Your report: Write a paper giving your observations and your reactions. You should have an introduction section that tells about the assignment and how you carried it out. Your introduction should define gender stereotyping. The body of the paper should summarize your observations and give many examples. The conclusion should highlight the main findings of your observations and should give your reactions as well as examples of gender neutral toys.

The paper:

1. Should be 4 to 6 pages long
2. Should be typed, double spaced, and have 1-inch margins
3. Should include a cover sheet giving your name, the title of your paper, your ID #, your course name, your section number, and the date

7. RESOURCES FOR INSTRUCTORS

Books and Journal Articles

Bettelheim, B. (1988). *A good enough parent: A book on childrearing*. New York: Random House.

Damon, W. (1988). *The moral child: Nurturing children's natural moral growth*. New York: The Free Press.

Rubin, Z. (1980). *Children's friendships*. Cambridge, MA: Harvard University Press.

Shaffer, D. R. (1988). *Social and personality development*, 2d ed. Pacific Grove, CA: Brooks/Cole.

Singer, J. L., & Singer, D. G. (1981). *Television, imagination, and aggression*. Hillsdale, NJ: Lawrence Erlbaum Associates.

Video resources

Preschool social development (IM, 1992, video, 30 min.). This program examines how children between the ages of 3 and 6 develop a sense of self, gaining greater self-control and self-reliance.

In the land of giants (IM, 1992, video, 57 min.). Urie Bronfenbrenner characterizes the family as "the most efficient means for making human beings human." This program examines models of behavior and codes of discipline used to mold children to a culturally desirable social image.

Adoption and assisted reproduction: A look at the children (FFHS, 1994, video, 26 min.). New biological options and shifting social mores have redefined traditional concepts about parenting and the average American family. This program looks at some examples and examines the effects of these choices on children.

Play and imagination (IM, 1992, video, 30 min.). By tracing the developmental course of play and imagination from infancy through adolescence, this program shows how play enhances social-emotional and cognitive skills. Footage of Mexican and American mothers playing with their children illuminates cultural differences in play. The program also considers the roles of toys and television in shaping imagination.

Sex roles: Charting the complexity of development (IM, 1991, video, 60 min.). Beginning with a look at the cultural ramification of sex roles and the myths associated with them, this program examines three theories of socialization: Freudian, social-learning, and cognitive-developmental. It analyzes how each theory views the nature versus nurture controversy. It explores the impact of sex-role stereotypes on the developing child.

LINKUPS

The middle years of childhood, from about age 6 to about age 11, are also called the school years. School is the central experience during this time---a focal point for physical, cognitive, and psychosocial development. As we see in Chapter 12, children grow taller, heavier, and stronger and acquire the motor skills needed to participate in organized games and sports. As we see in Chapter 13, they make major advances in thinking, in moral judgment, in memory, and in literacy. Individual differences become more evident and special needs more important, as competencies affect success in school.

Competencies also affect self-esteem and popularity, as we see in Chapter 14. Although parents continue to be important, the peer group is more influential than before. Children develop physically, cognitively, and emotionally, as well as socially, through contacts with other children.

Linkups to Look For:

o   Obese children often suffer social rejection.
o   Moral development may be linked to cognitive growth.
o   IQ can be affected by nutrition, socioeconomic status, culture, rapport with the examiner, and familiarity with the surroundings.
o   Parenting styles can affect school achievement.
o   Physical appearance plays a large part in self-esteem.
o   A decline in egocentric thinking permits deeper, more intimate friendships.
o   Children who are good learners and problem solvers tend to be resilient in coping with stress.

12 PHYSICAL DEVELOPMENT AND HEALTH IN MIDDLE CHILDHOOD

GROWTH AND PHYSIOLOGICAL DEVELOPMENT
Height and Weight
Nutrition and Oral Health
Obesity and Body Image

MOTOR DEVELOPMENT AND PHYSICAL PLAY
Rough-and-Tumble Play
Organized Sports
Gender Differences in Motor Skills

HEALTH AND SAFETY
Maintaining Health and Fitness
Medical Problems
Accidental Injuries

In This Chapter of Your Instructor's Manual You Will Find:
1. Total Teaching Package Outline
2. Expanded Outline (transparency-ready)
3. Guideposts for Study
4. Learning Objectives
5. Key Terms
6. Teaching and Learning Activities
   Lecture Topics
   Discussion Topics
   Independent Study
   Choosing Sides
   Knowledge Construction Activities
7. Resources for Instructors

1. TOTAL TEACHING PACKAGE OUTLINE

Chapter 12: Physical Development and Health in Middle Childhood

Growth and physiological development	**Guidepost for learning 12.1**
Height and weight	**Learning objectives 12.1, 12.2**
Nutrition and oral health	**Guidepost for learning 12.2** **Learning objectives 12.3, 12.4, 12.5**
Obesity and body image	**Learning objective 12.6**
Motor development and physical play	**Guidepost for learning 12.3** **Independent study 12.1**
Rough-and-tumble play	**Learning objectives 12.7, 12.8**
Organized sports	**Learning objective 12.9** **Lecture topic 12.2** **Choosing sides 12.1** **Knowledge construction activities 12.5, 12.6**
Gender differences in motor skills	**Knowledge construction activities 12.2, 12.4**
Health and safety	**Guidepost for learning 12.4**
Maintaining health and fitness	**Learning objective 12.10** **Box 12.1 (text p. 299)** **Lecture topic 12.1** **Discussion topics 12.2, 12.3, 12.4** **Knowledge construction activity 12.3**
Medical problems	**Learning objective 12.11** **Box 12.2 (text p. 301)** **Discussion topics 12.1, 12.5**
Accidental injuries	**Learning objective 12.12**

Please check out the online learning center located at www.mhhe.com/papaliacw9 for further information on these and other topics. There you can also access downloadable PowerPoint slides tailored to each chapter of the text and containing useful teaching notes as well as images and tables from the text itself.

2. EXPANDED OUTLINE (TRANSPARENCY READY)

I. Growth and Physiological Development
   A. Growth patterns
   B. Height and weight
   C. Nutrition
   D. Body Image
   E. Obesity

II. Motor Development and Physical Play
   A. Rough and tumble play
   B. Youth sports activity
      1. Organized play
      2. Children's games

III. Health And Safety
   A. Fitness
   B. Acute medical conditions
   C. Stuttering
   D. Asthma
   E. HIV and AIDS

3. GUIDEPOSTS FOR STUDY

12.1   What are normal growth patterns during middle childhood and how can abnormal growth be treated?

12.2   What are some nutritional and oral health concerns for school-age children?

12.3   What gains in motor skills typically occur at this age, and what kinds of play do boys and girls engage in?

12.4   What are the principal health and fitness concerns in middle childhood and what can adults do to make the school years healthier and safer?

4. LEARNING OBJECTIVES

After completing the study of this chapter, the student will be able to:

12.1   Summarize typical growth patterns of boys and girls in middle childhood and give reasons for variations.

12.2   Discuss the advisability of administering synthetic growth hormone to short children.

12.3   Discuss nutritional needs of school-age children.

12.4   Give a reason why health of permanent teeth has improved.

12.5   Describe effects of malnutrition and identify factors that may influence the long-term outcome.

12.6   Discuss possible causes of the increase in childhood obesity, tell how it can affect health in adulthood, and state recommendations for treatment.

12.7   Explain the significance of rough-and-tumble play.

12.8   Describe changes in the types of physical play children engage in, as they grow older.

12.9   Give reasons why fewer girls than boys participate in organized sports.

12.10 Explain the importance of adequate exercise and sleep and give some recommendations for parents.

12.11 Distinguish between acute and chronic medical conditions and discuss how chronic conditions can affect everyday life.

12.12 Identify factors that increase the risks of accidental injury.

5. KEY TERMS

Body image	Chronic medical conditions
Rough-and-tumble play	Stuttering
Acute medical conditions	Asthma

6. TEACHING AND LEARNING ACTIVITIES

LECTURE TOPICS

LECTURE TOPIC 12.1: UNFIT CHILDREN

In 1956 President Eisenhower created the President's Council on Youth Fitness because American children did more poorly than European children on tests of strength and flexibility. The council's work was a favorite cause of President Kennedy, and by 1965 President Johnson was able to report sizable gains in the fitness of youth. Since then, however, the physical fitness of American children has declined so much that many experts believe the current generation of children is more unfit than any other generation.

Despite the current emphasis among adults on physical fitness, the data on children are not encouraging. For example, one-third of all children over 12 years old may have elevated cholesterol levels. Using a skin-pinching test on nearly 9,000 youngsters from fifth through twelfth grade, researchers found that boys and girls today are much fatter than those in the 1960s.

It has been found that 10-year-old boys took an average of more than 10 minutes to run a mile and averaged fewer than 3 chin-ups. In Houston, about 50 percent of high school students scored "poor to weak" in the 600-yard run, an endurance test. More than one-third of third- and fourth-graders in low-income San Francisco schools were unable to do 10 minutes of moderate exercise. Finally, a study of elementary school children in Jackson County, Michigan, found that 98 percent showed at least one major risk factor for heart disease. Forty-two percent had high cholesterol levels; 28 percent had high blood pressure. In fact, more than half had at least three risk factors.

The main culprit in creating the "unfit generation" is the lifestyle of today's children. Eating habits have declined because of the accessibility of junk food and less supervision of eating at home. Today's child also exercises less and watches television more. The average teenager watches 7 hours of television per day! Also contributing to the problem is the lack of good physical education programs in the school. With budget cuts, support for physical education is still on the decline. Only 36 percent of students have daily physical education classes, and too many physical education programs still stress team sports over the development of fitness.

Some schools are attempting to reverse the decline in physical education programming. Many programs (such as Kutzleman's "Feelin' Good" regime, "Shapedown," and "Know Your Body") are being developed to teach students healthy lifestyles.

Reference

Cary, J., Hager, M., & Harrison, J. (April 1, 1985). Failing in fitness. *Newsweek*, 84-87.

LECTURE TOPIC 12.2: CHARACTERISTICS ASSOCIATED WITH PARTICIPATION AND NONPARTICIPATION IN ORGANIZED SPORTS

In the United States, a great deal of school district and community efforts are directed at organized sports activities for males and females. There is actually very little research on the physical, mental, and personality effects of this participation by children in grade school. Most research has looked at personality correlates with older athletes compared to nonathletes. The older athletes are a highly select group and have been found to vary in a number of ways. Although results from studies are not necessarily generalizable to older athletes, there is evidence that children in organized sports have good self-concepts, demonstrate good adjustment, and exhibit generally appropriate personality characteristics. Others have found that involvement in organized sports fostered aggression.

However, in France, where a 6-day academic school week is common, an experimental program placed children in academic classes two-thirds of the time and in physical exercise programs one-third of the time. Children in this experimental program improved their academic skills, improved their health, and exhibited fewer discipline problems. This program was instituted throughout France in 1979. However, the benefits of physical activity in a 6-day-a-week school system in France do not compare with those of the after-school sports programs typical in the United States.

A study by Richard Magill and Michael Ash compared academic, psychosocial, and motor characteristics of participants and nonparticipants in children's sports. These physical educators tested first-through-fifth-grade students in a middle-class grade school in Texas. Of the 321 students studied, 45 percent were sports participants (59 percent of first-graders were not included) in mostly football (48 percent), basketball (48 percent), and baseball (44 percent), but also in swimming (10 percent), judo, tennis, golf, and so on (combined 26 percent). A total of 83 percent of the children felt they participated in actual competition a great deal—that is, played in the games. Current or previous participation in sports on the part of their parents was not related to the children's participation. The experimenters measured perceptual motor ability (arm-hand speed and dexterity, balance, and manual dexterity), physical fitness (arm and shoulder strength, abdominal strength, and cardiovascular endurance (fourth- and fifth-graders only), self-concept, academic achievement, and anxiety about competition.

Complex statistical analyses yielded interesting results. In general, there were no differences between the participants and the nonparticipants. Thus, it appeared that those who took part in sports were not more perceptual-motorically adroit or physically fit, nor did they have better self-concepts and academic achievements. This is, of course, a blow to avid supporters of Little League and the like. However, as pointed out by Magill and Ash, at least sports participation (for an average of 5 hours per week) does not harm the children. However, Kolata showed that harm could occur if the children were younger than 9 or 10 years and were in highly competitive sports.

Although this result is statistically significant in only the fifth-graders, nonparticipants had more anxiety about sports competition than did participants. It must be remembered that these results are limited to the specific tests used. These were admittedly not so comprehensive as they could have been. Nevertheless, this is one of the few studies that has investigated broad aspects of organized sports among grade-school children.

References

Bailey, D. A. (1977). The growing child and the need for physical activity. In Russell C. Smart and Mollie S. Smart (eds.), *Readings in child development and relationships*, 2d ed. New York: Macmillan.

Kolata, G. (April 26, 1992). A parent's guide to kid's sports. *New York Times Magazine*, 12-15.

Magill, R. A., & Ash, M. (1979). Academic, psychosocial, and motor characteristics of participants and nonparticipants in children's sports. *Research Quarterly, 50*, 230-240.

DISCUSSION TOPICS

DISCUSSION TOPIC 12.1: THE USE OF GROWTH HORMONES

The text poses the following question: Just because height matters so much to so many people, should parents be free to give their children growth hormones? This topic can lead into a multifaceted discussion. What limits should there be on parental rights? Where is the line between parents seeking medical help with a child who may not be growing properly and parents who want (for whatever reason) to create a "super" child? What, if any, negative physical side effects occur from giving children growth hormones? Are there any negative psychological side effects for the children given the hormones? What rights should children age 6 to 12 have in terms of what hormones are injected into their bodies? To help control the problem, should we attempt to change people's attitudes about height in the direction of placing less emphasis on the advantages of height in social situations?

DISCUSSION TOPIC 12.2: THE SOCIAL IMPLICATIONS OF POOR NUTRITION

A series of studies described in the text points to the complex cycle of passive unsociability that stems from poor nutrition, a cycle that deserves extended discussion. Point out to your students the finding that poor nutrition from birth to age 2 is a good predictor of passive social behavior from ages 6 to 8. These children's poor interpersonal skills arise from their lack of enough energy to attract and maintain interactions with their mothers and is self-perpetuating. Brainstorm with your class ways to break this negative cycle. After brainstorming a list of possible solutions, evaluate each solution for its feasibility. This discussion can be turned into a class project in which the students investigate malnutrition in their local area and, where appropriate, try to implement their best solutions for the problem.

DISCUSSION TOPIC 12.3: PHYSICAL FITNESS IN CHILDREN

Children today are less physically fit than they were 20 years ago. Various explanations and remedies have been suggested. An interesting approach to this issue is to use it to review the major developmental perspectives presented in Chapter 1. Ask your class to discuss physical fitness from the psychoanalytic, behavioral, social learning, cognitive, and humanistic perspectives. They may have to speculate to some extent in some areas. You can bring out some of the following ideas in the discussion: Fitness activities should lead to ego development, in the psychoanalytic view. From the behavioral perspective, with sufficient rewards, all children should participate in fitness activities. With the prevalence of sports programs for young children and the media coverage of all types of sporting events, there should be no lack of models (social learning perspective). Fitness activities are another way to explore the world and learn about it through play (cognitive view). Fitness activities are growth oriented in the humanistic view. Continue the discussion by examining the reasons why today's children are less physically fit by seeing whether any of the perspectives offer explanations for children's lack of fitness. For example, the behavioral view would suggest that fitness activities entail too few rewards and too many punishments.

DISCUSSION TOPIC 12.4: FITNESS AND THE SCHOOLS

The decline in physical fitness among today's children has been partially blamed on the inadequacy of physical fitness programs in the schools. Many school systems have cut costs by decreasing the amount of physical education that is offered to children. With the understanding that physical fitness contributes to children's ability to learn, to their current and later health, and to their social relationships, ask the class for their opinions about whether schools can and should be responsible for supporting children's fitness. Should being physically fit be a sufficient reward in itself, or should society offer greater rewards to encourage fitness in its children? There is a current trend toward wellness programs in business and industry to reduce health care costs. Would a similar approach work with children?

DISCUSSION TOPIC 12.5: ILLNESS FEARS

Discuss with your class their recollections of their own ideas and fears about illness when they were children. Point out examples in their anecdotes of the different stages of cognitive development outlined in the section "Children's Understanding of Health and Illness." At an earlier time, many children had fears about polio. Discuss whether children today are developing similar fears about AIDS. You may want to have some students interview children of different ages about their understanding of the disease AIDS. (First discuss with your students the importance of guarding against any tendency to communicate to the children value judgments about sexual preference.)

INDEPENDENT STUDY

INDEPENDENT STUDY 12.1: OBSERVING PLAYGROUND BEHAVIOR

Have students observe school-age children on a school playground at recess. What types of activities do they engage in? How skilled are they in both gross and fine motor skills? Do boys and girls engage in the same activities? When both boys and girls are involved in the same game, how do they compare in skill? What kinds of skills and coordination are required to jump rope; play hopscotch, jacks, and marbles; catch, throw, and kick a ball; climb trees; climb on playground equipment; stand on one's head; turn cartwheels; and so on?

CHOOSING SIDES

CHOOSING SIDES 12.1: ORGANIZED SPORTS FOR CHILDREN

Are organized sports such as Little League good for school-age children, or would children be better off if they played less organized, informal neighborhood sports? Many students have strong opinions about this issue, and a lively debate often results when the following proposition is advanced:

Organized sports are good for children.

Pro: Organized sports such as Little League are good for children.

Con: Children are better off organizing their own games than participating in organized sports such as Little League.

The following lists give arguments that might be used to support each side of the debate.

Pro: Up with Organized Sports!

1. With 2.5 million participants worldwide in 120,000 United States teams and 20,000 international teams, something must be good about Little League baseball. If organized sports didn't work, children would refuse to participate in them.

2. Little League sports provide a wholesome, readily available activity for children who might otherwise turn to vandalism, drug experimentation, or idle activity.

3. Little League sports provide an avenue for joint parent-child activities. This type of experience brings families closer together.

4. In a world in which families are quite mobile, a national organization like Little League helps provide continuity and easy access to friends for children whose families move around the country.

5. The United States is a competitive country, and experience in Little League is a good way to introduce children to the positive aspects of competition.

6. Many American children are quite out of shape and need activities provided by organized sports to help become more physically fit.

7. Because of sprawling suburban neighborhoods, fears about crimes and drugs, and the impact of computer games and television, most individual kids just cannot get a group of other kids together at the same time for a game without the organized scheduling of Little League.

Con: Let's Hear It for Spontaneity!

1. Little League begins kids in T-ball when they are 6 years old, an age at which they are unable to understand the principles behind game rules and an age at which they don't have the attention span that sports such as baseball require.

2. Children who are pressured to participate in Little League activities but who do not feel ready and capable physically may suffer psychologically.

3. Although Little League may build some parent-child relationships in positive ways, it is also a setting in which some parents are overcritical of their children's efforts and abilities, model poor sporting attitudes, and often degrade the performance of other children.

4. In spontaneously organized neighborhood games, children learn to adapt rules to the number of players available, they learn to settle disputes, and they learn that they are responsible for how much fun they have. In Little League, rules are inflexible, adults settle disputes, and fun is often wanting.

5. Physical exercise is less in Little League games than in spontaneous neighborhood teams, because only so many children can play at a time on a Little League team.

6. Some children become too self-conscious when adults watch a game. They feel more free to try new behaviors when it's just friends having a lot of fun together.

7. Spontaneous teams enable parents to play with their children rather than merely watching or coaching them. This promotes better parent-child relationship building than does Little League.

8. Children, like adults, benefit from their own ability to turn idle time into unrestrained play. In our society, children are overscheduled into activities of all kinds.

KNOWLEDGE CONSTRUCTION ACTIVITIES

KNOWLEDGE CONSTRUCTION ACTIVITY 12.1: GENERATIVE TERMS

This activity will use the principles of generative learning as explained in the Introduction to assist students in gaining a better understanding of terms. Divide the class into groups of four or five. Assign each group the task of generating an example for a generative term from this chapter. The example that each group creates cannot be one that has been used in the class or in the book. They must think of a new application for the term that they are given. Groups are allowed to use their books and notes. By creating their own example of the term, they demonstrate an understanding of the term to the level of application. There are several approaches that can be used in this exercise. Students may be given the entire list at once, but often one group will finish far ahead of the others and topics will get out of sequence. Another strategy is to give all of the groups the same term to create an example and then go around the room to discuss outcomes. This has been very successful, but also takes the most time. A third approach is to give each group a different term and see what examples they can generate.

Some generative terms for Chapter 12 are listed below.

Body image	Girl's sport
Acute medical condition	Boy's sport
Chronic medical condition	

KNOWLEDGE CONSTRUCTION ACTIVITY 12.2: MOTOR DEVELOPMENT

Have students test school-age children on some of the motor skills listed in Table 12-2, Motor Development in Middle Childhood. Can any systematic sex differences be found? Are there gender differences in available activities for these children? Are there developmental differences from the beginning of the stage until the end of it?

KNOWLEDGE CONSTRUCTION ACTIVITY 12.3: MIDDLE CHILDHOOD NUTRITION

Keep a record of the eating habits of school-age children by having parents, teachers, and the children list foods consumed. Of particular concern might be preferences in food. Visit a school cafeteria to see what is chosen in hot lunch programs, what is packed in sack lunches, and what is thrown away. The school dietitian and cooks could be interviewed.

Have students watch television advertisements for "children's" foods. Students may collect nutrition labels for cereals or go to websites for fast-food restaurants to locate nutrition information. How well does a child's typical diet match the dietary needs of the child?

KNOWLEDGE CONSTRUCTION ACTIVITY 12.4: GENDER AND SPORTS

Women's sports have made tremendous gains in the past 30 years. More and more, young women are offered opportunities to participate in sports activities that their mothers never would have been allowed to experience. There are some sports, however that are still considered to be either for male or female participants. For a lively discussion, have the class list male sports and female sports, and gather opinions on whether females should be offered the opportunity to participate in sports competing against males. An example of this would be a school district that has a football team for males but not females. If a female athlete wishes to participate, playing against males, should she be allowed to? After the dust has settled from this discussion, ask the class if a male should be allowed to play on a female team if the district does not offer a male team for him to participate. An example of this would be a male who wishes to play field hockey and the only team that is available is a female team in a female league. Should the male be allowed to compete? Students will always have other examples that have happened locally to add to the conversation.

KNOWLEDGE CONSTRUCTION ACTIVITY 12.5: THE UNWRITTEN RULES OF SPORTS

One of the benefits that is mentioned in the section "Choosing Sides" is that when children are participating in unsupervised sports activities, they gain the responsibility of agreeing upon rules and then following those rules for the games that they are involved in. Pose a game scenario to the class and ask for a rules interpretation. One that works well is the "Ghost Man" scenario. Often, when children gather on their own to play a sport, they may not have enough players to follow the official rules. In this case, rules are created to make the game as realistic as possible. These rules are not written, but are handed down from older child to younger child in an undocumented, but continuous system. Ghost men are used when children are playing baseball or softball and there are not enough players to fill the bases with runners. Ghost men follow an established and very similar set of rules for advancement to the next base. Pose the following scenario to the class. There is a ghost man on first, and the batter hits a double. How many bases can the ghost man advance? You will be amazed by the common answers that are given by students who never played with each other or read a rule book regarding ghost men situations.

KNOWLEDGE CONSTRUCTION ACTIVITY 12.6: CHILDREN AND SPORTS

1. Interview children who are involved in youth sports to find out why they play sports. A potential format for questions may be based upon the following:
   a. What do you like the most about playing an organized sport?
   b. What is the thing that you like the least about playing an organized sport?
2. It may also be interesting to interview parents to ask them the same questions.
   a. What do they think their child enjoys the most about sports participation?
   b. What do they think their child enjoys the least about sports participation.
3. Have students compile their data in the classroom. Compare responses from parent to child and across genders.

Research has found the following in regard to children's participation in sports.

I. Motivation to continue sports participation
   A. Having fun. Children, like adults, choose leisure activities that they find enjoyable
      1. Greatest predictor of fun—post-game affective state
      2. Self-perceptions or how well the player believed he or she played the game.
      3. Perception that the contest was challenging.
   B. Fitness benefits.
   C. Affiliation needs
   D. Skill improvement and need for achievement.
   E. Self esteem
   F. Eustress
(Among boys, winning ranked 8th of 12. Among girls, winning ranked 12th of 12.)

II. Motivation to discontinue sports participation
   A. Loss of interest
   B. No longer having fun
   C. Too much emphasis upon winning (professional model of youth sports)
   D. Not enough playing time
   E. Too much pressure from parents
   F. Takes too much time
   G. Failure to fulfill needs for achievement
   H. Failure to gain self-esteem benefits
   I. Conflicts with other activities
   J. Poor coaching
      1. Poor teacher
      2. Plays favorites

References

Wann, D. L. (1998). *Sport Psychology.* Upper Saddle River, NJ: Prentice Hall.

Nixon, H. L., & Frey, H. H. (1996). *A Sociology of Sport.* Belmont, CA: Wadsworth.

7. RESOURCES FOR INSTRUCTORS

Books and Journal Articles

Eagleston, J. R., Kirmil-Gray, K., Thoresen, C. E., Wiedenfeld, S. A., Bracke, P., Heft, L., & Arnow, B. (1986). Physical health correlates of Type A behavior in children and adolescents. *Journal of Behavioral Medicine, 4,* 341-362.

Tanner, J. M. (1978). *Fetus into man: Physical growth from conception to maturity.* Cambridge, MA: Harvard University Press. A comprehensive and readable presentation of physical growth through the life span.

Murphy, S. (1999). *The cheers and the tears: A healthy alternative to the dark side of youth sports today.* San Francisco: Jossey-Bass.

220

13 COGNITIVE DEVELOPMENT IN MIDDLE CHILDHOOD

PIAGETIAN APPROACH: THE CONCRETE OPERATIONAL CHILD
Cognitive Advances
Influences of Neurological Development and Culture
Moral Reasoning

INFORMATION-PROCESSING APPROACH: MEMORY AND OTHER PROCESSING SKILLS
Basic Processes and Capacities
Metamemory: Understanding Memory
Mnemonics: Strategies for Remembering
Selective Attention
Information Processing and Piagetian Tasks

PSYCHOMETRIC APPROACH: ASSESSMENT OF INTELLIGENCE
Traditional Group and Individual Tests

The IQ Controversy
Is There More Than One Intelligence?
Alternative Directions in Intelligence Testing

LANGUAGE AND LITERACY
Vocabulary, Grammar, and Syntax
Pragmatics: Knowledge about Communication
Literacy

THE CHILD IN SCHOOL
Entering First Grade
Environmental Influences on School Achievement
Second-Language Education
Children with Learning Problems
Gifted Children

In This Chapter of Your Instructor's Manual You Will Find:
1. Total Teaching Package Outline
2. Expanded Outline (transparency-ready)
3. Guideposts for Study
4. Learning Objectives
5. Key Terms
6. Teaching and Learning Activities
     Lecture Topics
     Discussion Topics
     Choosing Sides
     Independent Study
     Generative Learning Activities
7. Resources for Instructors

1. TOTAL TEACHING PACKAGE OUTLINE

Chapter 13: Cognitive Development in Middle Childhood

Piagetian approach: The concrete operational child	
Cognitive advances	**Guidepost for study 13.1** **Learning objectives 13.1, 13.2** **Knowledge construction activity 13.2**
Influences of neurological development and culture	**Learning objective 13.3**
Moral reasoning	**Learning objective 13.4** **Lecture topic 13.1** **Discussion topics 13.1, 13.2** **Knowledge construction activity 13.3**
Information-processing approach: Memory and other processing skills	
Basic processes and capacities	**Guidepost for study 13.2** **Learning objective 13.5**
Metamemory: Understanding memory	**Learning objective 13.6**
Mnemonics: Strategies for remembering	**Learning objective 13.7**
Selective attention	**Learning objective 13.8**
Information processing and Piagetian tasks	**Learning objective 13.9** **Knowledge construction activities 13.1, 13.2**
Psychometric approach: Assessment of intelligence	
Traditional group and individual tests	**Learning objective 13.10**
The IQ controversy	**Guidepost for study 13.3** **Learning objective 13.11**
Is there more than one intelligence?	**Learning objective 13.13**
Alternative directions in intelligence testing	**Learning objectives 13.12, 13.14**
Language and literacy	
Vocabulary, grammar, and syntax	**Learning objectives 13.15, 13.16** **Lecture topic 13.3**
Pragmatics: Knowledge about communication	**Lecture topic 13.3**
Literacy	**Guidepost for study 13.4** **Learning objectives 13.17, 13.18**

The child in school	Learning objective 13.23 Box 13.1 (textbook p. 327) Box 13.2 (textbook p. 328) Discussion topic 13.4
Entering first grade	Learning objectives 13.19, 13.20 Choosing sides 13.1
Environmental influences on school achievement	Guidepost for study 13.5 Learning objectives 13.21, 13.22, 13.24 Discussion topic 13.3
Second-language education	Guidepost for study 13.6 Learning objective 13.25
Children with learning problems	Learning objectives 13.26, 13.27 Lecture topic 13.4 Choosing sides 13.2 Knowledge construction activities 13.4 Independent study 13.1
Gifted children	Guidepost for study 13.7 Learning objectives 13.28, 13.29 Lecture topic 13.2 Knowledge construction activity 13.5

Please check out the online learning center located at www.mhhe.com/papaliacw9 for further information on these and other topics. There you can also access downloadable PowerPoint slides tailored to each chapter of the text and containing useful teaching notes as well as images and tables from the text itself.

2. EXPANDED OUTLINE (TRANSPARENCY READY)

I. Piagetian Approach: The Concrete Operational Child
   A. Concrete operations
      1. Seriation
      2. Transitive inference
      3. Class inclusion
      4. Inductive reasoning
      5. Deductive reasoning
      6. Horizontal decalage
   B. Morality of constraint
   C. Morality of cooperation

II. Information-Processing Approach: Memory and Other Processing Skills
   A. Encoding, storage, retrieval
   B. Information-processing model
      1. Sensory memory
      2. Working memory
         a. Central executive
      3. Long-term memory
   C. Metamemory
   D. Mnemonic strategies
      1. External memory aids
      2. Rehearsal
      3. Elaboration

III. Psychometric Approach: Assessment of Intelligence
   A. Aptitude tests
      1. Otis-Lennon School Ability Test
      2. Wechsler Intelligence Scale for Children

B. Achievement tests
C. Cultural bias
    1. Culture free
    2. Culture fair
D. Theory of multiple intelligences
E. Triarchic theory of intelligence
    1. Componential element
    2. Experiential element
    3. Contextual element
F. Kaufman Assessment Battery for Children (K-ABC)
G. Sternberg Triarchic Abilities Test

IV. Language and Literacy
    A. Pragmatics
    B. Metacognition

V. The Child in School
    A. Self-fulfilling prophecy
    B. Social promotion
    C. English immersion
    D. Bilingual education
        1. Bilingual
    E. Two-way (dual-language) learning
    F. Learning problems
  1. Mental retardation
      2. Learning disabilities
        a. Dyslexia
        b. Attention deficit/hyperactivity disorder
    G. Convergent thinking
    H. Divergent thinking
    I. Enrichment
    J. Acceleration

3. GUIDEPOSTS FOR STUDY

13.1 How do school-age children's thinking and moral reasoning differ from those of younger children?

13.2 What advances in memory and other information-processing skills occur during middle childhood?

13.3 How accurately can schoolchildren's intelligence be measured?

13.4 How do communicative abilities and literacy expand during middle childhood?

13.5 What influences school achievement?

13.6 How do schools meet the needs of non-English-speaking children and those with learning problems?

13.7 How is giftedness assessed and nurtured?

4. LEARNING OBJECTIVES

After completing the study of this chapter, the student will be able to:

13.1 Identify five kinds of cognitive abilities that emerge or strengthen during middle childhood and explain how.

13.2 Name three principles that help school-aged children understand conservation and explain why children master different kinds of conservation at different ages.

13.3 Weigh the evidence for influences of neurological development and cultural experiences on Piagetian tasks.

13.4 Describe Piaget's two stages of moral development and explain their link to cognitive maturation.

13.5 Identify at least three ways in which information processing improves during middle childhood.

13.6 Describe the three steps in memory.

13.7 Name four of the most common mnemonic aids and discuss developmental differences in their use.

13.8 Explain the importance of metamemory and selective attention.

13.9 Give examples of how improved information processing may help explain cognitive advances that Piaget described.

13.10 Name and describe two traditional tests for schoolchildren.

13.11 Generate an argument for and one against IQ tests.

13.12 Assess various explanations that have been advanced for differences in the performance of children of various ethnic groups on psychometric intelligence tests.

13.13 Compare Gardner's and Sternberg's theories and name and describe the specific abilities proposed by each.

13.14 Describe several new types of intelligence tests.

13.15 Summarize improvements in language skills during middle childhood.

13.16 Compare and evaluate the whole-language and code-emphasis (phonetic) methods of teaching reading.

13.17 Tell how reading can best be taught and how comprehension can be improved.

13.18 Explain why writing is harder for younger children than for older ones and why social interaction may improve children's writing.

13.19 Explain the impact of the first-grade experience on a child's school career and identify factors that affect success in first grade.

13.20 Tell how parental beliefs and practices can influence school success.

13.21 Discuss the impact of socioeconomic status on school achievement.

13.22 Evaluate the effects of teachers' perceptions and expectations.

13.23 Trace major changes in educational philosophy and practice during the twentieth century including views about homework and teaching of math.

13.24 Give reasons for the superior achievement of children of East Asian extraction and identify some ways of addressing cultural differences in the classroom.

13.25 Describe and evaluate various types of second-language education.

13.26 Describe the causes and prognoses for three common types of conditions that interfere with learning.

13.27 Describe the impact of federal requirements for the education of children with disabilities.

13.28 Tell how gifted children are identified.

13.29 Discuss the relationships between giftedness and life achievements and between IQ and creativity.

5. KEY TERMS

Concrete operations
Seriation
Transitive inference
Class inclusion
Inductive reasoning
Deductive reasoning
Horizontal decalage
Morality of constraint
Morality of cooperation
Encoding
Storage
Retrieval
Sensory memory
Working memory
Central executive
Longer-term memory
Metamemory
Mnemonic strategies
External memory aids
Rehearsal
Organization

Elaboration
Aptitude tests
Achievement tests
Otis-Lennon School Ability Test
Wechsler Intelligence Scale for Children
    (WISC-II)
Cultural bias
Culture free
Culture fair
Theory of multiple intelligence
Triarchic theory of intelligence
Mental retardation
Dyslexia
Learning disabilities (LDs)
Attention deficit/hyperactivity disorder
    (ADHD)
Convergent thinking
Divergent thinking
Enrichment
Acceleration

6. TEACHING AND LEARNING ACTIVITIES
LECTURE TOPICS

LECTURE TOPIC 13.1: THE PRESCHOOLER AND MORALITY

Although we usually think of moral development as an important concept for elementary school children and older individuals, Jerome Kagan suggests that the emergence of moral standards unfolds through many steps during the preschool years. The following are some of the early factors that have an effect on our moral development.

1.   Children a bit older than 1½ years are beginning to become aware of standards and are also able to make causal inferences about events.
2.   Two-year-old children are anxiously interested in events that violate what they think is the normal appearance of things.
3.   Two-year-old children also have the capacity for empathy and the knowledge that they can use their own abilities to master something.
4.   Two- and three-year-olds reflect on the appropriateness of their behaviors before, during, and after the actions.
5.   During their third and fourth years, children begin to evaluate themselves as well as their behavior in terms of "good" and "bad." Behavior is now inhibited by the punishment. Also during this time period, children may believe that others are able to read their thoughts.
6.   By the fourth year, children can compare their psychological characteristics to those of others and experience pride and shame.
7.   Preschool children may believe that they should have all the qualities of the category in which they are a member.
8.   Three-year-old children have ideas about the qualities appropriate for different ages and tend to view the roles of older persons as more desirable.
9.   Young children believe that behaviors they are required to do must be good behaviors. Making a child practice a behavior increases the likelihood that that behavior will be evaluated positively.
10. Shame usually precedes guilt in development, and guilt develops around the fourth year.

Guilt, shame, and anxiety are emotional responses that children and adults experience when they violate moral standards. Which emotion we experienced depends on whether we had a choice about doing the behavior and on whether we think others will know about the violation. We experience guilt when we believe we had choice in our behavior but think no one will know about the violation. Shame is experienced when we neither had a choice in our behavior nor believe that anybody will be aware of our violation. When we have free will in our actions and no one knows about the violation, the probable emotional response is anxiety. Finally, if we feel we had a choice in our behavior and believe that others will know about the violation, we are likely to experience both shame and guilt.

References
Coles, R. (1990). *The spiritual life of children*. Boston: Houghton Mifflin.
Damon, W. (1988). *The moral child: Nurturings, children's natural moral growth*. New York: The Free Press.

Kagan, J. (1984). *The nature of the child.* New York: Basic Books.

LECTURE TOPIC 13.2: DEALING WITH GENIUS—AN IMPORTANT CASE HISTORY

Exceptional individuals to whom the label "genius" applies are the focus of much public fascination and stereotyping. During a lecture, ask the students to describe geniuses (or the brightest peers they have known). Mixed results often occur, but you will probably receive a stereotypic portrayal similar to the one presented by Townsend and Gensky. Geniuses are expected to have straight A's; to be in special programs; to enjoy science, music, reading; to be nonconforming; to be physically inept; to be harmed socially and emotionally by academic acceleration; to lack physical attractiveness; to present difficulties to parents and teachers; and not to live up to early predictions. On the contrary, in general it is found that geniuses are actually well adjusted, physically adept, and socially accepted individuals who attain high achievements. Public opinion has been much influenced by the unfortunate publicity concerning William James Sidis (1898-1944), a child genius who apparently exemplified the stereotyped genius.

Both of Sidis's parents, Russian immigrants attracted to the land of opportunity, believed that genius is a product of the early home life and education. Pushed especially by his father, William was able to spell and read before age 3, type at age 4, devise a calendar to predict what day of the week a date would fall on at age 5, and read Russian, French, and German at age 5. After age 6, he mastered Hebrew, Greek, and Latin. On his own, he became able at age 6 to pass a medical school student's examination on the human body. In 6 months, young William passed all 7 grades in grammar school. Home education and self-study made him a specialized math expert by age 8. By age 10 he had mastered math through integral calculus. Harvard enrolled the 11-year-old William, after refusing to for 2 years. As a 12-year-old, he gave an original mathematical lecture to Harvard professors that "remains the nonpareil of achievements by a child prodigy." Numerous magazines and books about him made his feats famous. During his adolescence, William seemed to have lost his direction. He dropped out of graduate school, was arrested for being in a radical demonstration, and lost a teaching job. He then dropped out of sight, refused to attend his father's funeral, and apparently became a cynical eccentric holding minor clerical jobs. Bad publicity and libelous misrepresentations abounded even after he died of a brain hemorrhage, destitute and unemployed, at age 46. Rumor spread that he committed suicide.

This spectacular example has been repeatedly used to prevent school acceleration, special programs, and acceptance of exceptional children. Apparently, adolescence is a critical time for these individuals to prosper or flounder, as is the case with any adolescent. Numerous documented accounts of geniuses have later demonstrated that a genius does not burn out and being one does not cause the problems William James Sidis experienced. Geniuses do not conform to stereotypes any more than other individuals do.

References

Montour, K. (1977). William James Sidis, the broken twig. *American Psychologist, 32,* 265-279.
Townsend, J. K., & Gensley, J. T. (1978). The experts react to stereotyping gifted children. *The Gifted Child Quarterly, 22,* 217-219.

LECTURE TOPIC 13.3: RIDDLES USED BY SCHOOL-AGE CHILDREN

The favorite form of joke for the school-age child is the riddle. It is also noted that the understanding and enjoyment of riddles are related to cognitive development. The early school-age child (7 or 8 years of age) has become aware of the fact that words can have several meanings. This awareness makes possible appreciation of the humor found in riddles. Riddles based on double meaning have several levels of complexity that are related to linguistic ambiguity. The four levels of linguistic ambiguity are lexical, phonological, surface-structure, and deep-structure.

Lexical ambiguity refers to the double meaning of a single word in the riddle. For example:

> Why did the farmer name his hog Ink?
> Because he kept running out of the pen.

Understanding of this joke depends on the knowledge that the word *pen* has several meanings, one that is related to pigs and one that is related to ink. Such ambiguous words, though used frequently in everyday language, are seldom seen as ambiguous because the context clarifies which meaning is intended.

Phonological ambiguity applies to situations where the sounds (or phonemes) can be interpreted in two ways. For example:

> Why did the cookie cry?
> Because its mother had been a wafer so long.

The humor here depends on the fact that the two alternatives, *a wafer* and *away for*, sound the same.

Surface-structure and deep-structure ambiguities are more complex, dealing with syntactic relationships between the words and the underlying meaning conveyed in a sentence.

Surface-structure ambiguity exists when a sentence can be diagrammed in several ways; that is, a particular word, depending on the interpretation, can be the subject, verb, or object of the sentence. For example:

> Tell me how long cows should be milked.
> They should be milked the same as short ones, of course.

In the initial interpretation, *how long* is an adverbial phrase modifying the verb *milked* and referring to a duration of time. The answer to the riddle implies the second method of diagramming this sentence. Here *how* is still an adverb modifying *milk*, but *long* becomes an adjective modifying *cows*. The reference now is to the size of the cow.

In *deep-structure ambiguity*, there is only one way to diagram the sentence, yet two underlying meanings still exist. For example:

> What animal can jump higher than a tree?
> All animals. Trees cannot jump.

Although this sentence is diagrammed in only one way (*higher than a tree* is an adverbial phrase modifying *jump*), there are still two interpretations. *Tree* can function either as the logical object, to be jumped over, or as the logical subject, to do the jumping.

Research by Schultz suggests that phonological ambiguity is the first form of riddle considered funny by a child, around age 6 or 7. The appreciation of lexical ambiguity soon follows. Jokes and riddles based on surface-structure and deep-structure ambiguity don't appear to be understood until age 11 or 12, about the age when interest in riddles begins to decrease.

The preschool child's humor is often based on perceptual and concrete aspects of a situation. Things look or sound wrong or funny because they are inconsistent with the child's past experience. First and second grade seem to mark a transition from focusing on perceptual qualities of humor to concern with underlying meanings. This parallels the cognitive stages outlined by Piaget (see Chapter 8 of the text). As shown by Piaget's conservation tasks, the preoperational child (from age 2 to age 7) is very egocentric and concentrates on perceptual features. The elementary schoolchild has lost most of his preoccupation with perceptual appearance and is more concerned with relationships.

Research on the cognitive aspect of humor is continuing, but much has yet to be discovered. We know what makes children laugh, but we have yet to truly discover why they are laughing.

References

McGhee, P. E. (1979). *Humor; Its origins and development.* San Francisco: Freeman.

Schultz, T. R. (1974). Development of the appreciation of riddles. *Child Development, 45,* 100-105.

Schultz, T. R., & Horibe, F. (1974). Development of the appreciation of verbal jokes. *Developmental Psychology, 10,* 13-20.

LECTURE TOPIC 13.4: EDUCATION FOR ALL HANDICAPPED CHILDREN ACT (PL 94-142)

The Education for All Handicapped Children Act (recently updated as the IDEA; Individuals with Disabilities Education Act) states that "a free appropriate public education will be available for all handicapped children between the ages of three and eighteen within the State not later than September 1, 1978." The upper-age range was expanded to 21 years of age by September 1980. Under the law a handicapped child is defined as any child who requires some form of special education and possibly related services such as transportation or speech therapy. This includes the mentally retarded, the physically handicapped, the emotionally disturbed, and any who have specific learning disabilities. (It does not cover the special needs of gifted children.) The handicap can be anywhere from mild to severe.

In 1975, when this law was drafted, reports to Congress estimated that only half of the handicapped children in the United States were receiving appropriate education. Nearly 1 million such youngsters were excluded entirely from the public school system. Those fortunate enough to be in school were often isolated and given inadequate instruction and inferior facilities. The cost of private schools was generally prohibitive for most. This law was meant to cope with these problems and inequalities.

Four basic principles are established in PL 94-142:

1. **Identification:** The schools must actively seek out handicapped children and provide free evaluation and testing to determine the needs of any specific child. This testing must be nondiscriminatory and multidisciplinary. If any school cannot or will not provide the necessary testing, it is obligated to pay for independent evaluation by others.

2. **Least-restrictive environment:** A handicapped child must be placed in a program that is as close as possible to that offered a nonhandicapped child. When such programs are not available, the school district must create them or pay for comparable services in another school district or a private school. For some children, this means being mainstreamed into a regular classroom with only 1 or 2 hours per week of special instruction. For others with severe handicaps, they might be placed in a self-contained classroom with other children who have similar problems; the handicapped children might join a regular class for some activities like music or physical education or perhaps not join a regular classroom at all. Education in special institutions or at home is also covered when it is considered to be in the best interest of the child.

3. **Individualized educational program (IEP):** For each child, a specific or individualized program must be written that states his or her current capabilities, lists the specific goals for that year, and details the services that will be provided. The IEP is created by a group of individuals that is likely to include the regular classroom teacher, the special education teacher, other professions when necessary (for example, a psychologist or speech therapist), a school administrator, the child, and the parents, who are encouraged to take an active part in planning. The parents must agree to the contents of the program and can challenge it if they choose. The IEP must be reviewed annually.

4. **Due process:** In situations where parents don't agree with the evaluation of their child, the classroom placement, or the IEP, hearing procedures are established in PL 94-142 so that grievances can be addressed. Procedures vary in different states but generally include informal hearings, formal district-level hearings, formal state-level hearings, and the availability of appeals to state courts.

For a discussion of the pros and cons of the process of mainstreaming and how it has been implemented, see "Choosing Sides."

References

Abeson, A., & Zettel, J. (1977). The end of the quiet revolution: The Education for All Handicapped Children Act of 1975. *Exceptional Children, 43*, 114-128.

Daly, M. (1979). Handicapped children in the classroom—What "mainstreaming" is all about. *Better Homes and Gardens, 57*, 38-49.

Weisz, V., & Tomkins, A. (1996). The right to a family environment for children with disabilities. *American Psychologist*, 1239-1245.

DISCUSSION TOPICS

DISCUSSION TOPIC 13.1: REASONS FOR OBEYING TRAFFIC LAWS

One of the problems with Kohlberg's classic moral dilemmas (such as the "poor Heinz" story) is that students may not view this as a "real" dilemma. To illustrate Kohlberg's six stages of moral reasoning, ask your class to discuss the various reasons why they obey (or fail to obey) traffic laws such as speed limits. First simply list the reasons on the chalkboard, and then ask the class to analyze them according to the six stages. Common responses are "I don't want to get into trouble" (Stage 1), "I can't afford the fine" (Stage 2), "What would the neighbors (parents, friends, etc.) think of me?" (Stage 3), "Because it's the law and my duty to" (Stage 4), "If I don't obey the law, I can't expect anyone else to" (Stage 5), and "I've decided that is what's best for me; I couldn't live with myself if I didn't" (Stage 6). If they do not notice it on their own, point out to the students that their responses vary not only between students, indicating different levels of development, but also from time to time within themselves, indicating that Kohlberg may be wrong in his ideas about an invariant sequence of development where individuals do not return to earlier stages of reasoning.

DISCUSSION TOPIC 13.2: DO OUR VALUES NEED CLARIFYING?

In recent years there has been an increase in fundamentalist religious views in our society. Generally, fundamentalists have reacted negatively to the idea of "values clarification." Their approach runs counter to the university ideal of "abhorring an unexamined idea." Therefore, it is worthwhile to spend some time examining the fundamentalists' argument against examining one's values and in favor of simply accepting certain given values. Class discussions of this topic need to be carefully monitored to allow presentation of all viewpoints and to prevent ridicule of any individual's religious beliefs.

DISCUSSION TOPIC 13.3: THE INFLUENCE OF TEACHERS

In the text the authors write that "a teacher becomes a parent substitute, an imparter of values, and a contributor to a child's self-esteem." Poll your class to elicit their opinions about each of these teacher roles. Do elementary school students view teachers as parent substitutes? Under what conditions do the teacher's values have a greater influence than those of the parents? Of the three roles mentioned, is "contributor to a child's self-esteem" the most important? Use the discussion to focus students' attention on the amount of influence teachers have had in their own lives.

DISCUSSION TOPIC 13.4: THE EDUCATION PARADOX

This chapter raises several issues related to schools and children's development. In our society, we still look to education as the basic way to affect our children's development. This is somewhat paradoxical in light of all the criticisms of our educational system (why Johnny can't read, write, spell, and do simple math). Explore this paradox by asking your class about their personal reasons for furthering their education. Do they merely see a college education as a way to earn more money or gain entry into certain careers, or do they also see further education affecting the way they live their lives? Do they share the opinion that U.S. schools are failing in their attempts to educate children?

INDEPENDENT STUDY

INDEPENDENT STUDY 13.1: SPECIAL EDUCATION

Have students investigate how a local school district is responding to the IDEA (Individuals with Disabilities Education Act). What special procedures have been started? Have any programs had to be terminated because of the change in emphasis? Has there been a shortage of teachers qualified to teach children with disabilities appropriately? What special qualifications do regular teachers as well as special teachers need? Visit a special-education or resource classroom. Discuss the uniqueness of these students and the opportunities and difficulties that arise in teaching them. What special methods does a teacher incorporate with these students?

CHOOSING SIDES

CHOOSING SIDES 13.1: FULL-DAY OR HALF-DAY KINDERGARTEN?

Are more benefits derived when kindergarten children attend school for full days or half days?

The Case for Full-Day Kindergarten
1. Children who attend full-day kindergarten have more opportunity to participate in activities and receive individual attention from teachers.
2. Only with full-day classes can schools utilize remedial and enrichment programs that benefit kindergarten-age children.
3. Disadvantaged children especially benefit from the full-day learning environment and from being included in school lunch programs.
4. Children with siblings travel to and from school at the same time.
5. Parents benefit from reduced day care costs and from not having to deal with morning or afternoon transportation and day care arrangements.
6. The school reduces bussing costs and utilizes classrooms for the whole day.
7. The teacher gets more time to run programs with the children rather than just preparing them to take part and to leave the school. ? Au: take part in what? How is this different than taking part in one of many programs? Clarify?

The Case for Half-Day Kindergarten
1. Half-day kindergarten provides a more gradual orientation to school.
2. Half-day kindergarten is helpful to the child who is having difficulty adapting to separation from parents.
3. This option allows parents who are in the home to spend more time with their young children.
4. Fewer teachers and supplies and less equipment and space are needed. Teachers can handle twice as many students.

5. Half-day kindergarten sets the appropriate pace for children; with more daily time, teachers often introduce formal academics that the majority of 5-year-olds cannot yet handle.

Reference

Jalongo, M. (January-February 1986). What is happening to kindergarten? *Childhood Education,* *62*, 154-160.

CHOOSING SIDES 13.2: INCLUSION

Mainstreaming, inclusion, or integrating handicapped children into regular school activities has been a reality since the passage of the Education for All Handicapped Children Act of 1975 (PL 94-142). In theory, each child is to receive the best education possible within the limits of her or his capabilities. However, considerable controversy has been generated over the implications of this law and its implementation. In theory, the law is to provide individualized instruction to and reach more handicapped children while at the same time reducing their isolation.

Some have felt that, in practice, this law threatens to be a comprehensive set of empty promises that may do more harm than good, harming the nonhandicapped child as well as the handicapped child. Students may want to debate the following proposition:

> *Inclusion (mainstreaming) is based on sound educational principles and benefits*
> *the educational community and the handicapped child.*

Pro: Throughout history, people's general response to the handicapped has been one of prejudice. The handicapped are systematically isolated from the mainstream of society and provided with inferior facilities and inadequate training. The stereotyping of handicapped children as being sharply different from normal children is wrong. They are entitled to the fundamental right of education, just as nonhandicapped children are.

Con: The Education for All Handicapped Children Act of 1975 provides naive empty promises that pay lip service to equal education for all, but in reality is very harmful. PL 94-142 requires schools to provide many special services without allocating the money to pay for them. Therefore, services for the nonhandicapped are cut and, even so, sufficient money is often not available to provide good services for the handicapped. This means that many handicapped children are "dumped" into regular classrooms as their segregated classrooms are closed. The result is poorer education for everyone.

The following lists give arguments that might be used to support each side of the debate.

Pro: Mainstreaming/Inclusion

1. Only about half of the estimated numbers of handicapped were receiving appropriate educational services, and many were excluded from public school prior to mainstreaming. Now more students are being reached.
2. PL 94-142 provides for the active involvement of parents in planning the educational program for their handicapped child.
3. The focus of mainstreaming is on providing an individualized education program for each handicapped child, thereby concentrating on the specific needs of individuals.

4. The law provides for education in the least-restrictive environment, which decreases the social isolation of handicapped children. To be successful adults, they must learn to function in as normal an environment as possible.
5. Nonhandicapped children have an opportunity to learn compassion for the disabled rather than harboring an attitude of fear, ridicule, and prejudice.
6. Mainstreaming decreases the stigma of labeling. Children are not identified as deviant, segregated into a special class, and maintained there in spite of a change in their status.
7. PL 94-142 requires that a battery of tests be administered and that the tests be nondiscriminatory. This should correct the existing situation, in which minority students are overrepresented in special-education classes.

Con: Segregated Education

1. School systems are required to provide programs, but they do not have access to sufficient funds for such programs. The law authorizes 20 percent of the average cost of educating a handicapped child to be allocated from the federal government. As yet, only 12 percent has actually been allocated.
2. The requirement to provide special programs affects school budgets to the extent that other programs (for example, art, music, and programs for gifted and talented children) are cut.
3. Nonhandicapped children receive less attention in the classroom because of the extra demands placed on the time and energy of the teacher by having handicapped children in attendance.
4. Teachers have no special training or experience in dealing with handicapped children.
5. The specially trained support staff necessary to supplement the regular classroom is not available in most school districts.
6. If funds are not available for diagnosis, individualized educational programs, and support services, children are mainstreamed into regular classrooms on a "sink or swim" basis.
7. In practice, parents are not included in the formation of individualized educational programs and are not informed of their legal rights to due process.
8. Peer acceptance and popularity of the handicapped is, in fact, below average. A protected environment would give them a better self-concept.

References

Jones, R. L., Gottlieb, J., Guskin, S., & Yoshida, R. K. (1978). Evaluating mainstreaming programs: Models, caveats, considerations, and guidelines. *Exceptional Children, 44,* 588-601.
Kirk, S. A. (1979). *Educating exceptional children,* 3d ed. Boston: Houghton Mifflin.
Reynolds, M. C. (ed.) (1975). *Mainstreaming: Origins and implications.* Reston, VA: The Council for Exceptional Children.
Wallis, C. (July 18, 1994). Life in overdrive. *Time.*

KNOWLEDGE CONSTRUCTION ACTIVITIES

KNOWLEDGE CONSTRUCTION ACTIVITY 13.1: GENERATIVE TERMS

This activity will use the principles of generative learning as explained in the Introduction to assist students in gaining a better understanding of terms. Divide the class into groups of four or five. Assign each group the task of generating an example for a generative term from this chapter. The example that each group creates cannot be one that has been used in the class or in the book. They must think of a new application for the term that they are given. Groups are allowed to use their books and notes. By creating their own example of the term, they demonstrate an understanding of the term to the level of application. There are several approaches that can be used in this exercise. Students may be given the entire list at once, but often one group will finish far ahead of the others and topics will get out of sequence. Another strategy is to give all of the groups the same term to create an example and then go around the room to discuss outcomes. This has been very successful, but also takes the most time. A third approach is to give each group a different term and see what examples they can generate.

Some generative terms for Chapter 13 are listed below.

Seriation	Metamemory
Transitive inference	Mnemonic strategy
Horizontal decalage	Convergent thinking
Inductive reasoning	Divergent thinking
Deductive reasoning	Working memory

KNOWLEDGE CONSTRUCTION ACTIVITY 13.2: SEEING CONCRETE OPERATIONS

Beginning students of child psychology often find it difficult to comprehend conservation, egocentrism, irreversibility, and other aspects of preoperational thinking unless they actually see and hear them. For example, (a) show the child two clay balls of equal mass; (b) after the child agrees that they are the same, mash one ball into a "pancake" shape; (c) ask the child which ball has more clay; (d) reverse the process by making the "pancake" a "ball" and the "ball" a "pancake" and ask the same questions. Perform this demonstration with both preoperational (5-year-old) and concrete operational (7- to 8-year-old) children. It is best to videotape the demonstration so the child is not distracted nor embarrassed.

With school-age children, students may choose a seriation task. For example, ask a group of first grades to get in line from tallest to shortest.

Class inclusion tasks can be constructed using toy dogs of different breeds. Are there more dogs or more collies?

Conservation of volume and area are very late appearing conservation skills, thus demonstrating the horizontal decalage. Using a ball of clay and a jar of water, put the clay in the water and ask the child to note the change in water level. Then fish out the clay, roll it into a snake and ask the child whether the snake of clay would make the water level rise more, less, or the same amount as the ball did.

Students who try these tasks out on children may be encouraged to write about their experiences, present them to their colleagues, or perhaps videotape the children they test to show in class.

KNOWLEDGE CONSTRUCTION ACTIVITY 13.3: EXPERIENCING DYSLEXIA

To experience some of the frustration of dyslexia (a reading disability), have students try one of the following: mirror writing (writing while watching their hands in a mirror), writing with the opposite hand, reading upside down, or reading a passage from which all the vowels have been removed. Discuss the possible reaction of teachers and parents confronted by a child who writes or reads as the students just did. Consider the effects on the child's self-concept caused by the ridicule of other students and by his realization that he is different.

KNOWLEDGE CONSTRUCTION ACTIVITY 13.4: TALENTED AND GIFTED EDUCATION

As schools have moved to meet the needs of all "special" students, "talented and gifted" (TAG) programs for creative and academically gifted students have become popular. Invite a TAG coordinator from your local school district to speak with your class. You may have, in your class, students or parents of students who have participated in TAG programs while in elementary school, junior high, or high school. Ask them to share their experiences with their classmates. Students may be assigned to investigate the TAG programs in their own communities and to present their findings in class. Some districts that lack the financial resources to fund such programs have discovered a very valuable asset in the talents of parents. Often, in elementary schools, parents will work together to provide enrichment opportunities for the children of the district. Students can investigate which options are being utilized in their district.

KNOWLEDGE CONSTRUCTION ACTIVITY 13.5: KOHLBERG'S THEORY FOR SCHOOL CHILDREN

Interview children who are relatives or friends and pose the following scenario to them:

In Europe, a woman is near death from a special kind of cancer. There is one drug that the doctors think might save her. It is a form of radium that a druggist in the same town has recently discovered. The drug is expensive to make, but the druggist is charging ten times what the drug cost him to make. He paid $200 for the radium and is charging $2000 for a small dose of the drug. The sick woman's husband, Heinz, goes to everyone he knows to borrow the money, but he can get together only about $1000, which is half of what it costs. He tells the druggist that his wife is dying and asks him to sell the drug cheaper or let him pay later. The druggist says, "No, I discovered the drug and I'm going to make money from it." Heinz is desperate and considers breaking into the man's store to steal the drug for his wife.

Ask children the following questions. In gathering your data, keep track of the age and gender of each of the respondents. In the class setting, compile your data with your classmates and look for patterns in responses.

a.   Should Heinz steal the drug? Why or why not?
b.   If Heinz doesn't love his wife, should he steal the drug for her? Why or why not?
c.   Suppose the person dying is not his wife but a stranger. Should Heinz steal the drug for a stranger? Why or why not?
d.   (If you favor stealing the drug for a stranger): Suppose it is a pet animal he loves. Should Heinz steal to save the pet animal? Why or why not?
e.   Why should people do everything they can to save another's life, anyway?
f.   It is against the law for Heinz to steal. Does that make it morally wrong? Why or why not?
g.   Why should people generally do everything they can to avoid breaking the law?
     (Story and questions reprinted from Hersh, R. H., Palitto, D. P., & Reimer, J. (1979). *Promoting moral growth: From Piaget to Kohlberg.* New York: Longman.

Using the children's answers, classify each child into the appropriate stage of Kohlberg's theory.

7. RESOURCES FOR INSTRUCTORS

Books and Journal Articles

Bettelheim, B., & Zelan, K. (1982). *On learning to read: The child's fascination with meaning*. New York: Knopf.

Bijou, S. W., & Ruiz, R. (1980). *Contribution of behavior modification to education*. Hillsdale, NJ: Lawrence Erlbaum Associates.

Bloom, B. S. (1985). *Developing talent in young people*. New York: Ballantine.

Boggiano, A. K., Main, D. S., & Katz, P. A. (1988). Children's preference for challenge: The role of perceived competence and control. *Journal of Personality and Social Psychology, 54,* 134-141.

Comer, J. P. (1988). Educating poor minority children. *Scientific American, 259,* 42-48.

Gearhart, B. R., & Weishahn, M. W. (1986). *The exceptional student in the regular classroom,* 3d ed. Columbus, OH: Merrill.

Kohlberg, L. (1986). *The staples of ethical development from childhood through old age*. New York: Harper & Row.

Miller, S. A. (1988). Parents' beliefs about children's cognitive development. *Child Development, 59,* 259-285.

Siegler, R. S.(1998). *Children's thinking*, 3d ed. Englewood Cliffs, NJ: Prentice Hall.

Sternberg, R. J. (1985). *Beyond IQ: A triarchic theory of human intelligence*. New York: Cambridge University Press.

Video resources

The elementary mind (IM, 1992, 30 min.).

IQ testing and the school (IM, 1991, 60 min.).

Language (IM, 1990, 30 min.).

Learning disabilities and self-esteem with Dr. Robert Brooks: Look what you've done (PBS, 1997, video, 60 min.).

Listening to children: A moral journey with Robert Coles (PBS, 1995, video, 90 min.).

Memory (IM, 1990, 30 min.).

Middle childhood: Physical growth and development (MS, 1997, video, 28 min.).

Middle childhood: Cognitive and language development (MS, 1997, video, 29 min.).

Moral development I –Concept and theory (MS, 1998, video, 29 min.).

Moral development II—Learning to be moral (MS, 1998, video, 29 min.).

Recognizing, understanding, and overcoming learning disabilities (IM, 1990, 33 min.).

14 *PSYCHOSOCIAL DEVELOPMENT IN MIDDLE CHILDHOOD*

THE DEVELOPING SELF
Representational Systems: A Neo-Piagetian View
Self-Esteem
Emotional Growth

THE CHILD IN THE FAMILY
Family Atmosphere
Family Structure
Sibling Relationships

THE CHILD IN THE PEER GROUP
Positive and Negative Effects of Peer Relations
Popularity
Friendship
Aggression and Bullying

MENTAL HEALTH
Common Emotional Disturbances
Treatment Techniques
Stress and Resilience

In This Chapter of Your Instructor's Manual You Will Find:
1. Total Teaching Package Outline
2. Expanded Outline (transparency-ready)
3. Guideposts for Study
4. Learning Objectives
5. Key Terms
6. Teaching and Learning Activities
    Lecture Topics
    Discussion Topics
    Independent Study
    Choosing Sides
    Generative Learning Activities
7. Resources for Instructors

1. TOTAL TEACHING PACKAGE OUTLINE

Chapter 14: Psychosocial Development in Middle Childhood

The developing self	**Discussion topic 14.3**
Representational systems: A neo-Piagetian view	**Learning objective 14.1**
Self-esteem	**Guidepost for study 14.1** **Learning objective 14.2**
Emotional growth	**Guidepost for study 14.2** **Learning objectives 14.3, 14.4**
The child in the family	
Family atmosphere	**Guidepost for study 14.3, 14.4** **Learning objectives 14.6, 14.7** **Lecture topics 14.1, 14.5** **Discussion topic 14.1** **Knowledge construction activity 14.3**
Family structure	**Guidepost for study 14.5** **Learning objectives 14.4-14.5, 14.8-14.13** **Lecture topics 14.2, 14.3, 14.6** **Discussion topic 14.4** **Box 14.1 (textbook p. 350)**
Sibling relationships	**Guidepost for study 14.6** **Learning objective 14.15**
The child in the peer group	
Positive and negative effects of peer relations	**Learning objective 14.16** **Lecture topic 14.4** **Knowledge construction activity 14.4**
Popularity	**Guidepost for study 14.7** **Learning objectives 14.17-14.20** **Discussion topic 14.1** **Knowledge construction activity 14.2** **Box 14.2 (textbook p. 356)**
Friendship	**Learning objectives 14.20-14.23** **Independent study 14.1**
Aggression and bullying	**Guidepost for study 14.8** **Learning objectives 14.24, 14.25** **Discussion topic 14.2**

Mental health	
Common emotional disturbances	**Guidepost for study 14.9** **Learning objective 14.26** **Knowledge construction activity 14.5**
Treatment techniques	**Knowledge construction activities 14.5, 14.6** **Choosing sides 14.1**
Stress and resilience	**Guidepost for study 14.10** **Learning objective 14.27**

Please check out the online learning center located at www.mhhe.com/papaliacw9 for further information on these and other topics. There you can also access downloadable PowerPoint slides tailored to each chapter of the text and containing useful teaching notes as well as images and tables from the text itself.

2. EXPANDED OUTLINE (TRANSPARENCY READY)

I. The Developing Self
   A. Representational systems
   B. Industry versus inferiority

II. The Child in the Family
   A. Coregulation
   B. Parents' work
   C. Poverty
   D. Traditional and nontraditional families
   E. Divorce

III. The Child in the Peer Group
   A. Positive and negative effects
   B. Friendship
      1. Selman
   C. Prejudice
   D. Aggression
      1. Bullying

IV. Mental Health
   A. Common emotional disturbances
      1. Oppositional defiant disorder (ODD)
      2. Conduct disorder (CD)
      3. School phobia
      4. Separation anxiety disorder
      5. Social phobia
      6. Generalized anxiety disorder
      7. Obsessive-compulsive disorder
      8. Childhood depression
   B. Treatment techniques
      1. Individual psychotherapy
      2. Family therapy
      3. Drug therapy
   C. Resilient children
      1. Protective factors

3. GUIDEPOSTS FOR STUDY

14.1   How do school-age children develop a realistic self-concept and what contributes to self-esteem?

14.2   How do school-age children show emotional growth?

14.3   How do parent-child relationships change in middle childhood?

14.4   What are the effects of parents' work and of poverty on family atmosphere?

14.5   What impact does family structure have on children's development?

14.6   How do siblings influence and get along with each other?

14.7   How do relationships with peers change in middle childhood and what influences popularity and choice of friends?

14.8   What are the most common forms of aggressive behavior in middle childhood and what influences contribute to them?

14.9   What are some common emotional disturbances and how are they treated?

14.10 How do the stresses of modern life affect children and what enables "resilient" children to withstand them?

4. LEARNING OBJECTIVES

After completing the study of this chapter, the student will be able to:

14.1   From a neo-Piagetian perspective, tell how the self-concept develops in middle childhood, comparing it with early childhood.

14.2   Compare Erikson's and Harter's views about sources of self-esteem.

14.3   Describe how the "helpless" pattern can affect children's reactions to social rejection.

14.4   Identify some aspects of emotional growth in middle childhood and tell how parental treatment may affect children's handling of negative emotions.

14.5   Describe how coregulation works and how discipline and the handling of family conflict change during middle childhood.

14.6   Identify ways in which parents' work can affect children.

14.7   Discuss effects of poverty on child raising.

14.8   Discuss trends in adoption and the adjustment of adopted children.

14.9   List the psychological "tasks" children face in adjusting to divorce and identify factors that affect adjustment.

14.10 Assess the impact of parental divorce on children.

14.11 Tell three ways in which a one-parent family can be formed and how living in such a household can affect children's well-being.

14.12 Discuss how parents and stepparents handle the issues and challenges of a stepfamily.

14.13 Discuss the outcomes of child raising by gay and lesbian parents.

14.14 Compare the roles and responsibilities of siblings in industrialized and nonindustrialized countries.

14.15 Discuss how siblings affect each other's development during middle childhood.

14.16 Tell some ways in which members of a peer group tend to be alike.

14.17 Describe characteristics of popular and unpopular children and tell how they may vary.

14.18 Identify family and cultural influences on popularity.

14.19 Discuss ways of helping unpopular children.

14.20 Distinguish between popularity and friendship.

14.21 List characteristics children look for in friends.

14.22 Summarize how friendships change with age.

14.23 Compare boys' and girls' friendships.

14.24 Tell how aggression changes in form during middle childhood and how social, information-processing, televised violence can contribute to it.

14.25 Describe how patterns of bullying and victimization become established and how they change.

14.26 Identify causes and symptoms of aggressive conduct disorders, social phobias, and childhood depression.

14.27 Explain Elkind's concept of the "hurried child."

5. KEY TERMS

Representational systems
Industry versus inferiority
Coregulation
Prejudice
Bullying
Oppositional defiant disorder
Conduct disorder
School phobia
Separation anxiety disorder
Social phobia

Generalized anxiety disorder
Obsessive-compulsive disorder
Childhood depression
Individual psychotherapy
Family therapy
Behavior therapy
Drug therapy
Resilient children
Protective factors

6. TEACHING AND LEARNING ACTIVITIES

LECTURE TOPICS

LECTURE TOPIC 14.1: CHILDREN OF THE NEW CENTURY

The children of the new century will experience a different childhood from earlier generations because of differences in lifestyles, livelihoods, and daily activities. At the turn of the nineteenth century, children were still regarded as "little adults," and child abuse, abandonment, and infanticide were common. Attitudes soon changed as child development became more frequently studied, leisure time expanded, medical treatments improved, and education became more widely available. The 1950s perhaps will be known as the "golden age of childhood." In the 1960s, the baby boom created new schools, experimental education, shifts in parenting styles, and struggles between old and new values. That same decade also saw the beginning of massive changes in family patterns and the decline in family size and on the importance placed on supporting children. If current trends continue, according to Frost, the following will be commonplace for the children of the 1990s:

1. **The typical child will experience the divorce of his or her parents:** Between 1960 and 1980, the divorce rate tripled and, in 1980, there was one divorce for every two marriages.

2. **The typical child will live with a single parent:** Currently, at least 60 percent of children live with just one parent sometime before the age of 18. One obvious effect of living in single-parent households is that financial problems are often greater. The emotional and adjustment problems may or may not be larger. Some studies indicate the problems are minor, and other studies find that children in single-parent families have higher rates of arrest, school disciplinary problems, smoking, and running away from home.

3. **The child's mother will work outside the home:** Currently, 60 percent of married women with preschool children are in the workforce, and some believe that this figure will be 80 percent by 1990. So far, as mothers have entered the workforce, fathers have not increased their contribution to home chores; this might result in fewer hours available to parent children.

4. **Watching television will be the child's major activity:** From age 6 to 18, the average child will watch 16,000 hours of television and will be in school 13,000 hours. The average child will see 18,000 murders on TV and view 350,000 TV commercials. The effects of so much TV viewing are suggested by the following research findings: (1) Over 2,500 studies support the conclusion that TV violence translates into aggression in children's behaviors. (2) Heavy TV viewing is associated with lower grades in school. (3) Heavy TV viewing is associated with obesity and poor physical health. (4) Many kids prefer TV to their parents.

5. **The typical female child will become pregnant before she is 18 years old:** American teenagers have the highest pregnancy rate among teenagers in all developed countries. Currently, 40 percent of females become pregnant during their teens. About one-third of all abortions are performed on teenagers.

6. **The typical child will use illegal drugs, alcohol, and tobacco:** Currently about 65 percent of high school seniors have tried some illicit drug, marijuana being the most prevalent and cocaine the drug showing the biggest increase in usage. Over 90 percent of the seniors have used alcohol (71 percent in the last month). Over 70 percent have smoked cigarettes.

7. **Suicides among children will increase:** In 1984, at least 5000 teenagers killed themselves and half a million teenagers made a suicide attempt. From 1970 to 1985, the number of suicides and homicides for white male teenagers doubled. Accidents and suicides are the two biggest killers of young people.

8. **A sizable number of children will be abused:** Current estimates of abuse suggest that 1 in 4 girls and 1 in 9 boys are sexually abused before the age of 18. A relative, neighbor, or friend is responsible 90 percent of the time. Physical abuse, emotional abuse, and neglect are even more common.

In addition to the foregoing concrete changes in the typical childhood experience, according to Henchey, these children will be affected by unique societal pressures and trends:

1. **The transformation of knowledge:** Research is generating more information that can be distributed in the world faster than ever before. Methods of working with and techniques of

gathering knowledge are improving. Knowledge is more quickly being transformed into technical applications. More careers are being developed in "knowledge industries."

2. **The communications revolution:** This includes televisions, computers, the World Wide Web, robots, and satellites, and artificial intelligence and symbionics (direct brain-computer connections).

3. **Economic turbulence:** Erratic shifts in inflation, unemployment, and economic development and a growing disparity between rich and poor nations are part of global economic uncertainties. Fewer have confidence in continuous progress in the world.

4. **Shifts in power structures:** New interest groups are affecting political parties, legal systems, health systems, educational systems, and business corporations.

5. **New concepts of work, education, and leisure:** The distinctions among these three areas are blurred and uncertain.

6. **The search for meaning:** People search for meaning in many ways from religion to cultural traditions; but, for some, a crisis in meaning leads to drugs, suicide, and other problems.

Discuss the effects of these statistics and trends on childhood and on other aspects of society.

References

Cootz, S. (1992). *The way we never were: American families and the nostalgia trap.* New York: Basic Books.

Frost, J. L. (March/April 1986). Children in a changing society: Frontiers of challenge. *Childhood Education,* 242-249.

Henchey, N. (January/February 1985). Looking at the future from 1984. *Childhood Education,* 162-168.

LECTURE TOPIC 14.2: DO CHILDREN OF DIVORCE HAVE ADJUSTMENT PROBLEMS AS ADULTS?

We have research that documents higher rates of depression, delinquency, antisocial behavior, and use of psychiatric services in children of divorce. But what happens to these children in the long run after they become adults has been poorly documented. A recent study by Kulka and Weingarten has attempted to investigate the adjustment and psychological functioning of a random sample of adults in America who either were raised by both their real parents or were raised in a family disrupted by divorce or marital separation. Each adult was interviewed for 90 minutes in his or her own home by a professional interviewer. Data were generated on these subjects' global adjustment, on specific aspects of their psychological adjustment, and on their evaluations of marital and parental roles.

Some of the measures of global adjustment included their evaluation of their present happiness (very unhappy to very happy), their morale about the future, and the extent of their worries (never to a lot or always). None of these measures showed a consistent significant difference between those adults from divorced backgrounds and those from intact families. One rather consistent finding on global adjustment was the tendency for adults from homes disrupted by divorce to identify childhood or adolescence as the most unhappy time of their lives. (As noted in the text, middle-aged women reported that their lowest point in life happiness came during early middle age, whereas men identified young adulthood as the unhappiest time.) Parental divorce was therefore a stressful event in the childhood of these respondents. One interesting exception was found among those currently divorced themselves. They were not so likely to identify their childhood as the unhappiest time of their lives, presumably because another, similar crisis in their later lives was "competing" with the earlier one.

On the psychological adjustment items, some interesting sex differences appeared. Men were more likely to report high anxiety, that bad things frequently happen to them, and that they frequently find things hard to handle. This corroborates other research data finding the negative effects of divorce to be more persistent for boys than for girls.

In looking at role adjustment, the investigators again found sex differences. Adults from divorced backgrounds were not so likely to say that marriage contributes to the fulfillment of their most important values. The women, compared with those women from intact families, were more committed to their parenting role as being their source of fulfillment. The men, on the other hand, were less likely to report parenthood as contributing to their most important value, but neither were they negative about parenthood. The conclusion drawn by the authors is that men from intact families have a stronger investment in the parental role than those from divorced backgrounds.

The results reported here are a few significant relationships that emerged from a much larger number of comparisons. The overall impression is that divorce has very little long term deleterious effect on children. There is some effect on the psychological well-being of men in adulthood. There are also some ramifications in the value placed on the marital and parental roles. However, as in most crises, the deleterious effects seem to fade over time as individuals develop methods of adjustment and coping.

References

Cherlin, A. (1991). Longitudinal studies of effects of divorce on children in Great Britain and the United States. *Science, 252.*

Kulka, R. A., & Weingarten, H. (1979). The long-term effects of parental divorce in childhood on adult adjustment. *Journal of Social Issues, 35,* 50-78.

LECTURE TOPIC 14.3: CHARACTERISTICS OF ADULTS RAISED IN SINGLE-PARENT FAMILIES

Mueller and Cooper did a survey of 19- to 34-year-olds and compared those who were raised in a single-parent household with those who were raised in a two-parent household. They sampled 1 percent of the young adults in a midwestern county and ended up with 123 respondents who were raised in single-parent households (Group A) and 1245 who were raised in two-parent households (Group B). In Group A, 112 were raised by their mothers and 11 were raised by their fathers. Twenty-six individuals in this group were reared in single-parent households because of the death of one parent. Comparison of Group A and Group B revealed the following differences:

1. A higher proportion of subjects in Group A (10 percent) did not have a high school diploma (it was 4 percent in Group B).
2. Group B subjects averaged one more year of education than Group A subjects.
3. Subjects in Group A had averaged more weeks of unemployment in the past year.

4. Group A subjects averaged lower occupational status.
5. The annual income for Group B subjects was higher than for Group A subjects.
6. Group A subjects were more likely to receive welfare assistance (AFDC or food stamps) than were Group B subjects.
7. Group B subjects were more likely to be homeowners.
8. A higher percentage of Group A subjects were separated, divorced, or not married.
9. A higher proportion of Group A subjects were parents.
10. Group A subjects tended to have their first child at a younger age than Group B subjects.

The researchers summarize their results as follows: "Persons raised by single parents . . . tended to have lower educational, occupational, and economic attainment during early adulthood than their counterparts raised in traditional two-parent families. Differences between the two groups were also observed in family formation and marital stability. . . . Those from single-parent family backgrounds were more likely to have their first child at a younger age and to be separated or divorced rather than married."

Reference
Mueller, D., & Cooper, P. (1986). Children of single-parent families: How they fare as young adults. *Family Relations, 35,* 169-176.

LECTURE TOPIC 14.4: SUBSTANCE USE AND ABUSE AMONG CHILDREN
Chapter 14 in the text presents information about emotional disturbances in middle childhood and about their treatment. Substance use and abuse are also significant issues in middle childhood. The following are some pertinent points about substance use and abuse among children:

1. The United States is a drug culture. Licit drugs (caffeine, nicotine, alcohol, prescription drugs, and over-the-counter drugs) as well as illicit drugs are widely available and highly publicized.
2. Children face the major task of sorting out all the images and messages about licit and illicit drugs that bombard them daily.
3. The concept of abuse requires careful formulation, and individual definitions of abuse vary widely.
4. However, any regular use of a psychoactive drug by a child is considered abuse.
5. Because of its ready availability, nicotine is the drug most widely experimented with by preadolescents. A substantial proportion of children at least experiment with smoking tobacco by age 9.
6. A boy's first drink typically occurs around age 12; girls typically take their first drink slightly later.
7. Preadolescents' first experiences with consciousness-altering substances usually involve inhalants.
8. Among high school seniors, 92 percent had experience with alcohol, and 66 percent had used alcohol within the last month; 20 percent were daily cigarette smokers.

9. Prescriptions for minor tranquilizers, barbiturates, and amphetamines over the past decade declined among adolescents.
10. More girls than boys smoke and take amphetamines.
11. Urban usage rates are typically higher than usage rates in rural areas.
12. Most individuals will become drug users at some point in their lives, whether they limit their use to alcohol, caffeine, and nicotine or extend it to cocaine, marijuana, other illicit drugs, and prescription medications.

References

Davies, J., & Coggans, N. (1991). *The facts about adolescent drug abuse.* London: Cassell.

Newcomb, M. D., & Bentler, P. M. (1989). Substance use and abuse among children and teenagers. *American Psychologist 44*, 242-248.

LECTURE TOPIC 14.5: SEXUAL ABUSE OF CHILDREN

Sexual abuse of children has a very long history. For example, in ancient Greece and Rome adult males (family members and teachers) would sodomize young boys. Several cultures used royal incest to preserve the purity of the royal line (pharaohs of Egypt, Peru's Incas, and the Hawaiian nobility into the nineteenth century). In the Middle Ages, male children were sometimes castrated before adolescence so that they would continue to have soprano voices for church choirs. Sexual abuse of children is a crime in most parts of the world now, but it was not a crime in England until 1908 and it is still not considered a crime in Turkey, Portugal, and Luxembourg.

Sexual abuse of children is the use of dependent, developmentally immature children in sexual activities they cannot completely comprehend or to which they cannot grant informed consent. The activities violate social taboos and sometimes family roles. There are many kinds of sexual abuse.

1. **Incest**—sexual activity between family members, including parents, siblings, grandparents, uncles and aunts, stepparents, and nonrelated siblings.
2. **Pedophilia**—the sexual preference of an adult for children.
3. **Exhibitionism (indecent exposure)**—the exposure of a male's genitals to children or women.
4. **Molestation (indecent liberties)**—a range of behaviors including touching, fondling, masturbating, or kissing the child.
5. **Statutory rape**—adult has sex with a child (fellatio, sodomy, or penile-vaginal intercourse) often under circumstances of seduction, bribery, persuasion, and authority. Each state determines the age of legal consent, which is from 12 to 18.
6. **Rape**—sexual intercourse or attempted intercourse without the victim's consent. Victims have been as young as 6 months, but they are usually over the age of 5 years.
7. **Child pornography**—pornography depicting children in sexual acts with other children, adults, or animals.
8. **Child prostitution**—children engaged in sex acts for profit.

Sexual abuse is widespread. Some studies suggest that there are a quarter of a million cases a year. Some believe that sexual abuse of children and adolescents is more common than physical abuse. A 1979 questionnaire of college students led to the conclusion that 1 in 5 females and 1 in 11 males had sexual activity with a much older person during their childhood. A 1981 Denver study revealed that 45 percent of sexually abused children were abused before their twelfth birthday. In fact, 16 percent were abused before they were 6 years old. It is estimated that 300,000 American children are involved in prostitution and pornography. Of children and adolescents put into psychiatric wards, 8 percent of the males and 37 percent of the females were incest victims. Of the 2 million children who run away from home in a year's time, about half have been sexually abused.

Sex abuse cases are being reported more now. Nationwide from 1976 to 1981, there was a 200 percent increase in reported cases of sexual child abuse. Public education plays a significant role here. In 1970, Florida received only 17 reports of child abuse. An education program was developed and, in 1971, Florida had 19,120 reports. More treatment programs and better research are now being instituted.

References

Haugaard, J., & Reppuccin, N. (1988). *The sexual abuse of children: A comprehensive guide to current knowledge.* San Francisco, CA: Jossey-Bass Publishers.

Kempe, R., & Kempe, H. (1984). *The common secret: Sexual abuse of children and adolescents.* San Francisco: Freeman.

LECTURE TOPIC 14.6: LIVING IN A STEPFAMILY

Stepfamilies do not immediately solve their problems and live "happily ever after" as depicted by some television shows. Stepfamilies take 4 to 7 years to adjust. Some of the more common problems faced are discussed below:

1. **Nuclear Family Myth:** The stepfamily will seldom act like a nuclear family. There are extra parents and other people involved.
2. **Communication:** Children, parents, and ex-spouses must develop methods to communicate without using the children to carry messages and spy for the parents.
3. **Respect for Difference:** Stepfamilies are filled with mixtures of discipline styles, parenting techniques, and past histories. The families must acknowledge these differences and work to solve conflicts.
4. **Immediate Parenting and Feelings of Failure:** Stepparents often take on the responsibility for children of a variety of ages without any prior experience. Remarried parents are often afraid that failures will reoccur and wait too long to confront problems.
5. **Need for Time:** Both the newly married couple and the children need time to form new relationships.
6. **Ex-spouses, Visitations, and Child Support:** The conflicts between ex-spouses often reappear along with new conflicts over visitation and child support.

These and other emotional conflicts make stepfamilies unique. Special support systems are needed to help these family groups adjust and care for the children.

Reference

Visher, E. B., & Visher, J. S. (1991). *How to win as a stepfamily*. New York: Brunner/Mazel, Publishers.

DISCUSSION TOPICS

DISCUSSION TOPIC 14.1: TEACHING SOCIAL SKILLS

The text suggests that there exist effective programs for teaching social skills to unpopular children. Children must both know the skills and have the opportunity to use them for the program to be successful. Remind your class that the negative effects of being an unpopular child are too great for us not to institute programs for teaching social skills to unpopular children. But should they be mandatory? There are many obvious side issues to this debate. Who will identify the children, and on what basis will the diagnosis be made? What role do self-fulfilling prophecies play in unpopularity? What standards of social skills must be met before children can leave the program? What constitutes popularity? Whose responsibility is it to teach social skills, the parents' or society's? Should parents and others be required to take "remedial social skills learning"?

DISCUSSION TOPIC 14.2: BULLIES

The text presents information about popular and unpopular children, but does not mention the age-old problem of peer group bullies. Invite your students to recall their own experiences with bullies (or being a bully?). Where do bullies fit in the system of popular and unpopular children? How was bullying dealt with when your students were younger? How is it dealt with today? What happens to bullies when they become older?

What advice should parents give their children who are victimized by a bully? Students may line up on either side of the argument: Should a child be encouraged to defend him or herself? Should he or she use adult resources? Is it always wrong to hit (such as in self-defense)? Are self-defense and retaliation different?

Some school districts have gone to a policy of zero-tolerance for aggressive behavior. How do these policies affect the social climate for children?

DISCUSSION TOPIC 14.3: HAS THE FOLKLORE CHANGED?

Explore with your class their opinions about the state of current childhood folklore. Do children still step on cracks in the sidewalk when angry with their mothers? Do children nowadays tell stories about the extraterrestrials in their closets? Is the tale about the prison escapee with the artificial hook for a hand still making the rounds? Help the class distinguish between their own personal recollections of childhood lore and the current lore shared by 6- to 12-year-olds. Many of these stories are called *urban myths*. This activity can easily be adapted into an interview or questionnaire project for the whole class or interested individuals.

DISCUSSION TOPIC 14.4: SUBJECTIVE/OBJECTIVE VIEWS OF DIVORCE

Much of the research presented in the text on the effects of divorce on children has attempted to obtain an objective description of those effects. It is useful to compare these objective findings with the actual subjective experiences that children have had when their parents divorce. If yours is an average class, fully half of the class will have had direct experiences with divorce—either their parents are divorced or they are. Explore with the class how well their own experiences match the more objective research findings reported in the text.

INDEPENDENT STUDIES

INDEPENDENT STUDY 14.1: FRIENDSHIP IN THE ONLINE AGE

What research has been done into children's online friendships? Many children spend a great deal of their time using instant messenger services and chat rooms. Many use these methods to keep in contact with friends from school and activities; some may create friendships through these media. Check published research and also internet sources for information on this topic. You may have interesting results by interviewing children you know about their online relationships.

CHOOSING SIDES

CHOOSING SIDES 14.1: BEHAVIOR MODIFICATION

The question of environmental determinism must be dealt with in any theory of development, philosophy of human nature, parenting technique, or teaching technique. The overriding importance that behaviorism places on the environment has won great support as well as created many detractors. Be sure the class understands the principles of behaviorism that underlie learning theory and behavior modification. In addition, point out the control this implies over our own and our children's lives—application in environmental contingencies results in controlled and predictable behavior in all organisms. There are many ways in which the nature-nurture controversy can be debated. Most issues in the controversy can be brought out in debating whether behavior modification really controls our lives.

Debate a statement similar to the following:

Systematic use of modern behavior modification on people is contrary to human nature and violates their individual rights or dignity. Therefore, strict applications of behavior modification should not be allowed in our society.

Pro: All humans, even children, have an inalienable right to choose their own behaviors and have responsibility for their actions. By structuring their environment such that they have no choice of either good or bad behavior, you thwart the very processes that make humans unique and creative. Genetic predispositions and ability to think unique thoughts would defeat any attempt at pure control, anyway. Rather than treating adolescents as miniature adults to be shaped and trained, it is better to respect their free will, cognitive motivation, and stage-wise development. These factors in an adolescent force the parent, teacher, and government to consider the teen-ager's rights and needs rather than the conveniences of the controllers of the society.

Con: There is no need to worry about assumed genetic dispositions, mental attributes, and internal causation when it can be shown that individual behavior dramatically adheres to basic environmental learning principles. Behavior modification works, as can be shown in case after case. Complex human behavior is really a matter of individual experience and environmental shaping. These are not new principles, but the recent detailing of these processes allows us to predict and control behavior much more effectively. By structuring the environment properly, human misery can be avoided and destructive behavior channeled into well-adjusted and productive behavior. Human behavior is a product of the environment, so the environment should be structured to produce individuals beneficial to society as well as to themselves.

Children would especially benefit more from an appropriately planned environment than from the haphazard and often cruel society we now have.

The following lists give arguments that might be used to support each side of the debate.

Pro: Antibehaviorism
1. Behaviorist descriptions of proper child-rearing techniques are severe and manipulating. See John B. Watson's advice on child rearing in Kessen. Read B. F. Skinner.
2. Focusing on environmental effects neglects thinking, dreaming, imagining, and other subjective experiences that do not lend themselves to easy objective analysis.
3. Feelings, love, and attachment are not products of primary and secondary reinforcement, as shown by experiments with infant animals and humans.
4. Misuse of behavior modification (for example, brainwashing or political coercion) is dangerous and not justified by the benefits.
5. Environmental determinism means that individuals are not responsible for their own behavior. It is difficult to explain why individuals from the same family and environment act so differently. Even children must have a sense of responsibility for their actions.
6. Behavior modification requires excessive control of the person's environment. This artificial environment is not natural, even though it may be temporarily effective.
7. Contrast the mechanistic, tabula rasa, behavioristic viewpoint with the more humanistic and appealing aspects of Freudian-Erikson and cognitive theory.

Con: Behaviorism
1. Environmental determinism is the only way for American democracy to succeed—all are created equal and given an equal chance to succeed if the environment permits.
2. Being in absolute control of a child's life is not new. All that is needed to prevent abuse is decisions about the moral principles to be followed in behavior modification.
3. Children cannot be given freedom of choice in critical life-death decisions until they have been trained and have learned habits such as honesty, service to others, diligence, and the like.
4. Behavior modification works when other therapies fail; for example, it often makes it possible to remove patients from the back wards of mental hospitals.
5. Behavior modification is reality oriented and forces an adolescent to bear the direct consequences of his or her immediate behavior and thus to assume greater responsibility for his or her own behavior.
6. Children have the right to the best possible environment; it is now possible to design such an environment and still prevent abuse by those in power.

7. The internal assumed constructs of other theories can be simply explained in terms of learning theory.

References

Kessen, W. (1965). *The child*. New York: Wiley.

Rogers, C. R., & Skinner, B. F. (1956). Some issues concerning the control of human behavior: A symposium. *Science, 124*, 1057-1066.

Skinner, B. F. (1979). *Beyond freedom and dignity*. New York: Knopf.

Skinner, B. F. (1948). *Walden Two*. London: Macmillan.

KNOWLEDGE CONSTRUCTION ACTIVITIES

KNOWLEDGE CONSTRUCTION ACTIVITY 14.1: GENERATIVE TERMS

This activity will use the principles of generative learning as explained in the Introduction to assist students in gaining a better understanding of terms. Divide the class into groups of four or five. Assign each group the task of generating an example for a generative term from this chapter. The example that each group creates cannot be one that has been used in the class or in the book. They must think of a new application for the term that they are given. Groups are allowed to use their books and notes. By creating their own example of the term, they demonstrate an understanding of the term to the level of application. There are several approaches that can be used in this exercise. Students may be given the entire list at once, but often one group will finish far ahead of the others and topics will get out of sequence. Another strategy is to give all of the groups the same term to create an example and then go around the room to discuss outcomes. This has been very successful, but also takes the most time. A third approach is to give each group a different term and see what examples they can generate.

Some generative terms for Chapter 14 are listed below.

Coregulation	Separation anxiety disorder
Oppositional defiant disorder	Obsessive-compulsive disorder
Conduct disorder	Childhood depression
School phobia	

KNOWLEDGE CONSTRUCTION ACTIVITY 14.2: YOUNG CHILDREN'S BELIEF ABOUT MYTHIC FIGURES

Conduct a survey on myths, fantasies, and beliefs of young school-age children. Develop a specific list of questions about such a figure as Santa Claus, the Easter bunny, the tooth fairy, or God. Ideas might include who these figures are, what they do, where they live, and so on. If children know the truth, find out how old they were when they found out and the manner in which they learned of it.

Investigate further to see what children's beliefs are about television figures or the heroes of video games and movies. Are these figures in the same category for children as the aforementioned Easter bunny, tooth fairy, and so on? What roles do parents, siblings, and television play in children's understanding of these figures?

KNOWLEDGE CONSTRUCTION ACTIVITY 14.3: POPULAR AND UNPOPULAR CHILDREN

Do a sociometric study on a single classroom of children. Have each child in the class write down the names of their three best friends in the class or the three they like least. (As mentioned in the text, these questions might be more specific; for example, "Which three children do you like to sit near?") Collect the data and determine several most-popular and several least-popular children by counting the number of votes each received. Be sure to have students list only names of children in their class, or you might end up with a single vote for someone's neighbor or someone's cousin whom no one else knows. If your classroom has young children, kindergartners for instance, you might use a class photograph, photocopy it, and ask children to circle their most favorite and cross out least favorite people to sit beside.

Prepare a list of descriptive adjectives (positive, negative, and neutral) such as those listed below. Have the classroom teacher check the descriptors that apply to the children your sociometric measure identified as most popular and least popular. How well do your results match the published research findings? That is, do the popular children fit the description in the text: healthy, vigorous, poised, capable of initiative but also adaptable and conforming, dependable, affectionate, considerate, original thinkers, moderate in self-esteem, self-confident without seeming conceited, mature dependence, and physically attractive? Are the unpopular children withdrawn, rebellious, aggressive, hostile, silly, babyish, immature, anxious, uncertain, lacking in confidence, unattractive, or slow learners?

What are the implications of these findings for the unpopular children in school? How can teachers, parents, and other interested people help them?

KNOWLEDGE CONSTRUCTION ACTIVITY 14.4: PEER PRESSURE

Have students interview third-, fourth-, fifth-, and sixth-graders about the influence of peer pressure. Possible areas for questioning include clothing, food preferences, values, friends, favorite music groups, and participation in athletics, academic performance, and hair styles. Alert students to observe carefully whether discrepancies exist between what the interviewees say and what they actually do. Toward this end, the students may want to visit schools and playgrounds to observe the children interacting with one another.

KNOWLEDGE CONSTRUCTION ACTIVITY 14.5: COMMON EMOTIONAL DISTURBANCES

Assign students to work in groups. Give each group the name of a common emotional disturbance that is listed in the chapter. For each of the disturbances, the group must create a family scenario with a hypothetical child that suffers from this disturbance. The group must say what behaviors characterize this disturbance and name different treatment techniques that are effective in dealing with the disorder. Be sure to include the families in the treatment plans.

KNOWLEDGE CONSTRUCTION ACTIVITY 14.6: TREATMENT TECHNIQUES—ATTENTION DEFICIT HYPERACTIVITY DISORDER

How do parents, teachers, and physicians identify children with ADHD? What treatment options are available?

Consider a scenario where you are the parent of a child in a local elementary school:

Third grade child, male
Extremely active
Average student in school—you think he could do better
Playground monitor suggests he is hyperactive
Teachers point out that he is impulsive, has difficulty staying on task
Sometimes acts out in school
Physician assesses and suggests a trial of stimulant medication

As a parent, you want the very best for your child. What options are there? Using the following resources, investigate treatment options for ADHD.

Make notes about the information you obtain from each type of source.

Professional Journal:

Textbook:

Magazine:

Internet Source:

Each type of reference provides a different level of information for the reader. What differences did you notice between them? Are some sources more credible than others? Write a 1- to 2-page summary of your findings, ending with your recommendation for treatment for your son.

7. RESOURCES FOR INSTRUCTORS

Books and Journal Articles

Alessandri, S. M., & Wozniak, R. H. (1987). The child's awareness of parental beliefs concerning the child: A developmental study. *Child Development, 58,* 315-323.

Anthony, E. J., & Cohler, B. J. (1987). *The invulnerable child.* New York: Guilford Press.

Caspi, A., Elder, G., & Bem, D. J. (1988). Moving away from the world: Life-course patterns of shy children. *Developmental Psychology, 24,* 824-831.

Demo, D. H. (1988). The impact of divorce on children. *Journal of Marriage and the Family, 50,* 619-648.

Kozol, J. (1995). *Amazing Grace.* New York: Crown Publishing.

Rubin, K. H., & Ross, H. S. (1982). *Peer relationships and social skills in childhood.* New York: Springer-Verlag.

Video resources

Eye of the Storm. (ABC, 25 min.) Shows a third-grade teacher's procedure for helping her children understand prejudice. Presents in a dramatic fashion the process by which children learn to discriminate and their reactions to being discriminated against.

Family Influences. (IM, 1992, 30 min.) This program illustrates how family background influences the way people view themselves and others. It defines four types of parents--authoritative, permissive, authoritarian, and uninvolved--and compares the characteristics of children raised by each. How parents can promote a sense of responsibility in children is discussed, and the role of siblings in a child's development is explored. The program examines the role of older siblings and presents opposing views on the influence of birth order on personality. It also considers nontraditional families and discusses recent findings on the effects of divorce on children.

Friendship, Gender, and Morality. (IM, 1992, 30 min.) Explores the functions of friendship in moral development and gender differences.

Gender Socialization. (IM, 1993, 60 min.) This video looks at interactions between gender, race, and class and their effects on self-esteem, emotions, behavior, and world view.

Helping Your Child Succeed. (IM, 1990, 50 min.) This presents six steps for anticipating and preventing problems and demonstrates how to use these steps to help children succeed. It shows how to instill self-esteem in a child, give effective praise, teach problem-solving techniques, and prepare a child to resist peer pressure.

Here Comes the Judge. (TLF, 26 min.) Reveals the relationship between cognitive and moral development as children and adults confront moral dilemmas.

Home and Away. (TLF, 26 min.) Shows how different children react to school and explores how children adapt to the new experience and their relationships with teachers. Suggests ways in which certain children may be helped to handle moral dilemmas.

Me and my Friends. (IM, 1992, 30 min.) Noted psychologists consider how children during the middle years prove their competence and how they develop durable, vital friendships. The program discusses children's perceptions of competence and identifies two patterns of how children deal with failure: the helpless pattern and the mastery pattern. What makes a child popular in his or her peer group and why certain children are rejected is examined.

Peer Culture. (IM, 1992, 30 min.) Examines conflicts as children move into greater involvement with their peers.

Peers in Development. (IM, 1991, 60 min.) Probing the importance of peer relationships in social and emotional development, this program examines the growth of peer relationships from the social interest of infants through the groupings of adolescence. It considers the importance of play in cognitive development, as explained by Piaget and Vygotsky, and describes Parten's six categories of social participation. Commentary from children of different ages provides insights into how the idea of friendship changes with age.

Self-esteem in School Age Children. (IM, 1990, 25 min.) Self-esteem affects mental health, motivation, and behavior. This video explores the components of the self: self-concept, self-control, and self-esteem. It outlines five criteria for self-perception and relates the way an individual ranks these five criteria to the individual's feelings of self-worth. It concludes with an exploration of how adults can enhance self-esteem in children.

Single Parenting. (IM, 1988, 20 min.) This program teaches single parents how to respond effectively to the difficulties of raising children alone. It details a four-step plan for raising children after a divorce. Vignettes illustrate ways to minimize the adverse effects on a child of the loss of a parent. The video also suggests ways to handle discipline, financial problems, and family crises.

Teaching Responsible Behavior. (IM, 1992, 54 min.) This video shows parents how to correct children's misbehavior and get them to accept responsibility. It teaches how to reinforce positive changes in behavior and how to help children set and achieve realistic goals.

The Conscience of a Child. (NET Film Service, 27 min.) Demonstrates moral development from a learning theory perspective.

LINKUPS

In adolescence, young people's appearance changes; as a result of the hormonal events of puberty, they take on the bodies of adults. Their thinking changes, too; they are better able to think abstractly and hypothetically. And their feelings change about almost everything. All areas of development converge as adolescents confront their major task: establishing an identity--- including a sexual identity---that will carry over to adulthood.

In Chapters 15, 16, and 17, we see how adolescents incorporate their drastically changed appearance, their puzzling physical yearnings, and their new cognitive abilities into their sense of self. We see how the peer group serves as the testing ground for teenagers' ideas about life and about themselves. We look at risks and problems that arise during the teenage years, as well as at characteristic strengths of adolescents.

Linkups to Look For:

o   Both hormonal and social influences may contribute to heightened emotion and moodiness in adolescence.
o   Early or late physical maturation can affect emotional and social adjustment.
o   Conflict between adolescents and their parents may sometimes stem from immature aspects of adolescent thinking.
o   Parental involvement and parenting styles influence academic achievement.
o   The ability of low-income adolescents to do well in school may depend on the availability of family and community resources.
o   Physical characteristics play an important part in molding adolescents' self-concept.
o   Girls who are knowledgeable about sex are most likely to postpone sexual activity.
o   The intensity and intimacy of adolescent friendships is in part due to cognitive development.

15 PHYSICAL DEVELOPMENT AND HEALTH IN ADOLESCENCE

ADOLESCENCE: A DEVELOPMENTAL TRANSITION
Markers of Adolescence
Opportunities and Risks of Adolescence

PUBERTY: THE END OF CHILDHOOD
How Puberty Begins
Timing, Sequence, and Signs of Maturation
Psychological Effects of Early and Late Maturation

PHYSICAL AND MENTAL HEALTH
Physical Activity
Sleep Needs
Nutrition and Eating Disorders
Use and Abuse of Drugs
Sexually Transmitted Diseases (STDs)
Abuse and Neglect
Death in Adolescence
Protective Factors: Health in Context

In This Chapter of Your Instructor's Manual You Will Find:
1. Total Teaching Package Outline
2. Expanded Outline (transparency-ready)
3. Guideposts for Study
4. Learning Objectives
5. Key Terms
6. Teaching and Learning Activities
   Lecture Topics
   Discussion Topics
   Independent Studies
   Choosing Sides
   Knowledge Construction Activities
7. Resources for Instructors

1. TOTAL TEACHING PACKAGE OUTLINE

Chapter 15: Physical Development and Health in Adolescence

Adolescence: A developmental transition	**Guidepost for study 15.1**
Markers of adolescence	**Learning objective 15.1** **Choosing sides 15.1**
Opportunities and risks of adolescence	**Guidepost for study 15.2** **Learning objective 15.2** **Discussion topic 15.3**
Puberty: The end of childhood	**Guidepost for study 15.3** **Lecture topic 15.1**
How puberty begins	**Learning objective 15.3**
Timing, sequence, and signs of maturation	**Learning objective 15.4** **Lecture topic 15.2** **Knowledge construction activity 15.3**
Psychological effects of early and late maturation	**Learning objectives 15.5, 15.5** **Knowledge construction activities 15.1, 15.2, 15.6**
Physical and mental health	**Guidepost for study 15.4** **Learning objective 15.6**
Physical activity	**Learning objective 15.7** **Independent study 15.1**
Sleep needs	**Learning objective 15.8**
Nutrition and eating disorders	**Learning objectives 15.9, 15.10** **Lecture topic 15.3** **Knowledge construction activity 15.4**
Use and abuse of drugs	**Learning objectives 15.11, 15.12** **Lecture topic 15.4** **Discussion topic 15.1** **Knowledge construction activities 15.1, 15.5**
Sexually transmitted diseases (STDs)	**Learning objectives 15.13, 15.14** **Discussion topics 15.2, 15.4** **Box 15.1 (text p. 388)**
Abuse and neglect	**Learning objective 15.15**
Death in adolescence	**Learning objective 15.16** **Box 15.2 (text p. 390)**
Protective factors: Health in context	**Learning objective 15.17** **Knowledge construction activity 15.1**

Please check out the online learning center located at www.mhhe.com/papaliacw9 for further information on these and other topics. There you can also access downloadable PowerPoint slides tailored to each chapter of the text and containing useful teaching notes as well as images and tables from the text itself.

2. EXPANDED OUTLINE (TRANSPARENCY READY)

I. Adolescence: A Developmental Transition
    A. Markers of adolescence
        1. Puberty
        2. Secular trends

II. Puberty: The End of Childhood
    A. Adolescent growth spurt
    B. Primary sex characteristics
        1. Spermarche
        2. Menarche
    C. Secondary sex characteristics
    D. Gonadarche
    E. Adrenarche

III. Physical and Mental Health
    A. Nutrition and eating disorders
        1. Obesity
        2. Body image
        3. Anorexia nervosa
        4. Bulimia nervosa
    B. Use and abuse of drugs
        1. Substance abuse
        2. Substance dependence
        3. Gateway drugs
    C. Sexually transmitted diseases
    D. Abuse and neglect
    E. Death in adolescence
        1. Accidents and firearms
        2. Suicide

3. GUIDEPOSTS FOR STUDY

15.1   What is adolescence and when does it begin and end?

15.2   What opportunities and risks does adolescence entail?

15.3   What physical changes do adolescents experience and how do these changes affect them psychologically?

15.4   What are some common health problems and health risks of adolescence and how can they be prevented?

4. LEARNING OBJECTIVES

After completing the study of this chapter, the student will be able to:

15.1   Distinguish among three ways of defining entrance into adulthood.

15.2   Identify some risky behavior patterns common during adolescence.

15.3   Tell how puberty begins and how its timing and length vary.

15.4   Describe typical pubertal changes in boys and girls and identify factors that affect psychological reactions to these changes.

15.5   Identify the age of the first sexual attraction and discuss its implications for the timing of puberty.

15.6   Summarize the status of adolescents' health and health care.

15.7   Explain why physical activity is important in adolescence and discuss risks and benefits of athletic activity for adolescent girls.

15.8   Explain why adolescents often get too little sleep and how sleep deprivation can affect them.

15.9   Summarize the normal nutritional needs and typical dietary deficiencies of adolescent boys and girls.

15.10 Discuss risk factors, effects, treatment, and prognosis for obesity, anorexia, and bulimia.

15.11 Summarize recent trends in drug use among adolescents.

15.12 Discuss factors and risks connected with use of drugs, specifically alcohol, marijuana, and tobacco.

15.13 Identify and describe the most common sexually transmitted diseases.

15.14 List risk factors for developing an STD during adolescence and state effective prevention methods.

15.15 Tell how maltreatment of adolescents differs from maltreatment of younger children.

15.16 Name the three leading causes of death among adolescents and discuss the dangers of firearm injury.

15.17 Assess risk factors and prevention programs for teenage suicide.

5. KEY TERMS

Puberty
Secular trend
Adolescent growth spurt
Primary sex characteristics
Secondary sex characteristics
Spermarche
Menarche
Gonadarche

Adrenarche
Anorexia nervosa
Bulimia nervosa
Substance abuse
Substance dependence
Gateway drugs
Sexually transmitted diseases

6. TEACHING AND LEARNING ACTIVITIES

LECTURE TOPICS

LECTURE TOPIC 15.1: THE SECULAR TREND

As mentioned briefly in the textbook, recent history has shown a secular trend in physical development. Humans in modernized countries are maturing earlier and attaining greater physical stature. Malina points out that, in all probability, the modern menarche maturation trends are very similar to those of classical Greek and Roman adolescents. Mean age of menarche then was 12 to 15 years, and in the United States today it is 12.8 years. For some unknown reasons, menarche in nineteenth-century Europe occurred at about 15.5 to 16.0 years of age. Skeletal height in Japan rose from 159 centimeters in the year 100 B.C. to 169 centimeters in 1970. The cause of the secular trend is most often thought to be elimination of growth-inhibiting factors rather than addition of growth-stimulating factors. The following are possible explanations for the secular trend.

1. **Nutrition:** The quality as well as the composition of American food consumption has changed. In particular, fat consumption increased from 32 percent of the diet in 1909-1913 to 43 percent in 1972. A dramatic drop in cereal consumption, down 75 to 90 percent, has occurred since 1880. Relevant to bone construction, calcium intake has increased. Metabolism and even endocrine functions may have been affected by increases in sugar consumption. Interestingly, refined-sugar consumption per capita has not risen dramatically since 1920, but a larger proportion of sugar is being consumed in the form of processed foods and beverages (mainly soft drinks). The effect of infant nutrition is still a matter of controversy (fat babies do not necessarily make fat adults), but in the period 1926-1930 about 81 percent of first-born babies were breastfed. In 1961-1965, approximately 32 percent of first-borns were breastfed.

2. **Improved Environment:** There has been a significant increase in per capita income. This and the concomitant luxuries of modern life have drastically changed lifestyles and life spans. In particular, the secular trend may be a reflection of the overall better health of individuals.

This is readily apparent from mortality rates of children. In 1840, only 70 percent of the children lived past 5 years of age, whereas in 1960, 97 percent survived age 5. (Several European countries have better survival rates.) Elimination of childhood and adult epidemics is mainly responsible for increased survival and perhaps for increases in adolescent growth.

3. **Urbanization-Industrialization:** Although the early industrial revolution was a regression, today's youth do not suffer harsh working conditions.
4. **Reduction in Family Size:** Children from smaller families generally mature earlier and are larger than children from larger families.
5. **Genetic Hypothesis:** Selective breeding, in that taller mates are more fertile or that persons are seeking taller mates, is not a viable hypothesis. Outbreeding (hybrids) has been promoted by modern transportation (for example, the bicycle) or immigration and has been shown to have only a slight overall effect on the secular trend.
6. **Additional Hypotheses:** Additional hypotheses cite changes in physical activity, different and less-restrictive clothing, and biological 150-year cycles.

Determining the exact cause of the secular trend is impossible but it cannot be denied. There are several important effects of the secular trend on adolescents and on society as a whole.

1. **Lengthened Reproduction Span:** Since 1950, menarche has been rather stable at 12.8 years and menopause at 50 years. Only 130 years ago, menarche at 16 years meant that females had fewer years of fertility (the age of menopause has not changed).
2. **Increased Births to Teenagers:** Early maturation results in earlier reproduction and in more births—legitimate as well as illegitimate—to teenagers. (Earlier-maturing individuals also tend to marry earlier.) The median marrying age for females in 1890 was 22.0 years; in 1970 it was 23.3 years (first marriages), a nonsignificant increase. However, most females are now fertile at 15 years of age. Indicative of this, as well as other cultural factors, is the fact that the birthrate in 10- to 14-year-olds has increased since 1940. This is not good for either babies or mothers. Currently about 15 percent of the deliveries from mothers under age 15 are premature, whereas only 7 percent of the babies of 20- to 24-year-old mothers are premature.
3. **Diets:** Pubescence in girls is associated with accumulation of body fat. Earlier-maturing young adolescents have a tendency to engage in crash fad diets that have ill effects on their health.
4. **Strength:** Pound for pound, individuals today are less strong than their ancestors. However, greater weight and stature result in an overall greater strength in today's youth.
5. **Normative Data:** Growth charts used by industries from medicine to furniture manufacturing (classroom desks and so on) must make allowances for current increases in body size.
6. **Educational and Social Implications:** Females must be prepared for earlier menstruation and its accompanying psychological implications. Both early maturers and late maturers must be sensitively dealt with. There is now a longer period of sex taboo when an individual is physiologically but not psychologically ready. Parent-child relationships are strained. The child is big too early and can successfully intimidate the parents and even outperform them in physical sports and activities.

The secular trend needs to be recognized and dealt with more effectively by all, particularly by industrialized nations.

Reference

Malina, R. M. (1979). Secular changes in size and maturity: Causes and effects. In A. F. Roche (ed.). Secular trends in human growth, maturation, and development. *Monographs of the Society for Research in Child Development, 44* (3-4, Serial no. 179), 59-102.

LECTURE TOPIC 15.2: EARLY VERSUS LATE MATURATION

Hold a mini-debate about the benefits of early versus late maturation. The discussion in the text suggests that there are more benefits for early-maturing boys than for late-maturing boys. However, the picture is not so clear for girls. Discuss the mixed messages that are given early-maturing girls and boys. Discuss with your class the effects of early-maturing teens not having so much time as others to prepare for the impact of puberty.

Sexuality/Health. With extensive growth during this stage in life, nutrition is an important issue. Adequate protein level, calcium intake, and mineral supplies are needed for good health now and later. Obesity continues to increase for adolescents, with physical, social, and emotional consequences.

Eating disorders, such as anorexia nervosa and bulimia, have become more common, especially in girls. A person suffering from anorexia nervosa may begin to lose a few pounds and continue to diet far beyond a healthy limit. Bulimia is characterized by episodes of binge eating followed by purging. Treatment is available, and a variety of techniques are used.

Alcohol, marijuana, and tobacco are the drugs most frequently used by adolescents. The rate for sexually transmitted diseases (STDs, also called venereal diseases) such as gonorrhea, pelvic inflammatory disease (PID), syphilis, chlamydia, herpes, and acquired immune deficiency syndrome (AIDS) has soared recently. Regular medical checkups, protective measures, and knowledge of symptoms can minimize vulnerability to STDs.

The extent of abuse and neglect of adolescents is greatly underestimated. Abuse and neglect is a health problem, particularly for females who are less able to fight back. Tragic death can also be part of adolescence. Although they are basically healthy, cuts short some adolescents have their' lives cut short by accidents and suicides.

LECTURE TOPIC 15.3: EATING DISORDERS

Eating disorders are prevalent in the United States, especially among adolescent and college-age females. Some estimate that one in three college-age females has anorexia or bulimia. An eating disorder is a gross disturbance in eating behavior that jeopardizes a person's physical and psychological health. Here are some facts about each of the three major eating disorders.

Anorexia Nervosa

1. Anorexia nervosa is self-starvation and obsessive fear of weight gain.
2. Ninety-five percent of those with anorexia nervosa are females, and it is more common in the middle and upper socioeconomic strata.

3. The typical onset of a female's period is puberty, but it can occur at other ages groups.? Au: Due to anorexia? Add to make sentence explicit?
4. The general behavior pattern involves severe weight loss, extensive fasting, obsessive exercise, and persistent obsession with being overweight.
5.   Food is a control issue in the family. The anorexic patient often cooks the meals for the family.
6. The patients deny hunger pains.
7. Adolescent anorexia nervosa patients tend to avoid adult responsibilities and to have childlike dependencies.
8. Anorexia nervosa patients usually avoid sexual relationships.
9. There is amenorrhea.
10. About two-thirds have hypotension, hyperthermia, dry skin, and lanugo hair.
11. The most serious complications are electrolyte imbalance and cardiac abnormalities.
12. The mortality rate may be as high as 20 percent.

Bulimia
1. The main symptom of bulimia is binge eating, the rapid consumption of large amounts of food in a short period of time. There is intense preoccupation with food; 15,000 to 20,000 calories may be eaten in a couple of hours.
2. Males and females of all ages may be bulimics.
3. There is usually progressive weight gain with periods of weight loss due to diets, fasting, and sometime amphetamine abuse.
4. The binge eating is usually secretive.
5. Most bulimics want very much to be liked and accepted.

Treatment for eating disorders is similar to chemical dependency treatment. There needs to be (1) relief of symptoms, (2) education about the disease and treatment, (3) counseling to break through defense mechanisms, (4) family therapy, (5) group therapy to learn assertiveness and to control anger, and (6) emotional honesty. Most patients with eating disorders suffer from the emotional lies of terminal uniqueness (private, unshared, misunderstood, but special life) and terminal nobility (one will need to suffer alone and forever). Through professional support and support from other eating-disordered patients, the individual learns to take control of life and give up control-of-eating disorders.

References
Cousin, A. (November-December 1983). Anorexia nervosa and bulimia: An overview. *Journal of Emergency Nursing,* 343-345.
Harris, R. T. (1983). *Bulimarexia and related serious eating disorders with medical complications.* Condensed from *Annals of Internal Medicine, 99,* 800-807.

LECTURE TOPIC 15.4: FACTS ABOUT AIDS

AIDS (Acquired Immune Deficiency Syndrome) was first reported in the United States in 1981, and now thousands have AIDS and thousands more are infected with HIV (human immunodeficiency virus), which precedes the development of AIDS. Over one-third of those infected with HIV develop AIDS within 6 years.

In the summer of 1989, doctors estimated that more than 500,000 individuals worldwide had AIDS and that about 10 million individuals were infected with HIV. New York City has more reported AIDS cases than the next four largest cities combined; as of 1989, that translated into 288 cases per million population. San Francisco is second with 254 cases per million population, and Los Angeles is third with 98 per million. Yet no part of the United States nor the rest of the world is free of the danger of the AIDS epidemic.

AIDS also hits a wide range of the population. In Africa, a sizable number of the heterosexual population has contracted HIV; in America, a higher percentage of homosexuals than heterosexuals have contracted HIV. In 1989, homosexual men made up 65 percent of all Americans with AIDS. However, people of any sexual orientation are at risk, especially adolescents and young adults, who are likely to have several sex partners. In a study involving one Brooklyn and one Newark hospital, nearly 8 percent of low-risk male and female patients had been exposed to the HIV virus. Males age 25 to 44 who were hospitalized for other conditions were found to have a risk of 1 in 5 of being HIV positive.

Persons who use needles to inject drugs are also at increased risk for AIDS because many users share dirty needles. Intravenous drug use is considered the number-one reason for the high rate of AIDS in New York City. Hemophiliacs make up 5 percent of all AIDS victims because blood transfusions were not screened in the early stages of the epidemic. Finally, many babies are being born with HIV: at least 3000 in 1987 alone. Babies whose mothers have contracted HIV may become infected during the pregnancy and especially during the birth process.

People do not die from AIDS itself. AIDS causes a defect in the patient's natural immune system because the AIDS virus attacks the white blood cells. This makes an AIDS patient vulnerable to diseases that other individuals can fight, such as those caused by bacteria and viruses and some forms of cancer. Common symptoms for an AIDS patient include fever, diarrhea, dry cough, yeast infections in the mouth, loss of weight, skin rashes, tiredness, sweating, and swollen lymph glands—a pattern referred to as ARC (AIDS-Related Complex).

Among adult victims, two diseases are quite common: Kaposi sarcoma (KS) and pneumocystic carinii pneumonia (PCP). KS is a type of cancer in which tumors of blood vessels occur on the skin surface, inside the body, or in the mouth. These tumors can be purple, blue-violet, or brownish spots. Common among AIDS patients, KS is otherwise a rare form of cancer. PCP is a parasitic infection with symptoms typical of all severe pneumonias: persistent cough, fever, and shortness of breath. Some AIDS patients experience memory loss, indifference, poor coordination, mental problems, and partial paralysis because the AIDS virus can affect the brain and nervous system.

Children affected with AIDS are less likely to have KS or PCP. These children have enlarged livers and spleens, poor growth, and a form of pneumonia in which huge numbers of white blood cells are found in the lungs.

Society has taken some important precautions to slow down the spread of AIDS. Blood donations are very carefully screened, educational efforts are being increased, and condoms are being pushed as one type of protection (condoms need to be used every time from start to finish; condoms should not be reused; and condoms should be used with a spermicide called nonoxynol-9, which can kill the AIDS virus). Still many at-risk individuals refuse to acknowledge that their

273

habits could result in AIDS, and little behavior change is occurring in the sexual habits of teenagers and heterosexual adults.

In 1992 AIDS became the sixth leading cause of death among 15- to 24-year-olds, with teens being diagnosed in every state in the United States. In Washington DC, blood tests for all 13- to 20-year-olds at a public hospital has shown an increase in the number of AIDS infected, from one in 250 in 1989 to one in 90 in 1992. Teens are at risk because of more partners and fewer precautions, along with the egocentrism of "It can't happen to me."

References

Aids: A guide for survival. (1987). Houston: The Harris County Medical Society and the Houston Academy of Medicine.

HIV infected youth speaks about needs for support and health care. (Summer 1995). *Target 2000*.

Teenagers and AIDS. (August 3, 1992). *Newsweek*, 45-50.

DISCUSSION TOPICS

DISCUSSION TOPIC 15.1: MADD AND SADD

Invite representatives of Mothers Against Drunk Driving and Students Against Drunk Driving to discuss their organizations with your class. Explore your students' opinions about the effectiveness of these groups in reducing alcohol abuse among teenagers.

DISCUSSION TOPIC 15.2: COLLEGE STUDENTS' KNOWLEDGE OF STDS

A major concern of our society is adequate sex education for teenagers, but even many college students do not possess accurate, up-to-date information about sexually transmitted diseases. Conduct a miniquiz and a discussion of STDs to assess the level of knowledge of your students and to ensure that they have accurate information about these diseases. The county public health department typically provides information and lectures, or the health center on your campus may have resources for you.

DISCUSSION TOPIC 15.3: RITES OF PASSAGE AND THE MATURITY TEST

Ask your class to create a list of modern-day rites of passage in our society. It may be useful to arrange the events on a time line, beginning with events such as religious confirmation and a driver's permit at age 14 and including things like a driver's license, solo dating, the first job, and various legal eligibilities (voting, signing contracts, purchasing alcoholic beverages, marrying without consent of parents, and so on). The class should be able to generate a long list. Then discuss whether some of the problems teenagers encounter are a result of this confusing pattern of signs and signals of adult status. A lively discussion may ensue from a debate on the proposition that everyone should be required to pass a national comprehensive maturity test before being granted adult status. Side issues: What constitutes maturity? Can you measure maturity with a pencil-and-paper test? Who will create the test, and will it be subject to the same problems of bias that are associated with IQ tests? What will happen to those who fail the test? What is the appropriate punishment for those individuals caught acting illegally as adults?

DISCUSSION TOPIC 15.4: DEALING WITH AIDS

You may wish to ask a speaker from an organization such as Planned Parenthood to talk on AIDS and to hold a discussion with your class. Otherwise, it is recommended that you provide some facts and statistics about AIDS either before or after your discussion. Many students still harbor misconceptions about AIDS, such as "You can get AIDS from a mosquito bite or by donating blood."

Because many teenagers are sexually active and are experiencing adolescent egocentrism (the personal fable, or sense of invulnerability), it is difficult to Change? get adolescents to believe that they are at risk for contracting HIV. How can parents, teachers, and medical practitioners encourage adolescents to delay engaging in sex or to practice safe sex? At what age should sex education classes discuss AIDS and include information about condom use?

College students also seem to deny the reality of the AIDS epidemic. One research study found that college students have barely reduced the number of sexual partners they have and that only a minority regularly use condoms. Knowing about AIDS and having had formal sex education did not predict the use of condoms—the only predictive variable was seat belt use. That is, the students who always used a seat belt were highly likely to practice safe sex. Why don't more college students practice safe sex? Can you design an educational or media promotion that would increase safe-sex practices among the sexually active on campus? What misconceptions about AIDS, AIDS victims, or safe-sex practices might contribute to the low level of reliable practice of safe sex?

INDEPENDENT STUDY
INDEPENDENT STUDY 15.1: GENDER AND MOTOR SKILLS

After puberty, the physical differences between boys and girls become more apparent. Boys can throw harder and farther, run faster, and have more strength and endurance. Two generations ago, girls were even less able to compete. In fact, in the old days when there was disparity between boys' and girls' sports, girls were expected to do much more poorly than boys. This discrepancy was considered to be due to biology, to the degree that the Army's physical training requirements for women were much less stringent than those for men. Women were not allowed to enter marathons because of a presumption that they were not capable of running the distance.

Things have changed, however. One significant effect of the equalization of resources spent on sports for boys and for girls is that girls' motor skills, strength, and endurance are much better than in previous generations. This is a stunning example of how a variable thought to be biological and therefore immutable can be dramatically affected by social context.

Your students might be interested in examining the real and perceived gender differences in motor skills. At what age do boys typically become stronger and faster than girls? How does training affect these abilities? This is a great opportunity to tease out the relative effects of nature and nurture over time.

CHOOSING SIDES

CHOOSING SIDES 15.1:COULD WE DO WITHOUT ADOLESCENCE?

The text observes that adolescence only recently emerged as a developmental stage. Discuss with the class whether we really need this stage as part of our development. Explore with your students the societal changes and influences that have lengthened the time period of adolescence. An interesting case may be made that adolescence emerged as a result of the industrial revolution and the resulting need to limit the number of people in the workforce. The requirement of more education is a manifestation of the underlying need to delay entry into the workforce. As people's longevity increases, mandatory retirement will be the corresponding effect on the other end of the life span. Ask the class to speculate about how our society would change if teenagers were allowed to compete for jobs with adults on an equal basis.

Pro: Adolescence is a recent created concept: adolescents are capable of making their own decisions, accepting responsibility, and thus should have all of the rights and responsibilities of adults.

Con: Adolescents maybe mature physically but have not had sufficient experience in the world to take on all the responsibilities of adulthood. They need a protected period of development in which to practice making decisions, gain the skills they need for adult life, and gradually separate from their parents.

KNOWLEDGE CONSTRUCTION ACTIVITIES

KNOWLEDGE CONSTRUCTION ACTIVITY 15.1: GENERATIVE TERMS

This activity will use the principles of generative learning as explained in the Introduction to assist students in gaining a better understanding of terms. Divide the class into groups of four or five. Assign each group the task of generating an example for a generative term from this chapter. The example that each group creates cannot be one that has been used in the class or in the book. They must think of a new application for the term that they are given. Groups are allowed to use their books and notes. By creating their own example of the term, they demonstrate an understanding of the term to the level of application. There are several approaches that can be used in this exercise. Students may be given the entire list at once, but often one group will finish far ahead of the others and topics will get out of sequence. Another strategy is to give all of the groups the same term to create an example and then go around the room to discuss outcomes. This has been very successful, but also takes the most time. A third approach is to give each group a different term and see what examples they can generate.

Some generative terms for Chapter 15 are listed below.

A youth who demonstrates psychological effects of early maturation
A youth who demonstrates psychological effects of late maturation
Secular trend
Substance abuse
Substance dependence

Risk factors for drug abuse
Risk factors for suicide
Protective factors for suicide prevention

KNOWLEDGE CONSTRUCTION ACTIVITY 15.2: IDEAL MALE AND FEMALE

In class have students write down their personal descriptions of the physical characteristics of the ideal male and the ideal female. Limit them to physical characteristics. Ask them to be sure to include height, weight, and physical proportions. Suggest that they consider such things as hair and eye color, length of hair or hair style, amount of body hair, facial characteristics, and the like. After they have completed their lists, ask them to estimate (realistically!) how close they come to the physical ideal that they described for their own sex. You can use a scale from 0 to 100, where 100 indicates that they are the living, breathing ideal. Using the same scale, ask them to indicate how closely someone they know or know of comes to matching their ideal description of the opposite sex. You can collect these descriptions and estimates and have a group of students summarize the results.

Some useful descriptive statistics to calculate are the average heights and weights and the frequency with which different physical characteristics are named. Typically, the averages for the ideal descriptions are somewhat different from the actual averages in the population. For example, the ideal male is often described as 2 or more inches taller than the average male actually is. The estimates for how close they come to their descriptions are typically low, whereas their estimates of how close someone they know is to the ideal are fairly high. Discuss with the class the origins of these ideals and how they are affected by the media and advertising. Discuss the implications these ideals have for our body images and feelings of self-esteem. Bring a Barbie doll and have the students convert her measurements to a real person.

KNOWLEDGE CONSTRUCTION ACTIVITY 15.3: EARLY AND LATE BLOOMERS

Elicit case history information from students about whether they were early or late maturers. What effect do they feel this had on their adolescence? Some areas to include: popularity, social acceptance, self-confidence, athletic participation, dating, overall adjustment, and happiness with their lives. One non-threatening way to do this is to ask students to write a "puberty memory," while in class. Those who choose to may share theirs m, while (others will probably prefer to keep their personal experiences confidential). The shared memories tend to generate enthusiastic discussion and increase empathic understanding of early adolescence.

KNOWLEDGE CONSTRUCTION ACTIVITY 15.4: EATING DISORDERS COUNSELOR

Invite a counselor who works with anorexic or bulimic teenagers to discuss with your class his or her work and experiences. There is much interest in this topic, so (if possible) it would be good to allow students to invite other interested students to attend. Many hospitals now have eating-disorder units, and it may be possible for you to arrange a tour of their facilities for your class.

KNOWLEDGE CONSTRUCTION ACTIVITY 15.5: SUBSTANCE ABUSE COUNSELOR

Invite a local community representative who works in the area of drug abuse to speak to your class. Students might be interested in the actual incidence of drug abuse, as well as in the effects on the victim and his or her family. What programs are available to help the abuser? Are support groups available to assist the families of abusers? Some possible contacts include local law enforcement officers, Alcoholics Anonymous, Al-Anon Family Groups (for families of alcoholics), and the Palmer Drug Abuse Program (PDAP).

KNOWLEDGE CONSTRUCTION ACTIVITY 15.6: MEDIA IMAGES OF TEENS

The goal of the activity is to systematically examine television images of adolescence, compare them to real teens, and draw some conclusions.

Get together with three or four other students to do this activity.

Brainstorm a list of television shows that are explicitly aimed at teens. From your brainstormed list, choose four shows that represent different content: comedy, realism, drama, etc. Divide them up among group members and go watch TV!

While you are watching, list the characteristics of the adolescent characters you see. Include physical characteristics and personality traits. Be sure to include demographic information: that is, race or ethnicity, social class, education level. Remember that you are trying to describe the character on the program, not the actor (although with reality-style shows, it may be hard to tell the difference).

Bring your lists to the group and compile a group list of television images of teens. How well do these images fit with what you know about real life? Are television teens smarter, prettier, richer, less likely to get in trouble, more or less likely to drink or use drugs, more or less likely to be sexually active than real teens?

Make a poster with two columns. On one side, list the characteristics of TV teens. On the other, list characteristics of real teens. How realistic are the media images? Share your data with the class.

What purposes do the media images of teen serve? Why does television show teenagers in these particular ways?

7. RESOURCES FOR INSTRUCTORS

Books and Journal Articles

Baldwin, J. D., & Baldwin, J. I. (1988). Factors affecting AIDS-related sexual risk-taking behavior among college students. *The Journal of Sex Research, 2,* 181-196.

Dawson, D. A. (1986). The effects of sex education on adolescent behavior. *Family Planning Perspectives, 18,* 162-170.

Hatfield, E., & Sprecher, S. (1986). *Mirror, mirror . . . The importance of looks in everyday life.* Albany: State University of New York Press.

Hayes, D., & Ross, C. E. (1987). Concern with appearance, health beliefs, and eating habits. *Journal of Health and Social Behavior, 28,* 120-130.

Johnston, L., Bachman, J., & O'Malley, P. (January 31, 1994). Drug use rises among American teenagers. News release, Institute of Social Research, University of Michigan, Ann Arbor.

Video resources

Adolescence: The Prolonged Transition (IM, 1992, 30 min.). Uses historical and cross-cultural comparisons to question the view of adolescence as a social construction.

Adolescent Development (IM, 1990, video, 30 min.). Covers diverse aspects of physical, social, and psychological development. Discusses developmental tasks, puberty, and self-image, Elkind on social cognition, formal operations, and Kohlberg's theory of moral development.

Bulimia: The Binge-Purge Obsession (RP, 20 min.). Explores the causes and effects of bulimia and the way that this type of behavior is routine for many high school and college students.

Eating Disorders (FFHS, 1994, video, 19 min.). This program covers the personality profiles of those people most likely to be anorexic and shows how anorexia develops and can be cured.

Kids under the Influence (FFHS, 1989, 58 min.). Examines the long-term psychological and physical disorders caused by alcohol consumption among teenagers.

Menstruation: Understanding Your Body (From Women's Health Series, Video Learning Library, 1993, 28 min.). This is one part of an 8-part series , which provides clear, concise answers to the health issues facing every woman at every age. It is designed to empower through self-examination, self-assessment, and education. Hosted by Holly Atkinson, MD, NBC News' *Today* Medical Correspondent

Rich Kids on Drugs (FFHS, 1994, video, 28 min.). In this specially adapted Phil Donahue program, a teenager tells his story about how he got hooked on drugs.

Teenage Suicide (FFHS, 1994, video, 19 min.). This documentary explores some of the reasons teens commit suicide and the recent increase in suicide and describes some of the behavior patterns of which family and friends should be aware.

16 COGNITIVE DEVELOPMENT IN ADOLESCENCE

ASPECTS OF COGNITIVE MATURATION
Piaget's Stage of Formal Operations
Language Development
Elkind: Immature Characteristics of Adolescent Thought

MORAL REASONING: KOHLBERG'S THEORY
Kohlberg's Levels and Stages
Evaluating Kohlberg's Theory

EDUCATIONAL AND VOCATIONAL ISSUES
Influences on School Achievement
Dropping Out of High School
Educational and Vocational Preparation

In This Chapter of Your Instructor's Manual You Will Find:
1. Total Teaching Package Outline
2. Expanded Outline (transparency-ready)
3. Guideposts for Study
4. Learning Objectives
5. Key Terms
6. Teaching and Learning Activities
    Lecture Topics
    Discussion Topics
    Choosing Sides
    Knowledge Construction Activities
7. Resources for Instructors

1. TOTAL TEACHING PACKAGE OUTLINE

Chapter 16: Cognitive Development in Adolescence

Aspects of cognitive maturation	Guidepost for study 16.1
Piaget's Stage of Formal Operations	**Learning objectives 16.1, 16.3** **Knowledge construction activity 16.2**
Language development	**Learning objective 16.4** **Box 16.1 (text p. 399)**
Elkind: Immature characteristics of adolescent thought	**Learning objective 16.5** **Lecture topic 16.1** **Knowledge construction activities 16.1, 16.3** **Discussion topic 16.1**
Moral reasoning: Kohlberg's theory	**Guidepost for study 16.2** **Learning objective 16.2** **Box 16.2 (textbook p. 404)** **Lecture topic 16.2** **Knowledge construction activity 16.1**
Kohlberg's levels and stages	**Learning objective 16.6** **Knowledge construction activity 16.4**
Evaluating Kohlberg's theory	**Learning objective 16.7**
Educational and vocational issues	**Guidepost for study 16.3, 16.4**
Influences on school achievement	**Learning objectives 16.8-16.11,16.9, 16.10, 16.11** **Discussion topic 16.2** **Choosing sides 16.2**
Dropping out of high school	**Learning objective 16.12** **Knowledge construction activities 16.5, 16.6** **Independent study 16.1** **Choosing sides 16.3**
Educational and vocational preparation	**Learning objectives 16.13, 16.14** **Lecture topic 16.3** **Knowledge construction activity 16.5** **Choosing sides 16.1**

Please check out the online learning center located at www.mhhe.com/papaliacw9 for further information on these and other topics. There you can also access downloadable PowerPoint slides tailored to each chapter of the text and containing useful teaching notes as well as images and tables from the text itself.

2. EXPANDED OUTLINE (TRANSPARENCY READY)

I. Aspects of Cognitive Maturation
    A. Formal operations
        1. Hypothetical-deductive reasoning
    B. Adolescent egocentrism
        1. Imaginary audience
        2. Personal fable

II. Moral reasoning: Kohlberg's Theory
    A. Preconventional morality
    B. Conventional morality
    C. Postconventional morality

III. Educational and Vocational Issues
    A. Academic success and failure
        1. Self-efficacy
    B. Social capital
    C. Parental issues
    D. Social issues
    E. Gender issues

3. GUIDEPOSTS FOR STUDY

16.1 How do adolescents' thinking and use of language differ from younger children's?

16.2 On what basis do adolescents make moral judgments?

16.3 What influences affect success in secondary school and why do some students drop out?

16.4 What factors affect educational and vocational planning and preparation?

4. LEARNING OBJECTIVES

After completing the study of Chapter 16, students should be able to

16.1 Explain the difference between formal operational and concrete operational thinking, as exemplified by the pendulum problem.

16.2 Cite factors influencing adolescents' development of moral reasoning.

16.3 Evaluate strengths and weaknesses of Piaget's theory of formal operations.

16.4 Identify several characteristics of adolescents' language development that reflect cognitive advances.

16.5 Describe Elkind's six proposed aspects of immature adolescent thought and explain how they may grow out of the transition to formal operational thought.

16.6 List Kohlberg's levels and stages and discuss factors that influence how rapidly children and adolescents progress through them.

16.7 Evaluate Kohlberg's theory with regard to the role of emotion and socialization, family influences, gender, and cultural validity.

16.8 Explain how self-efficacy beliefs can contribute to adolescents' motivation to learn.

16.9 Assess the influences of parents and peers on academic achievement.

16.10 Discuss ethnic differences in attitudes toward school.

16.11 Give examples of educational practices that can help high school students do better.

16.12 Give reasons why some students drop out of school.

16.13 Discuss influences on educational and vocational planning.

16.14 Give evidence as to the value of part-time work for high school students.

5. KEY TERMS

Formal operations

Hypothetical-deductive reasoning

Imaginary audience

Personal fable

Preconventional morality

Conventional morality (or morality of conventional role conformity)

Postconventional morality (or morality of autonomous moral principles)

Social capital

3. TEACHING AND LEARNING ACTIVITIES

LECTURE TOPICS

LECTURE TOPIC 16.1: IS THERE AN IMAGINARY AUDIENCE?

It is a common assumption that adolescents become extremely self-conscious and critical of themselves. This can be manifest in many ways, such as prolonged primping before a mirror, reluctance to be in front of groups, dissatisfaction with certain body parts (nose, breasts, hair, and so on), embarrassment at being seen in public with family members, and even hypercritical remarks about others. This behavior is too pronounced and widespread to be due merely to situational factors. Elkind hypothesized that cognitive development allowed adolescents to lose egocentrism at the expense of gaining an imaginary audience. In other words, the adolescent feels as though an audience of perfect attributes is constantly watching and making judgments on his or her appearance and behavior. Thus, when this "audience" appears in a child's life, we should see an excess of the aforementioned self-critical behaviors.

There is actually very little evidence that an "imaginary audience" exists. It has been a convenient explanatory term, but little effort has been expended to empirically support it. David Elkind and Robert Bowen tested 697 fourth-, sixth-, eighth-, and twelfth-graders with a new Imaginary Audience Scale (IAS). This scale was designed to measure self-consciousness with regard to two aspects of the self—the transient self and the abiding self. The transient self consists of temporary appearances and behaviors (new haircut, accidentally dirtied clothes, slips of the tongue, awkward behavior, and so on). The abiding self refers to rather stable characteristics and abilities (intelligence, personality traits, and so on).

The 12-item test consisted of potentially embarrassing or self-revealing situations in which the subjects rated their willingness to participate. One transient-self item was "Suppose you went to a party that you thought was a costume party, but when you got there, you were the only person wearing a costume. You'd like to stay and have fun with your friends, but your costume is very noticeable. Would you stay or go home?" One abiding-self item was "If you went to a party where you did not know most of the kids, would you wonder what they were thinking about you?"

The results were generally consistent with Elkind and Bowen's predictions. The younger adolescents (eighth-graders) scored significantly higher on the IAS. That is, they were more self-conscious than the younger children and the older adolescents. The transient self and the abiding self were truly separate constructs; they did not correlate highly with each other. In addition, only the abiding self correlated with the lasting personality trait of self-esteem. As was expected, girls consistently were more self-conscious on both transient-self and abiding-self measures.

Further research with this technique will yield more evidence of the power the imaginary audience has on adolescent behavior. As suggested by the researchers, this may be useful for dealing with delinquents, unwed mothers, or even extreme introverts. Perhaps delinquents have no imaginary audience, whereas introverts are playing to an audience of thousands.

References

Elkind, D. (1967). Egocentrism in adolescence. *Child Development, 38,* 1025-1034.

Elkind, D., & Bowen, R. (1979). Imaginary-audience behavior in children and adolescents. *Developmental Psychology, 15,* 38-44.

LECTURE TOPIC 16.2: HISTORICAL DEFINITIONS OF MORALITY

It is a human characteristic to evaluate one's own actions and the actions of others. Yet the criteria for calling something good or bad vary from era to era. At times the meanings of good and bad emphasize the person's intentions, feelings, knowledge, or actions. During other historical periods, the emphasis is on the consequences of the act for others rather than on the actor's internal processes.

For example, in the seventeenth century the primary criterion for good and bad was the individual's feeling of pleasure and displeasure; Hume believed that one's own feelings were the basic guide to moral evaluation. In time, conflict grew between libertarians and those of traditional ethic. Libertarians are those who emphasize personal freedom and self-interested wishes for power, wealth, and beauty; individuals who subscribe to the traditional ethic believe in universal standards, suppress their own desires, and conform to the rules of benevolent authority. In the eighteenth century Kant argued that there were universal standards to which everyone was morally bound.

The dominant concept of the nineteenth century was that good and bad behaviors should be defined in terms of consequences, regardless of the actor's feelings, knowledge, or intentions. Note that one must still decide which consequences are relevant: effects on health, self-esteem, feelings, resources, or freedom.

Currently we seem to be emphasizing both individual freedom and the intention to be fair and honest. This is reflected in Kohlberg's Theory of Moral Development. Kagan suggests that both Piaget and Kohlberg are popular because their stages of moral development do not address specific situations.

There are significant cultural differences in defining morality. For example, in Western societies we emphasize that one should always be honest. However, in Japan it is considered ethically desirable to avoid telling the truth in order to preserve social harmony. Telling a lie under these circumstances is called *tatemae* by the Japanese. There are so many different values in Japan that, whatever one's personal values, someone will disapprove. It is important to be able to rely on a personal ethic to avoid self-condemnation.

Reference

Kagan, J. (1984) *The nature of the child.* New York: Basic Books.

LECTURE TOPIC 16.3: EMPLOYMENT IN ADOLESCENCE

Throughout history, opinions have diverged on the value of adolescents being employed. The most recent argument is that children in school are segregated from the rest of society, increasing the conflict and alienation they feel. According to the 1974 Panel on Youth of the President's Science Advisory Committee, holding a job "teaches adolescents responsibility and develops positive attitudes in them toward work, brings them into closer contact with adults from whom they can learn, and keeps them out of trouble." From this philosophy, the panel recommended: flexible school hours to allow for part-time jobs, lowering the minimum wage, and setting up more work/study programs.

How many high school students are actually working? In 1970, 16 percent of the girls aged 16 and 27 percent of the 16-year-old boys were attending high school and working part time. Current estimates are much higher: 30 percent of ninth and tenth graders and 50 percent of juniors and seniors in high school work. The hours worked by these young people are also increasing; 46 percent of the females and 56 percent of the males (age 16) worked more than 14 hours per week.

As yet, however, there is very little meaningful information on the effects of employment in adolescence. Does working build moral fiber and keep children out of trouble, or does it disrupt school achievement, educational plans, friendships, and family relationships? The data compiled here are from a survey of four California high schools conducted by Greenberger and Steinberg in 1978 and from interview information obtained from across the country by Sheila Cole. In some respects their findings were contrary to commonly held opinions on this topic. For instance, they found that youngsters do not get on-the-job training that is technically useful. This may be partially a result of the types of jobs available to adolescents. The six most frequent job categories were food service, retail sales and cashiering, manual labor, clerical work, operative and skilled labor, and cleaning. These jobs either require little training or call for skills that teens learned elsewhere before they are hired.

Another seemingly false notion is that, through working, teenagers will improve their rapport with adults. The surveys indicated that young people rarely feel close to the adults they work with.

To determine whether young people learn useful information about business on the job, Greenberger and Steinberg administered a questionnaire. One sample question was "When the owner of a record store talks about the store's market, she is referring to: (a) the place where she buys her records; (b) the people who are likely to buy records from her store; (c) the newspaper in which the store advertises record prices; (d) the place in which the records are actually displayed and sold." Students who had worked scored higher than students who had not. The higher scores seemed to be due to the work experience. The whole process of seeking a job teaches things about how society functions and what characteristics are necessary for success. Sometimes a great deal of ingenuity and perseverance is needed to get a job. Once a job is obtained, the employee must obtain a work permit and Social Security number and must fill out withholding-tax forms.

Jobs offer a chance to explore the possibilities of a career in a certain field. An aspiring veterinarian might get a job in a veterinary clinic, a potential banker might be a bank teller, and so on. However, few adolescents take or can find such opportunities.

One important aspect of students' employment is learning to deal with competing demands on their time. They must accept the responsibility of being at work while still meeting their obligations at school, at home, and to their friends. Working adolescents must often give up athletics, school activities, and outings with both friends and family. Meanwhile, on the job, they must learn not to let these demands distract them. They must be polite to rude customers, work even when they are tired, take over when someone else is sick or doesn't show up, and so on.

The main motivation to the teenagers themselves is, of course, the money they earn. With the money comes a freedom not enjoyed by those who must ask their parents for money. However, very few adolescents have any goals for which they are saving money. Working high school students have bought, sold, and used marijuana and alcohol more than their nonworking classmates. The researchers speculate that this is due to their having more money to spend.

One of the costs of employment is that working students have lower grade-point averages than nonworkers. Workers also reported disliking school more, being absent more often, and feeling less involved in school.

There are obvious benefits when adolescents work in society and contribute to it; there are also drawbacks. To prevent exploiting adolescents and to avoid "souring" them on society, both the positive and negative aspects need to be considered.

Reference

Greenberg, E., & Steinberg, L. (1986). *When teenagers work: The psychological and social costs of adolescent employment.* New York: Basic Books.

DISCUSSION TOPICS

DISCUSSION TOPIC 16.1: CONTRACEPTION AND THE PERSONAL FABLE

That teenagers are more sexually active today than in the past is an accepted fact of contemporary society. Elkind has argued that one reason why many teenagers fail to use contraception when engaging in sexual intercourse (even though they know about and have access to contraceptives) is that, as part of their cognitive development, they believe in a personal fable that gives them immunity not available to others. Discuss ways in which our society can deal with this problem. Two possibilities are to institute programs designed to teach more responsible sexual behavior or ones designed to accelerate cognitive development so that children experience the personal fable period before they are sexually mature. Discuss the implications and the feasibility of each approach.

DISCUSSION TOPIC 16.2: HIGH SCHOOL THEN AND NOW

Use this discussion topic to illustrate how the high school experience has changed over the past couple of generations and to establish what features of high school have remained the same. You will undoubtedly have students who are recent graduates, some who graduated more than 10 years ago, and perhaps some who graduated more than 20 years ago. If you have few students in the latter categories, ask students to prepare for the discussion by interviewing their parents and grandparents about their high school experiences. The object of this discussion is to sensitize students (particularly the younger ones) to the enduring features of the high school experience, while establishing what is truly different about the high school experience today.

INDEPENDENT STUDY

INDEPENDENT STUDY 16.1: ALTERNATIVE HIGH SCHOOL PROGRAM

If you have an alternative high school nearby for students at risk of dropping out, invite a teacher or counselor from that school to talk with your class about the dropout problem. In conjunction with the presentation, ask students to find high school dropouts and tape-record interviews with each about her or his experiences as a dropout and her or his thoughts and attitudes about education. Adult education facilities that offer GED (General Equivalency Diploma) training could serve as a resource for interviewees.

CHOOSING SIDES

CHOOSING SIDES 16.1: THE VALUE OF HIGHER EDUCATION

It is becoming increasingly apparent that the role of college education is being reevaluated by large segments of our population. The United States went through a period in the 1940s and 1950s in which college was the panacea for our economic and social ills. The student riots of the 1960s and 1970s alienated not only students but also the tax-paying public. Economic climate, unemployment, college costs, and declining enrollment are having drastic effects on college and postgraduate education. Have the students evaluate the lifelong implications of higher education by debating the following proposition.

> *The value of higher education has been exaggerated. College and graduate education are of little value in the individual's efforts to achieve personal and societal development and success.*

Pro: Several generations have been victimized by the myth that higher education will lead to higher incomes, higher values, and overall success. As shown by current social inequities, economic disasters, and political chicanery, we cannot solve all our problems by sitting at the feet of wise college professors and applying their solutions. It is time to limit the influence of self-perpetuating educational systems that fabricate unrealistic solutions and do little to train students for life situations and occupations. The ivory towers, if they continue to exist, need to solve real problems and train students for the real world. For far too long, universities have served as baby-sitters to keep young people out of the job market and to distort moral, religious, and political value systems. College limits the possible growth of individuals by requiring unnecessary classes and majors. Once out of college, the graduates have difficulty finding jobs. Personal satisfaction and economic success do not depend on a college education.

Con: The elimination of ignorance has been responsible for the tremendous advances in medicine, technology, human relations, and the standard of living in general. Even without the materialistic advantages attributable to education, the immeasurable literary, humanistic, artistic, and other cultural advances fostered by higher education and educational institutions are invaluable. Seeking knowledge itself is a higher goal than the materialistic benefits that such knowledge might bring. The aims of higher education should be to train minds, remove ignorance, present natural and human-made wonders, and promote the movement to more perfect social, cultural, economic, and political conditions. As imperfect as higher education might be today, it is of lifelong value to all participants.

The following lists give arguments that might be used to support each side of the debate.

Pro: Skeptical of the Value of a College Education
1. Graduates are having difficulty finding jobs after undergraduate and graduate school.

2. The university system is not providing the right kind of education. The classes are either so faddish that they are quickly outdated or so theoretical that they are irrelevant. In many schools the emphasis is on sports, not academics.
3. The publish-or-perish syndrome results in inferior instruction, graduate students teaching classes, and emphasis on research grants rather than students.
4. College is too expensive for the state and for the student. Income differences attributable to college duration are no longer substantial.
5. Most businesses and professions could design their own training and education programs. Research could similarly be privately fostered.
6. College isolates students from the problems and benefits of interacting in general society. This prolongs adolescence and distorts the "facts of life."
7. Higher education fosters an elitism based on prestige of one's school, type of degree, grade point average, fraternity or sorority membership, having the right connections or recommendations, and so on.

Con: In Support of a College Education
1. General education preserves the cultural heritage of our civilization.
2. College degrees are required for most leadership, business, and technological positions in the job market.
3. The isolation of college allows for exploring alternatives and developing oneself more fully and creatively. Discussing different ideas and philosophies will not cost a person a job.
4. Compared to the long-term gains (economic, inventive technology, culture, and the like), the cost of college is relatively small.
5. The greatest minds and forgers of world policy teach or are educated and stimulated at colleges.
6. The research at universities may or may not have practical applications. Basic research is the foundation of later technology. The libraries needed to support such research and education are themselves invaluable.

References
College in 2000: Is less more? (Jan. 26, 1980). *Science News, 117*, 55.
Engel, P. (January 1980). Harvard's soft core. *The Washington Monthly,* 43-50.

CHOOSING SIDES 16.2: ADOLESCENCE AND WORKING

What are the pros and cons of high school students' holding jobs? Would you encourage a teenager who did not have to get a job to wait or, by all means, to get a part-time job now?

The majority of high school students are members of the workforce, and "having a job" currently has more status than athletics or academics. In fact, some educators are worried about the number of students who do not have school as an important priority; they find that these students have had to cut back on homework assignments because their long working hours keep them from completing the school work at more than a poor level.

Many people feel that teenagers should go to work in order to increase the family income. Interestingly, more middle class teenagers than low-class teenagers are working. More part-time jobs are available in the affluent suburbs, and poor teenagers have more difficulty arranging transportation to work.

Some individuals maintain that teenagers should work because working teaches responsibility, reliability, teamwork, and the value of the dollar. Others disagree and believe that work disrupts the students' planning for future careers by encouraging them to devalue school learning. Because many working teenagers do not need money, they may learn "premature affluence" rather than the dollar's value—they learn about spending and immediate gratification rather than economy. Some experts even believe the availability of money and the stress that arises from having a job contribute to the high rate of alcohol and drug use among teenagers.

One definable position would be to suggest that work is a positive growth experience as long as the teenager keeps his or her work hours down to a reasonable level, such as 12 hours during the week and 6 more hours during the weekend. The state of Florida has officially taken an "all things in moderation" approach by passing in 1986 a law that limits high school students to 30 hours of work a week. What do you think?

KNOWLEDGE CONSTRUCTION ACTIVITIES

KNOWLEDGE CONSTRUCTION ACTIVITY 16.1: GENERATIVE TERMS

This activity will use the principles of generative learning as explained in the Introduction to assist students in gaining a better understanding of terms. Divide the class into groups of four or five. Assign each group the task of generating an example for a generative term from this chapter. The example that each group creates cannot be one that has been used in the class or in the book. They must think of a new application for the term that they are given. Groups are allowed to use their books and notes. By creating their own example of the term, they demonstrate an understanding of the term to the level of application. There are several approaches that can be used in this exercise. Students may be given the entire list at once, but often one group will finish far ahead of the others and topics will get out of sequence. Another strategy is to give all of the groups the same term to create an example and then go around the room to discuss outcomes. This has been very successful, but also takes the most time. A third approach is to give each group a different term and see what examples they can generate.

Some generative terms for Chapter 16 are listed below.

Formal operational thinking
Hypothetical-deductive reasoning
Imaginary audience
Personal fable
Preconventional morality

Conventional morality
Postconventional morality
Self-efficacy in the school setting
Social capital

KNOWLEDGE CONSTRUCTION ACTIVITY 16.2: PIAGET'S PENDULUM PROBLEM

The text describes Piaget's pendulum problem. Have students present this problem to a school-age child, a high school student, and a college student. The object of the task is to determine which of the following factors (alone or combined) directly affect(s) the speed of the oscillation: (a) length of string, (b) weight of object, (c) height from which object is dropped, and (d) force used to push it. Materials necessary include string and several different weights. To exhibit formal operations, it is not necessary to correctly solve the problem (length of string) but only to eliminate alternatives systematically.

KNOWLEDGE CONSTRUCTION ACTIVITY 16.3: PERSONAL EXPERIENCES WITH EGOCENTRISM

Ask students to write about their own experiences with adolescent egocentrism, and ask them to share their writings with the class. In conjunction with this project, you can provide excerpts from Salinger's *The Catcher in the Rye*. Ask students to compare Holden's experiences with adolescent egocentrism with their own.

KNOWLEDGE CONSTRUCTION ACTIVITY 16.4: HEINZ' DILEMMA

If you have not used Kohlberg's moral dilemmas in earlier units, do so now. The classic poor Heinz dilemma in which the man's wife is dying can be used, or you can devise a dilemma that is more relevant to students. For example, ask students what should be done with a student who is failing a course and cheats on an exam in order to obtain the passing grade that will enable him or her to retain financial aid and thus remain in school. Collect the responses, and ask a group of students to classify them according to Kohlberg's stages. Summarize the results for later class discussion.

KNOWLEDGE CONSTRUCTION ACTIVITY 16.5: SCHOOL DROPOUTS

Some statistics about student dropouts follow. The task for students is to decide what they would do to keep students in schools. In other words, what can be done to improve these statistics?

The national dropout rate is between 25 and 30 percent of students. The typical high school graduation includes only 70 percent of its ninth-grade class members. One result is that approximately one-third of the adult population is functionally illiterate.

States with the lowest dropout rates:		States with the highest dropout rates:	
North Dakota	5%	Louisiana	43%
Minnesota	9%	Florida	35%
Delaware	11%	Mississippi	35%
Iowa	12%	Tennessee	35%
South Dakota	15%	Georgia	34%

It is possible to spot regional differences in dropout rates, but even more noticeable is the effect of family economics on dropout statistics.

Dropout rates by family income:

Low income	22.3%	Low middle	13.2%
High-middle	10.7%	High	7.0%

Reference

U.S. Dept. of Education, Education Commission of the States, National Center for Education Statistics

KNOWLEDGE CONSTRUCTION ACTIVITY 16.6: CAREER ASPIRATIONS OF HIGH SCHOOL STUDENTS

With your classmates, create a survey for high school seniors. Try to get answers to the following questions:

1. What are your plans for next year?

2. How did you decide which direction to go into?

3. What are you hoping for in the next year?

4. What do you expect college or a job to be like?

5. What are your long-term goals in life?

6. How do your plans for next year fit into those long-term goals?

7. Who helped you to make your decisions?

After creating your survey, collect data from a variety of locations. This is a good activity to do over a semester break when you might be at home and high schoolers are still in school.

Compile your data with your classmates' to develop a picture of contemporary students' plans.

Do urban, rural, and suburban seniors have different expectations and aspirations?

How realistic or idealistic do these students seem to be about their own futures?

If you were a high school guidance counselor, what might you tell seniors to expect from college?

How are high school seniors different than when you were in that position? How are they the same?

7. RESOURCES FOR INSTRUCTORS

Books and Journal Articles

Crockett, L., & Crouter, A. (1995). *Pathways through adolescence.* Mahwah, NJ: Lawrence Erlbaum Associates.

deRosenroll, D. A. (1987). Early adolescent egocentrism: A review of six articles. *Adolescence, 22,* 791-802

Elkind, D. (1984). *All grown up and no place to go.* Reading, MA: Addison-Wesley.

Greenberger, E., & Steinberg, L. (1986). *When teenagers work: The psychological and social costs of adolescent employment.* New York: Basic Books

Inhelder, B., & Piaget, J. (1958). *The growth of logical thinking, from childhood to adolescence.* Boston: Little, Brown.

Sandberg, D. E., Ehrhardt, A. A., Mellins, C. A., Ince, S. E., & Meyer-Bahlburg, H. F. L. (1987). The influence of individual and family characteristics upon career aspirations of girls during childhood and adolescence. *Sex Roles, 16,* 649-668.

Sternberg, R. J. (1988). *Intelligence applied.* San Diego, CA: Harcourt.

Wagner, J. A. (1987). Formal operations and ego identity in adolescence. *Adolescence, 22,* 23-25.

Video resources

Cognitive Development (IM, 1990, 30 min.). Focuses on Piaget's theory and criticisms of that theory to describe stages of cognitive development. Looks at development of thought, reasoning, memory, and language.

Culture, Time, and Place (IM, 1992, 30 min.). Shows how language, school, and relationships bring about acculturation about attitudes, values, and beliefs.

Development and Diversity (IM, 1992, 30 min.). Explores historical and cultural definitions of childhood. Probes the prolongations of infancy and childhood; looks at children in different countries.

Dialogues: Dr. Jean Piaget with Dr. Barbel Inhelder (Association Films, 1969, 2 parts, 40 min. each). In Part 1, Piaget and Inhelder discuss their theories and relationship to American psychology. Part 2 focuses on Freud, the Jensen controversy, and applications of Piaget's theory in various countries.

Jean Piaget (IM, 1969, 2 parts, 40 min. each). This 2-part interview with the developmental psychologist illuminates key concepts of his theory.

Learning (IM, 1990, 30 min.). Presents information about classical and operant conditioning. Includes a special focus on helping hyperactive children with operant conditioning.

Shortchanging Girls, Shortchanging America (IM, 1992, video, 19 min.). This program interviews educators and business leaders to illuminate the devastating effects of gender bias in schools. It calls upon educators to encourage girls to develop math and science skills.

Teenage Mind and Body (IM, 1992, video, 30 min.). Looks at Elkind's ideas about the contrast between teenagers' abilities and interests and parents' hopes, formal operations, social cognition, and moral development.

17 PSYCHOSOCIAL DEVELOPMENT IN ADOLESCENCE

THE SEARCH FOR IDENTITY
Erikson: Identity versus Identity Confusion
Marcia: Identity Status—Crisis and Commitment
Gender Differences in Identity Formation
Ethnic Factors in Identity Formation
Elkind: The Patchwork Self

SEXUALITY
Sexual Orientation
Sexual Behavior
Sexual Risk Taking
Teenage Pregnancy and Childbearing

RELATIONSHIPS WITH FAMILY, PEERS, AND ADULT SOCIETY
Is Adolescent Rebellion a Myth?
How Adolescents Spend Their Time—and with Whom
Adolescents and Parents
Adolescents and Siblings
Peers and Friends
Antisocial Behavior and Juvenile Delinquency

IS THERE A "UNIVERSAL ADOLESCENT"?

In This Chapter of Your Instructor's Manual You Will Find:
1. Total Teaching Package Outline
2. Expanded Outline (transparency-ready)
3. Guideposts for Study
4. Learning Objectives
5. Key Terms
6. Teaching and Learning Activities
    Lecture Topics
    Discussion
    Independent Studies
    Choosing Sides
    Knowledge Construction Activities
7. Resources for Instructors

1. TOTAL TEACHING PACKAGE OUTLINE

Chapter 17: Psychosocial Development in Adolescence

The search for identity	**Guidepost for study 17.1**
Erikson: Identity versus identity confusion	**Learning objective 17.1** **Lecture topic 17.1** **Knowledge construction activity 17.2**
Marcia: Identity status—Crisis and commitment	**Learning objective 17.2** **Discussion topic 17.4** **Lecture topic 17.2** **Knowledge construction activity 175** **Knowledge construction activity 17.1**
Gender differences in identity formation	**Learning objective 17.3**
Ethnic factors in identity formation	**Learning objective 17.3**
Elkind: The patchwork self	**Learning objective 17.4**
Sexuality	**Lecture topic 17.4**
Sexual orientation	**Guidepost for study 17.2** **Learning objective 17.5**
Sex Behavior	**Learning objective 17.6, 17.7** **Choosing sides 17.1** **Lecture topic 17.5**
Sexual risk taking	**Guidepost for study 17.3** **Learning objective 17.8**
Teenage pregnancy and childbearing	**Guidepost for study 17.4** **Learning objectives 17.9-17.11** **Box 17.1 (textbook p. 429)** **Discussion topic 17.1** **Knowledge construction activity 17.3**
Relationships with family, peers, and adult society	**Guidepost for study 17.6**
Is adolescent rebellion a myth?	**Guidepost for study 17.5** **Learning objective 17.12** **Lecture topic 17.6** **Discussion topic 17.2** **Independent study 17.1**
Adolescents and parents	**Guidepost for study 17.6** **Learning objectives 17.14, 17.15** **Lecture topic 17.1** **Knowledge construction activity 17.4**
Adolescents and siblings	**Guidepost for study 17.6**
Peers and friends	**Learning objectives 17.16, 17.17** **Lecture topic 17.2**

Antisocial behavior and juvenile delinquency	**Guidepost for study 17.7** **Learning objectives 17.18, 17.79** **Box 17.2 (textbook p. 438)** **Discussion topic 17.4** **Knowledge construction activities 17.1, 17.5** **Independent study 17.2**
Is there a "universal adolescent"?	**Guidepost for study 17.8** **Learning objective 17.20**

Please check out the online learning center located at www.mhhe.com/papaliacw9 for further information on these and other topics. There you can also access downloadable PowerPoint slides tailored to each chapter of the text and containing useful teaching notes as well as images and tables from the text itself.

2. EXPANDED OUTLINE (TRANSPARENCY READY)

I. The Search for Identity
    A. Identity versus role confusion
    B. Identity statuses
        1. Crisis
        2. Commitment
        3. Identity achievement
        4. Foreclosure
        5. Moratorium
        6. Identity diffusion
    C. Gender differences
    D. Patchwork self
II. Sexuality
    A. Sexual orientation
        1. Heterosexual
        2. Homosexual
        3. Bisexual
        4. Teenage pregnancy
III. Relationships with Family, Peers, and Adult Society
    A. Adolescent rebellion
    B. Adolescents and parents
    C. Family conflict
    D. Siblings
    E. Peers and friends
    F. Antisocial behavior and juvenile delinquency
    G. Youth violence

3. GUIDEPOSTS FOR STUDY

17.1 How do adolescents form an identity?

17.2 What determines sexual orientation?

17.3 What sexual practices are common among adolescents and what leads some to engage in risky sexual behavior?

17.4 How common is teenage pregnancy, and what are its usual outcomes?

17.5 How typical is "adolescent rebellion"?

17.6 How do adolescents relate to parents, siblings, and peers?

17.7 What are the root causes of antisocial behavior and juvenile delinquency and what can be done to reduce these and other risks of adolescence?

17.8 How does adolescence vary across cultures and what are some common psychosocial features?

4. LEARNING OBJECTIVES

After completing the study of Chapter 17, the student should be able to:

17.1 List the three major issues involved in identity formation, according to Erikson.

17.2 Describe four types of identity status found by Marcia.

17.3 Discuss how gender and ethnicity can affect identity formation.

17.4 Distinguish the two paths of identity development described by Elkind and explain how he links risky behavior with the patchwork self.

17.5 Discuss theories and research regarding origins of sexual orientation.

17.6 Describe trends in sexual attitudes and activity among adolescents.

17.7 Discuss factors in homosexual identity and relationship formation.

17.8 Identify and discuss factors that increase the risks of sexual activity.

17.9 Identify ways to prevent teenage pregnancy.

17.10 Summarize trends in teenage pregnancy and birthrates.

17.11 Discuss problems and outcomes of teenage pregnancy.

17.12 Assess the extent of adolescent rebellion and of storm and stress during the teenage years.

17.13 Identify age and cultural differences in how young people spend their time and discuss their significance.

17.14 Identify factors that affect conflict with parents.

17.15 Discuss the impact on adolescents of parenting styles and of marital status, mothers' employment, and socioeconomic status.

17.16 Describe characteristics that affect adolescents' popularity.

17.17 Discuss important features of adolescent friendships.

17.18 Explain why parental and peer influences on antisocial behavior interact to promote delinquency.

17.19 Give examples of programs that have been successful in preventing or stopping delinquency and other risky behavior.

17.20 Identify cross-cultural commonalities and differences in adolescents' self-image, attitudes, and personalities.

5. KEY TERMS

Identity versus identity confusion

Identity statuses

Crisis

Commitment

Identity achievement

Foreclosure

Moratorium

Identity diffusion

Patchwork self

Sexual orientation

Heterosexual

Homosexual

Bisexual

Adolescent rebellion

6. TEACHING AND LEARNING ACTIVITIES

LECTURE TOPICS

LECTURE TOPIC 17.1: ABSENCE MAKES THE HEART GROW FONDER: PARENTS AND ADOLESCENTS

One of the individual's major decisions in adolescence is whether to go to college. As far as uprooting and finances are concerned, the decision of whether to live at home and commute to college, or to board away from home on or near the college campus is also difficult. Staying at home may offer emotional stability, continuance of old friendships (or love), better access to jobs, and perhaps the last long-term chance to be with the family. Moving away to college, however, may foster independence, self-sufficiency, interaction with a broader cross-section of persons, and a chance to avoid everyday family conflicts. Interesting comparisons were made between parents and their commuting versus college-boarding sons in a study by Sullivan and Sullivan. These researchers investigated how separation affected the communication, independence, satisfaction, affection, and mother-father relationship of parents and their boys who either stayed at home or lived at college.

The boys, from 12 New York, Massachusetts, and New Jersey high schools, and their parents were tested during the boys' senior year in high school (college choices having already been completed). Of those tested, a total of 104 boys boarded at college, with 51 of their mothers and 36 of their fathers also participating in the study. The remaining 138 tested were commuters, and 41 of their mothers and 29 of their fathers took part in the study. After approximately one month at college in the fall, parents and sons again filled out the questionnaires they had answered the previous spring.

The most consistent finding was that going away to college changed the reported perceptions of affection between parents and sons. The boarder sons reported, "increases in their parents' affection toward them, their own affection toward their parents, and the total affection in their relationships with their parents." The mothers of boarders similarly reported sensing more affection from their sons. The fathers did not report noticing any difference. The commuter sons and their parents did not indicate any effectual changes. In the spring pretest, no differences in affection were found among any of the groups. This does appear to be an emotional benefit attributable to separation. Perhaps the boarders were a bit homesick after one month at school.

Boarders also thought that the total communication between them and their parents had improved. Parents of boarders, however, did not perceive any great change. There were again no reported differences between spring and fall testing for the commuter group. Boarders were not any different from commuters in the spring communication pretest. A lack of actual measures of communication (letters, phone calls, visits, and so on) makes it impossible to know whether communication actually changed with the boarders.

The results of growth of independence were not strongly supportive of any feeling of greater independence by the boarders or the commuters. The boarders reported that their feelings of independence from their parents increased, but the increase was not substantial. Also, the mothers and most fathers did not think that there was a higher degree of independence in their relationships with their sons. The exception was the group of fathers whose sons moved at least 200 miles away. They thought their sons were more dependent!

With regard to satisfaction with their independence, both boarders and commuters were more satisfied after one month at college. The boarders, however, had higher scores on this point, while both at high school and at college. Perhaps the eventual boarding students were looking forward to independence away from home.

Adolescence puts an individual in the paradoxical position of wanting to increase her or his independence, but at the same time wanting to improve or maintain emotional and communication bonds with parents. As pointed out by Sullivan and Sullivan, parents have this same perplexing problem. Perhaps going away to college helps develop individuality and strengthens or at least maintains bonding relationships. In order to strengthen these findings, the study needs to be conducted with females and after a longer period of separation from home.

Reference

Sullivan, K., & Sullivan, A. (1980). Adolescence-parent separation, *Developmental Psychology, 16,* 93-99.

LECTURE TOPIC 17.2: PARENTAL AND PEER INFLUENCE ON ADOLESCENT ATTITUDES

A survey was administered to samples of teenagers in 1963, 1976, and 1982, to assess whether parents or peers are turned to for advice on 18 social issues. A total of 570 subjects were used in this research.

Rather than finding that adolescents turn only to the peer group or only to parents for advice, Sebald found that different issues were addressed to each group. On the whole, parental advice was sought for financial, educational, and career concerns, and peer advice was sought for social concerns. The issue on which both boys and girls were most likely to seek parental advice was whether or not to attend college (over 60 percent asked their parents), and the next highest amount of parental advice was sought about future career concerns (averaging 57 percent). How to spend money and which courses to take in school were also issues on which much parental advice was sought.

Teenagers were unlikely to seek parental advice on which magazines to buy, what clubs to join, how to dress, what social events to attend, what hobbies to pursue, what books to read, and how intimate to be on a date (parents were asked about these issues by only 5 to 11 percent of the subjects).

The opposite picture emerged on peer advice—friends were consulted frequently about social events (over 70 percent), club memberships (over 63 percent), and clothing (about 55 percent). At least half of the subjects consulted peers about magazine buying, whom to date, and whether to drink. Peers were seldom asked about future careers, college decisions, finances, and course selections.

In the 1976 data, the girls were more parent oriented on 17 of the 18 issues than were the boys. For example, 55 percent of the girls, but only 31 percent of the boys, thought it was important to get parental opinions about spending money, and 17 percent of the girls, but only 4 percent of the boys, thought parental opinion was important in deciding whom to date. However, the 1982 data indicated a shift in gender differences—girls were only more parent oriented on 6 of the 18 issues, and the gender differences were quite small. Girls had become somewhat less parent oriented, and boys had become somewhat more parent oriented on several issues. Boys sought parental advice on personal problems, choosing a spouse, choosing a career, and how to dress.

In 1976, boys were more peer oriented in 16 of 18 scales; in 1982, boys were more peer oriented in only 6 of 18 scales. Girls were more likely to seek peer advice than were boys on personal problems, sex information, and clothing decisions. Boys were more likely than girls to seek peer advice on money issues, dating, hobbies, intimacy decisions, and drinking.

Sebald suggests that parental orientation has increased over the last two decades, especially for boys. He also concludes that there is little conflict on orientation issues—the split in parental or peer advice depends on the social issue topic. The dual reference groups for advice on issues also reflect how adolescents spend their time—they do more work activities with parents and more recreational activities with peers. Finally, Sebald concludes that the fewest gender differences were found in the most recent sample because gender roles are changing significantly.

Reference

Sebald, H. (1986). Adolescents' shifting orientation toward parents and peers: A curvilinear trend over recent decades. *Journal of Marriage and the Family, 48*, 5-13.

LECTURE TOPIC 17.3: THE BIOLOGY BEHIND SEXUAL BEHAVIOR PATTERNS

One approach to understanding sexual behavior is to see our sex organs as evolving from our social habits, which were partly structured by our food-gathering style. Sociobiologists are fairly good at predicting the sexual behaviors of species from either their genital anatomy or from their food-gathering techniques. There are a few general guidelines.

1. In species where the males are much larger than the females, there is more male promiscuity.
2. There are more differences in secondary sexual characteristics in polygynous species.
3. Males of species that have frequent intercourse and/or are promiscuous tend to have bigger testes.

Using these guidelines, let us look at the typical patterns for humans and some primates:

1. **Gibbons** are basically monogamous. The male and female are about the same size, and their secondary sexual characteristics are very similar.

2. **Gorillas** are a species in which the males weigh twice as much as the females. A male gorilla is likely to have from three to six females. Size is an advantage in getting rid of other males who want to compete for females. The testes of a gorilla are small. Even though the male has several females, the sex act occurs only a few times a year; the female gorilla doesn't resume sexual intercourse for at least 3 years after giving birth.

3. **Chimpanzees** of both sexes weigh about the same, yet the chimpanzees are promiscuous creatures. They exist in a group of females attended by a group of the mates. Chimpanzees have the biggest testes, which weigh about 4 ounces (compared to about 1½ ounces for human males, and about 1¼ ounces for the gorilla).

4. **Humans** are a species in which males are slightly bigger than females. Depending on social norms, human males marry one or more women. Because the human female is receptive year round, the male's testes are larger than average. It is harder to explain why human males have the largest penis of all primates, or why only the human female has large breasts that are noticeable even before the first pregnancy.

Part of the sociobiology theory is that natural selection causes animals to evolve anatomically and behaviorally such that organisms maximize the numbers and viability of their offspring. The more controversial part of sociobiology is the belief that natural selection has also shaped our social behavior, such as monogamy, marriage, and extramarital affairs. And even here, our human reasoning power lets us make moral choices that override our genes.

Reference
Weisser, W., & Coleman, B. (April 1985). Everything else you always wanted to know about sex. *Discovery*, 70-82. ? Au: vol no?

LECTURE TOPIC 17.4: TEENAGE SEXUALITY

In recent years sexual activity among young teenagers has increased. Currently, it is estimated that one-third of the females and nearly half of the males are sexually active before their sixteenth birthday. Let us look both at the factors influencing this trend and at the concerns this trend produces.

The factors that have apparently tended to promote earlier sexual activity include biological changes, changes in family structure and atmosphere, peer influences, media influences, and philosophical changes. The most significant biological change has been earlier menarche, but because this has decreased slowly over generations and the trend toward earlier sexual activity is more sudden and recent, it probably plays a small role in developing the trend. It does, of course, have a considerable effect on the possible consequences of early sexual activity.

There are many changes in family styles that can influence this trend. Parents, for example, have a greater tendency to spend time with other adults and expect their children to find their own things to do. More adolescents are lonely, are put in pseudo-adult roles, and turn to peers for support. It has also been found that teenage girls in fatherless homes are more likely to be sexually active than those in two-parent homes.

Peers may put a lot of pressure on teenagers to be sexually active. Some feel a lot of pressure to lose their virginity, reversing the emphasis of two previous generations. Because of mass technology, today's teenagers have a huge peer group to communicate with through the media. The media also use sexuality to sell merchandise to adolescents and, therefore, affect how much and what teens think about sex.

Concerns focus on three major areas: pregnancy, sexual health, and sexual readiness. Teenage *pregnancy* is very common: This year one million females under the age of 20 will become pregnant. Some of them will be elementary school students. Studies suggest that 6 out of 10 adolescents do not use contraceptives the first time they have intercourse.

Moreover, one in five teens who do not want to get pregnant are still not using birth control. Concerns about *sexual health* include the amount of venereal disease in the adolescent population. Research findings suggest early sexual intercourse is correlated with the incidence of cervical cancer.

The biggest issue of all is probably *sexual readiness*. Adolescents may be having sexual intercourse when they have knowledge but not understanding, and before they are emotionally ready. Jane Loevinger has a scale of ego development that suggests that the average sixth grader is operating on an impulsive level and that most ninth graders are in a conformist stage. A third stage is the conscientious stage, when individuals think about long-term goals and responsibilities. Some junior high students are in this stage, but this level of maturity has still not been reached by the majority of high school seniors. Our sexual biology and societal pressure seem to ready us for sexual activity long before we are emotionally ready.

Reference

Thornton, A. (1990). The courtship process and adolescent sexuality. *Journal of Family Issues, 11*, 239-273.

LECTURE TOPIC 17.5: THE CASE FOR SEX EDUCATION IN THE SCHOOLS

The following 1985 statistics suggest a need for sex education in the schools:

1. More than one million teenage girls will be pregnant this year.
2. Four in 10 girls will get pregnant at least once during their teen years.
3. Of the 29 million young people between the ages of 13 and 19, approximately 12 million are sexually active.
4. The average age for becoming sexually active is 16 years old.
5. Of 13- to 14-year-olds, 6 percent of girls and 18 percent of boys are sexually active.
6. Female teenagers make up 18 percent of the females of childbearing years, but they account for 46 percent of all single-parent births, and for 31 percent of all abortions.
7. Approximately 1.3 million children are being raised by teenage mothers; about half of these teenage mothers are unmarried.
8. Only 11 percent of teenage mothers ages 13-15 graduate from high school. One-third live in poverty.
9. Teenage mothers make seven times as many suicide attempts as teenage girls without children.
10. The infant mortality rate is twice as high for babies born to mothers under 15 than for babies born to mothers in their twenties.

11. One in seven pregnancies of teenage mothers involves a girl who has already given birth to at least one child.
12. In a 1980 Gallup poll, 87 percent of Americans were found to support sex education and courses in marriage and family living for the public schools.
13. Sex education does not seem to affect the amount of sexual activity, but teenagers who have had sex education are more likely to use birth control and less likely to become pregnant.

For sex education programs to be successful and accepted by the public, four general guidelines are suggested:

1. Sex education should include instruction on attitudes and values as well as factual information.
2. Sex education should be presented in a family context.
3. Precise, dignified language and presentation style are important. An effort should be made to debunk myths.
4. Sex education should begin in kindergarten and progress in a developmental fashion through the school years. However, current law requires sexuality to focus upon abstinence-only models or the school faces the loss of funds.

References

Gullotta, T., Adams, G., & Montemayor, R. (eds) (1992). *Adolescent sexuality*. Newbury Park, CA.

Vance, P. C. (March/April 1985). Love and sex: Can we talk about that in school? *Childhood Education, 61,* 272-276.

LECTURE TOPIC 17.6: VALUE SYSTEMS OF ADOLESCENCE

As pointed out in the text, judgments about adolescents' behaviors and attitudes tend toward polar stereotypes. On the one hand, adolescence is thought of as a time of idealism, of struggling for principles, and of seeking truth. On the other hand, adolescents are thought to be rebellious, emotional, selfish, and inconsiderate. Unfortunately, the latter viewpoint is the more prevalent. This lecture will nevertheless focus on the ideals or values thought to be important by adolescents.

Adelson believes that neither viewpoint is correct and points out his studies, which suggest that the political ideology of adolescents does not conform to any simple stereotype. He bluntly states that, because they lack cognitive maturity, very few adolescents up through high school have any consistent ideologies from which specific structured attitudes follow. Adolescents do not have the introspective-reflective power that many "idealists" attribute to adolescents. Adelson found adolescents to be reflective of parental attitudes and values rather than rebellious (see also Gallatin).

Developmental studies of adolescents' value systems do show interesting consistencies. Feather summarizes the relatively scant amount of ? Au: Add Feather to ref list? developmental literature available from both the United States and Australia. One notable study by Beech and Schoeppe ? Au: Add to ref list? had fifth, seventh, ninth, and eleventh graders rank, in order of importance, 18 terminal values (goals to accomplish in life) and 18 instrumental values (personality characteristics). This value survey was developed by Rokeach. The terminal values included a comfortable life, an exciting life, a sense of accomplishment, a world at peace, and a world of beauty, equality, family security, freedom, happiness, inner harmony, mature love, national security, pleasure, salvation, self-respect, social recognition, true friendship, and wisdom. The instrumental values included being ambitious, broad minded, capable, cheerful, clean, courageous, forgiving, helpful, honest, imaginative, independent, intellectual, logical, loving, obedient, polite, responsible, and self-controlled. Have your class rank the items in these lists from most important to least important, and see whether they agree with Beech and Schoeppe's 1969 New York City and Feather's 1971 Australian findings.

Beech and Schoeppe found consistencies and differences between the boys and the girls. In general, boys and girls highly valued peace, freedom, equality, honesty, love, and family security, whereas salvation, logicality, and imagination were devalued by both sexes. As far as general differences are concerned, family security rankings were similar for younger but not for older boys and girls. Older boys and girls agreed on equality and social recognition more than younger boys and girls did. It was suggested that all these rankings are influenced by current events and situations (for example, the Vietnam War) and therefore can change. However, Feather found similar results with his later study in a different Western culture.

References

Adelson, J. (ed.) (1980). *Handbook of Adolescent Psychology*. Somerset, NJ: Wiley.
Greenspan, S., & Pollock, G. (1991). *The course of life: Adolescence*. Madison, CT: International Universities Press, Inc.
Kurtines, W., & Gewirtz, J. (Eds) (1991). *Handbook of moral behavior and development*. Hillsdale, NJ: Lawrence Erlbaum Associates.

DISCUSSION TOPICS

DISCUSSION TOPIC 17.1: EVALUATING PREGNANCY-PREVENTION PROGRAMS

Ask your class for their evaluations of the three suggestions made in Box 16-1 about ways in which we can lower the high rate of teenage pregnancy. What do they see as the major problems of each approach? Each of these suggestions has been advocated for a number of years. Why, then, have we made so little progress? Are the programs ineffective, or have we been ineffective in implementing them? Do class members have other suggestions for curbing teenage pregnancies? If your class seems reluctant to discuss this issue, try an outlandish suggestion as a way to spark discussion. Suggest that all children from the age of 9 onward should be tested every 6 months for sexual maturity. When they reach sexual maturity, suggest that they be surgically implanted with a beeper mechanism to alert their parents when they engage in sexual activity.

DISCUSSION TOPIC 17.2: STORM AND STRESS

Adolescence is a broad period of development during which individuals change considerably. Although many adolescents do not exhibit outright rebellion against their parents, frequent arguments and conflicts between teenagers and their parents are a nearly universal experience. Discuss Hall's concept of adolescence as "storm and stress" by asking your class to pinpoint the age at which they experienced the greatest amount of conflict with their parents. Is the point closer to the early teen years (12, 13, 14), the middle years (14, 15, 16) or the later years (16, 17, 18)? Does the point correspond less to a specific year and more to a developmental time period (prepubertal, puberty, postpuberty)?

DISCUSSION TOPIC 17.3: IS FORECLOSURE SUCH A BAD THING?

The discussion of identity formation in the text leaves the impression that the only way to achieve a "true" identity is by working through the arduous process yourself. The impression is given that the identity achieved through foreclosure is somehow a lesser or a false identity. Discuss with your class the differences between societies where roles are highly fixed and, therefore, identities are very stable and determined mostly through foreclosure, and societies such as our own where you can be almost anything you want to be. Nostalgically we often long for the earlier times in our society, where we assume (probably mistakenly) that problems were fewer and solutions simpler. Would anyone in your class like to go back to the times when women grew up to become wives and mothers only, and men grew up largely to follow in their fathers' footsteps? Are there people for whom foreclosure is a better way to achieve an identity?

DISCUSSION TOPIC 17.4: VIOLENT TEENAGERS

Juvenile delinquency has always been around, but many experts believe that the amount and degree of violence among youth are increasing. For example, some youths are enjoying participation in "wilding," which involves finding people to torment and hurt for no purpose other than to brutally harm others. Nearly 90 percent of the American people think that teenage violence is a bigger problem today than it was in the past. Do you agree? If so, why? Have students discuss the causes of teen violence (you may wish to list their ideas on the blackboard) and what can be done about these contributing factors. Here's a list of potential causes: genetic factors (among males, testosterone rises rapidly during puberty), family violence (both for modeling violence and for causing neurological damage that may increase violent tendencies), poverty (one in five teens is raised below the poverty level; they may perceive that there are fewer avenues out of poverty now), family neglect (young parents, career parents), failure of education (more than 25 percent of teens drop out of school; even some graduates are functional illiterates), violent television (by age 16, children have seen 33,000 murders and at least 200,000 acts of violence on TV), movies (the increase in sadistic films), recorded music (especially heavy-metal lyrics that encourage violence, including rape and incest), comic books (lots of bondage, torture, and killings), sex in advertising, and lack of positive alternatives. What can help to reduce teenage violence?

References

Eron, L., Gentry, J., & Schlegel, P. (Eds.) (1994). *Reason to hope: A Psychological Prospective on violence and youth.* Washington, DC: American Psychological Association.

Goldstein, A. (1991). *Delinquent gangs: A psychological perspective.* Champaign, IL: Research Press.

INDEPENDENT STUDIES

INDEPENDENT STUDY 17.1: GANG ACTIVITIES

Have students research gang activity in the area and then discuss how gangs are involved in the identity process with teenagers. What alternatives would need to be provided for teens to counteract the impact of gangs? What parts of the identity process can be linked to gang membership?

INDEPENDENT STUDY 17.2: HIGH SCHOOL ACTIVITIES

Have your students go to a high school and observe typical adolescent activities. For example, attend a pep rally, a football or basketball game (or whatever sport is important in your local area), a school dance, graduation ceremonies, and so on. What is important to teenagers? What is their typical dress? What types of behavior were observed? What is their language like?

CHOOSING SIDES

CHOOSING SIDES 17.1: DOUBLE STANDARDS

It is clear from Freud's and Erikson's discussion of adolescent personality development that much greater emphasis is placed on the process of sexual development as it occurs in males than as it occurs in females. Though the dramatic rise over the last generation in the sexual activity of teenage girls has diminished the basis for the double standard in sexual behavior, there apparently still remains somewhat a double standard of attitudes (girls think they should not engage in sexual activity even though they do). Ask the class for their opinions on when, if ever, will the underlying attitudes that have led to the biases in psychoanalytic theory, and also to the double standard, change. Will it ever be possible for our society to value males and females equally?

Pro: Society is working toward valuing men and women equally. This can be seen in the equalization of educational programs, non-discrimination policies in the workplace, and the emphasis on women as consumers in the marketplace.

Con: Society will always struggle with true equality between the sexes because of fundamental biological/reproductive differences. Females will always be valued for appearance more than ability: men will always be valued for their achievement rather than nurturance and caring.

It may be interesting to steer the discussion toward considering the issue of "comparable worth," the idea that women and men should receive equal pay for equal work. Will fundamental attitudes change when women across the board all have the same access to jobs and the same pay scale as men?

KNOWLEDGE CONSTRUCTION ACTIVITIES

KNOWLEDGE CONSTRUCTION ACTIVITY 17.1: GENERATIVE TERMS

This activity will use the principles of generative learning as explained in the Introduction to assist students in gaining a better understanding of terms. Divide the class into groups of four or five. Assign each group the task of generating an example for a generative term from this chapter.

The example that each group creates cannot be one that has been used in the class or in the book. They must think of a new application for the term that they are given. Groups are allowed to use their books and notes. By creating their own example of the term, they demonstrate an understanding of the term to the level of application. There are several approaches that can be used in this exercise. Students may be given the entire list at once, but often one group will finish far ahead of the others and topics will get out of sequence. Another strategy is to give all of the groups the same term to create an example and then go around the room to discuss outcomes. This has been very successful, but also takes the most time. A third approach is to give each group a different term and see what examples they can generate.

Some generative terms for Chapter 17 are listed below.

Role confusion   Moratorium
Crisis   Identity diffusion
Commitment   Patchwork self
Identity achievement   Antisocial behavior
Foreclosure   Adolescent rebellion

KNOWLEDGE CONSTRUCTION ACTIVITY 17.2: ERIKSON'S ROLE CONFUSION

To allow your students to experience a different aspect of Erikson's role confusion, ask them to identify all the different hats (roles) that they now wear (play). Some will produce a fairly short list of 10 or fewer roles. Some will be more creative and list cook, maid, dishwasher, taxi driver, and other roles they perform within their home setting. Encourage them to create as long a list as possible. Lists of 30 or 40 roles should not be unusual for most of your students (and yourself!). Remind them of their relationship roles: son, daughter, aunt, uncle, husband, wife, lover, grandchild, niece, nephew, cousin, friend, enemy, neighbor, client, customer, patient, and so on. Mention their legal roles: citizen, resident, taxpayer, registered voter, and so on. Check their lists for occupational roles: student, teacher, worker, homemaker, colleague, boss, employee, and the like. Be sure to add vocational roles: tennis player, knitter, musician, singer, actor, woodworker, gardener, reader, poet, and so on. By now you should have the idea of how to get them to expand their lists. After they have created their expanded lists, ask them to identify those roles that they actively chose for themselves and to determine how many were conferred as a result of the circumstances of their birth and other events. When you consider the expanded list, is it any wonder that teenagers are sometimes confused about who they are and who they will be?

KNOWLEDGE CONSTRUCTION ACTIVITY 17.3: PLANNED PARENTHOOD SPEAKER

The local incidence of adolescent sexual awareness, sexual activity, and teenage pregnancy may best be presented by a community resource person. Someone from an organization such as Planned Parenthood would make a good speaker. Might there be someone from your college Health Center or Counseling Center? Have students formulate ideas and questions ahead of time to facilitate maximum information exchange.

KNOWLEDGE CONSTRUCTION ACTIVITY 17.4: COMMUNICATION GAP

A common reference to the communication difficulties between parents and adolescents is the *generation gap*. This term refers to just about any observable differences between parents and teens. Have students document the existence or nonexistence of a generation gap by observing young people and middle-aged persons (the age range of parents of adolescents). Collect data on these two groups of subjects in several areas, including styles of dress, language or slang used, eating habits, exercise habits, hobbies and interests, taste in music, and so on.

KNOWLEDGE CONSTRUCTION ACTIVITY 17.5: IDENTITY STATUS

Based on the work of Marcia, there are four general areas in which a person needs to make commitments in order to achieve an identity. These include career identity, sexual beliefs and values, religious beliefs and values, and political beliefs.

Interview a young teenager about his or her plans and commitments in these four areas. You do not have to ask about specific behaviors, but ask generally what the person believes.

Career:

Religion:

Sexual behavior:

Politics:

How committed is this young person to his or her beliefs? Now think about yourself at the same age. What did you believe? Have you maintained your commitments to those beliefs from early adolescence?

What kind of identity status do you think your respondent has achieved? What is your identity status?

Write a brief (1-2 page) summary of your findings.

7. RESOURCES FOR INSTRUCTORS

Books and Articles

Apter, T. (1990). *Altered loves: Mothers and daughters during adolescence.* New York: St. Martin's.

Baker, S. A., Thalberg, S. P., & Morrison, D. M. (1988). Parents' behavioral norms as predictors of adolescent sexual activity and contraceptive use. *Adolescence, 23,* 265-282.

Csikszentmihalyi, M., & Larson, R. (1984). *Being adolescent: Conflict and growth in the teen-age years.* New York: Basic Books.

Diamont, L. (ed.) (1987). *Male and female homosexuality.* Washington DC: Hemisphere.

Ellis, L., & Ames, M. A. "Neurohormonal functioning and sexual ? Au: Year? orientation: A theory of homosexuality-heterosexuality." *Psychological Bulletin, 101,* 233-258.

Erikson, E. (1968). *Identity: Youth and crises.* New York: Norton.

Harris, L. (1987). *Inside America.* New York: Vintage.

Lancaster, J. B., & Hamburg, B. A. (eds.) (1986). *School-age pregnancy and parenthood: Biosocial dimensions.* New York: Aldine.

Schlein, S. (ed.) (1987). *A way of looking at things: Selected papers from 1930 to 1980. Erik H. Erikson.* New York: Norton.

Sternberg, R., & Barnes, M. L. (eds.) (1988). *The anatomy of love.* New Haven: Yale University Press.

Video resources

Adolescence: Current issues I (MS, 1995, video, 32 min.). Realistic examination of teen issues including STDs, sexual abuse, sexual harassment, and substance abuse from viewpoints of the experts and the teens.

Adolescence: Current issues II (MS, 1995, video, 24 min.). Explores the subjects of depression, suicide, delinquency, violence, runaways, and dropouts from the viewpoints of the authorities in the field as well as the teens.

Adolescence: Social and emotional development (MS, 1995, video, 38 min.). Explores the search for identity in relationship to parents, parenting styles, and peer support.

AIDS, teens, and Latinos (FFHS, 1994, video, 28 min.). This program profiles a Cuban-American teenager with AIDS who is dedicating his life to public awareness efforts and the education of Miami Latinos.

Coping with peer pressure (FFHS, 1994, video, 15 min.). Viewers learn to cope with peer pressure by looking ahead to the consequences of their actions and being honest with themselves.
Does TV kill? (PBS, 1995, video, 90 min.). Explores the impact of the media upon violence.

Educating pregnant teens (FFHS, 1994, video, 25 min.). This program takes a candid look at teenage pregnancy and attitudes toward it through the forthright views of a young group of women.

Ignoring the risks: Teenage pregnancy and AIDS (FFHS, 1994, video, 28 min.). In this specially adapted Phil Donahue program, teens themselves explain why they ignore the warning that unprotected sex can cost them their lives.

Parents' views and teenagers' rights (FFHS, 1994, video, 28 min.). In this program, teens tell of their battles with their parents. Young women tell how they feel they must lie to their parents to stand up for their own rights. Muslim girls, in particular, are unhappy when their parents try to prevent them from becoming part of wWestern culture.

Reviving Ophelia: Saving the selves of adolescent girls (MEF, 1999, video, 38 min.). Dr. Mary Pipher discusses the challenges of teens with concrete ideas for helping young women counteract the influences culture.

Straight talk with Derek McGinty: Kids in trouble (PBS, 1998, video, 60 min.). Discusses the issues facing troubled teens including the shooting sprees in schools.

Street gangs of Los Angeles (FFHS, 1994, video, 44 min.). This program looks at the thrills and dangers of life for black and Hispanic gang members and their parents.
Struggle for identity: Issues in transracial adoption (FL, 1999, video, 21 min.). Teenagers discuss the problems and solutions associated with race, culture, and identity in adoptive and foster families.

Teens, sex, and AIDS (FFHS, 1994, video, 28 min.). This program combines an open discussion among teens about their AIDS concerns, with dramatizations of teens dealing with decisions about sex.

When a kid is gay (WGBH, 1995, video, 60 min.). Discusses sexual identity for adolescents who must also struggle with being gay or lesbian in a world that provides few supports.